Lecture Notes in Computer Science 10995

Commenced Publication in 1973
Founding and Former Series Editors:
Gerhard Goos, Juris Hartmanis, and Jan van Leeuwen

More information about this series at http://www.springer.com/series/7409

Muhammad Younas · Irfan Awan
George Ghinea · Marisa Catalan Cid (Eds.)

Mobile Web and Intelligent Information Systems

15th International Conference, MobiWIS 2018
Barcelona, Spain, August 6–8, 2018
Proceedings

 Springer

Editors
Muhammad Younas
Oxford Brookes University
Oxford
UK

George Ghinea
Brunel University London
Uxbridge
UK

Irfan Awan
University of Bradford
Bradford
UK

Marisa Catalan Cid
i2CAT
Barcelona
Spain

ISSN 0302-9743   ISSN 1611-3349   (electronic)
Lecture Notes in Computer Science
ISBN 978-3-319-97162-9   ISBN 978-3-319-97163-6   (eBook)
https://doi.org/10.1007/978-3-319-97163-6

Library of Congress Control Number: 2018949142

LNCS Sublibrary: SL3 – Information Systems and Applications, incl. Internet/Web, and HCI

This Springer imprint is published by the registered company Springer Nature Switzerland AG
The registered company address is: Gewerbestrasse 11, 6330 Cham, Switzerland

Preface

The 15th International Conference on Mobile Web and Intelligent Information Systems (MobiWis 2018) was held in Barcelona, Spain, during August 6–8, 2018. Barcelona is the capital of Catalonia and one of the largest cities in Spain. It is also one of the leading tourist and economic centers in the world. Barcelona also hosts one of the largest technological events, GSMA Mobile World Congress, which is attended by a large number of participants from various industries and organizations across the world.

With the tremendous growth in the use of mobile devices such as smart phones, tablets, and wearable devices, mobile web has created new ways for producing and consuming web information. Mobile web plays an increasingly important role in modern society giving people ubiquitous access to relevant information anytime and anywhere. More and more people are accessing web information through mobile devices as compared with desktop computers.

The International Conference on Mobile Web and Intelligent Information Systems (MobiWis) aims to advance research on and practical applications of mobile web, intelligent information systems, and related mobile technologies. It provides a forum for researchers, developers, and practitioners from academia, industry, and the public sector to share research ideas, knowledge, and experiences in the areas of mobile web and information systems. The call for papers of MobiWis 2018 included interesting and timely areas such as: mobile web systems, recommender systems, security and authentication, context-awareness, mobile web and advanced applications, cloud and IoT, mobility management, mobile and wireless networks, and mobile web practice and experience.

MobiWis 2018 attracted a good number of submissions from different countries across the world. This year, 50 papers were submitted to MobiWis 2018. All submitted papers were reviewed by multiple members of the Program Committee. Based on the reviews, 17 papers were accepted for the conference — with 15 full and 2 short papers. This shows an acceptance rate of 34%. The accepted papers covered a range of topics related to the theme of the conference. These include: mobile web and apps, wireless sensor networks, web services, cloud services, web applications, and various web technologies.

The MobiWis 2018 program also included two keynote talks delivered by Prof. Gottfried Vossen (University of Münster, Germany) and Prof. Luis Muñoz (University of Cantabria, Spain). These talks were delivered in conjunction with the co-located conferences of the IEEE 6th International Conference on Future Internet of Things and Cloud (FiCloud 2018) and the 4the International Conference on Big Data Innovations and Applications (Innovate-Data 2018), IEEE-TCI. We would like to thank the keynote speakers for delivering interesting and thought-provoking talks.

We thank all the Program Committee members, who provided valuable and constructive feedback to the authors. We also thank Dr. Aneta Poniszewska-Maranda (Workshop

Coordinator), Dr. Barbara Masucci (Publicity Chair), and Dr. Farookh Hussain (Special Issues Chair for International Journals) for their help and support. We would like to thank the local organizing team of the i2Cat Foundation, Spain, for their great help and support.

Our sincere thanks also go to the Springer LNCS team, Alfred Hofmann, and Anna Kramer for their valuable support in the production of the conference proceedings.

August 2018

Muhammad Younas
Irfan Awan
George Ghinea
Marisa Catalan Cid

Organization

General Chair

George Ghinea   Brunel University, UK

Program Chair

Muhammad Younas   Oxford Brookes University, UK

Local Organizing Chair

Marisa Catalán Cid   i2Cat Foundation, Spain

Publication Chair

Irfan Awan   University of Bradford, UK

Workshop Coordinator

Aneta Poniszewska-Maranda   Lodz University of Technology, Poland

Journals Special Issues Chair

Farookh Hussain   University of Technology Sydney, Australia

Publicity Chair

Barbara Masucci   University of Salerno, Italy

Program Committee

Agnis Stibe   Massachusetts Institute of Technology (MIT), USA
Ali M. Aseeri   King Khalid University, Saudi Arabia
Andrea Omicini   University of Bologna, Italy
Aneta Poniszewska-Maranda   Lodz University of Technology, Poland
Bryan A. Knowles   Western Kentucky University, USA
Carlos Calafate   Technical University of Valencia, Spain
Carmela Comito   ICAR-CNR, Italy
Chi (Harold) Liu   Beijing Institute of Technology, China
Ciprian Dobre   Politehnica University of Bucharest, Romania
Costas Mourlas   University of Athens, Greece
Dan Johansson   Umea University, Sweden

Fatma Abdennadher	National School of Engineering of Sfax, Tunisia
Florence Sedes	Paul Sabatier University, France
Ivan Demydov	Lviv Polytechnic National University, Ukraine
John Lindström	Luleå University of Technology, Sweden
Jorge Sa Silva	University of Coimbra, Portugal
Jozef Juhar	Technical University of Košice, Slovakia
Jung-Chun Liu	TungHai University, Japan
Nor Shahniza Kamal Bashah	Universiti Teknologi MARA, Malaysia
Lidia Ogiela	AGH University of Science and Technology, Poland
Maher Ben Jemaa	ReDCAD-ENIS, Tunisia
Marek R. Ogiel	AGH University of Science and Technology, Poland
Maria Luisa Damiani	Università degli Studi di Milano, Italy
Masahiro Sasabe	Nara Institute of Science and Technology, Japan
Novia Admodisastro	Universiti Putra Malaysia, Malaysia
Ondrej Krejcar	University of Hradec Kralove, Czech Republic
Pablo Adasme	University of Santiago de Chile, Chile
Paolo Nesi	University of Florence, Italy
Perin Unal	METU, Turkey
Philippe Roose	IUT de Bayonne, France
Pınar Kirci	Istanbul University, Turkey
Rafidah Noor	University of Malaya, Malaysia
Riccardo Martoglia	University of Modena and Reggio Emilia, Italy
Sameera Abar	King Khalid University, Saudi Arabia
Sergio Ilarri	University of Zaragoza, Spain
Shinsaku Kiyomoto	KDDI R&D Laboratories Inc., Japan
Stephan Böhm	RheinMain University, Germany
Thanh Van Do	Telenor, Norway
Tony Wasserman	Carnegie Mellon University, Silicon Valley, USA
Viet-Duc Le	University of Twente, The Netherlands

Contents

Web and Mobile Applications

Mobile Web and Apps

Towards Model-Driven Business Apps for Wearables

Christoph Rieger$^{(\boxtimes)}$ and Herbert Kuchen

ERCIS, University of Münster, Münster, Germany
{christoph.rieger,kuchen}@uni-muenster.de

Abstract. With the rise of wearable devices expected to continue in the near future, traditional approaches of manually developing apps from scratch for each platform reach their limits. On the other hand, current cross-platform approaches are usually limited to platforms for smartphones and tablets. The model-driven paradigm seems well suited for developing apps for novel and heterogeneous devices. However, one of the main challenges for establishing a model-driven framework for wearables consists of bridging the variety of user interfaces and considering different capabilities of device input and output. This paper seeks to investigate the challenges of app development for wearable devices regarding user interfaces and discusses a possible mapping of typical application building blocks in the domain of business apps. Ultimately, apps modelled on a task-oriented level of abstraction using platform-independent notations such as MAML or CTT can then be transformed into code that adopts device class specific representations.

Keywords: Cross-platform · Model-driven software development
Multi-platform · Wearables · Mobile app · Business app

1 Introduction

Wearables have seen a drastic increase in popularity in the last years, with most major vendors providing software platforms and hardware products such as smartwatches and fitness devices for the mainstream consumer market. According to Gartner, the wearable device market is expected to grow significantly in the forthcoming years to more than 500 million devices sold in 2021 [23]. Many of these devices will be app-enabled and accessible to third-party developers.

For now, many available wearable applications – so-called apps – are of rather exploratory nature, providing only a limited set of companion functionality compared to a main app running on a smartphone. However, traditional approaches to app development are limited with regard to the plethora of input and output capabilities by current and announced wearable devices such as smartwatches and smart glasses. In addition, not all cross-platform approaches can be used for developing apps for wearables due to technical limitations. Many devices do not provide web views or support JavaScript execution, excluding hybrid frameworks such as the popular Apache Cordova.

© Springer International Publishing AG, part of Springer Nature 2018
M. Younas et al. (Eds.): MobiWIS 2018, LNCS 10995, pp. 3–17, 2018.
https://doi.org/10.1007/978-3-319-97163-6_1

Therefore, new methods are needed in order to extend app development to these different device classes. Model-driven software development (MDSD) seems particularly suitable for targeting a large range of devices and ease the development as opposed to the repetitive manual implementation. When extending existing model-driven mobile development approaches to wearables, adapting business logic is probably not the most pressing issue and transpiling approaches such as ICPMD [6] may be applied. One of the main challenges consists of bridging the heterogeneity of user interfaces (UI) regarding input capabilities and information visualisation according to the platform's user experience (UX).

In addition, wearable devices are not used in isolation but often considered as connected devices – although they might technically run standalone apps such as with Google's Wear OS (formerly Android Wear 2.0). Most likely, wearable apps in the near future will co-exist with other device counterparts or interact with their environment such as with smart personal agents or cyber-physical sensor networks. With regard to these scenarios, MDSD can play out its strengths even more when apps are jointly modelled for multiple devices using a single, abstract representation, and individually transforming the models to device-specific interfaces.

This paper seeks to investigate the challenges of app development for wearable devices, in particular related to the diversity issue of device interfaces. As a building block on the path towards extending model-driven development approaches to wearable devices, it contributes a conceptual mapping of UI representations across multiple device classes for typical operations in the domain of business apps. The eventual aim is to spark discussion on the long-standing issues of cross-platform UI modelling. The structure of this paper follows these contributions: after discussing related work in Sect. 2, we highlight the current challenges and our proposed mapping of user interfaces and suitable modelling approaches in Sect. 3. Section 4 discusses the applicability of model-driven development for wearable devices before we conclude in Sect. 5.

2   Related Work

In this work, we focus on the domain of business apps, i.e. form-based, data-driven applications interacting with back-end systems [13]. Using this definition, business apps not only refer to smartphone applications but also apply to a broader scope of *app-enabled* devices. These can be described as being extensible with software that comes in small, interchangeable pieces that are usually provided by third parties unrelated to the hardware vendor or platform manufacturer and increase the versatility of the device after its introduction [19]. Although related to the term *mobile computing*, app-enablement also considers stationary devices such as smart TVs, smart personal assistants, or smart home devices.

Cross-platform overview papers such as [11] typically focus on a single category of devices and apply a very narrow notion of mobile devices. [19] provides the only classification that includes novel device classes. Furthermore, few papers provide a technical perspective on apps *spanning multiple device classes*. Singh and Buford [21] describe a cross-device team communication use case for desktop, smartphones, and wearables, and Esakia et al. [8] performed research on Pebble smartwatch and smartphone interaction in computer science courses. In the context of Web-of-Things devices, Koren and Klamma [12] propose a middleware approach to integrate data and heterogeneous UI, and Alulema et al. [1] propose a DSL for bridging the presentation layer of heterogeneous devices in combination with web services for incorporating business logic.

With regard to commercial cross-platform products, Xamarin[1] and CocoonJS[2] provide Android Wear support to some extent. Whereas several other frameworks claim to support wearables, this usually only refers to accessing its data by the main smartphone application or displaying notifications on coupled devices.

Together with the increase in devices, new software platforms have appeared, some of which are either related to established operating systems for other device classes or are newly designed to run on multiple heterogeneous devices. Examples include Wear OS, watchOS, and Tizen. Although these platforms ease the development of apps (e.g., reusing code and libraries), subtle differences exist in the available functionality and general cross-platform challenges remain.

3 Creating Business App UIs for Wearable Devices

To pave the way towards model-driven software development for wearable devices, we provide a possible mapping of typical tasks in this domain to different app-enabled devices and present a model-driven app development approach.

3.1 Challenges of Wearable UIs

From development and usage perspectives, two main categories of UI/UX challenges related to app development across different device classes can be identified.

Diversity of Input and Output Capabilities. Traditionally, mobile apps are designed for rectangular screen sizes between 4" and 10" to cover smartphones and tablets with similar visual characteristics. However, wearables vary greatly in terms of screen size or provide completely different means of output such as audio or projection. In addition, current interface design considerations such as device orientation and pixel density are aggravated due to the introduction of different aspect ratios (e.g. ribbon-like fitness devices worn around the wrist), positions (e.g. objects at different angles and depths within the field of view for smart glasses) or form factors (e.g. round smartwatches) [19].

---

[1] https://www.xamarin.com.
[2] https://docs.cocoon.io/article/canvas-engine/.

Correspondingly, novel app-enabled devices provide different possibilities for user interaction which span from hardware buttons to handling graphical UI elements on touch screens, using auxiliary devices (e.g., stylus pens), and voice inputs [19]. Moreover, multiple input alternatives may be available on one device and used depending on user preferences or usage context.

Multi-device Usage Patterns. Until now, cross-platform approaches were mainly designed to provide equivalent functionality for similar devices with different operating systems. However, novel app-enabled devices usually do not replace smartphone usage but represent complementary devices which are used contextually (e.g. location- or time-based) or depending on user preferences. This might occur *sequentially* when a user switches to a different device, e.g., using an app with smart glasses while walking and switching to the in-vehicle app when boarding a car. Alternatively, a *concurrent* usage of multiple devices for the same task is possible, for instance in second screening scenarios in which one device provides additional information or input/output capabilities for stationary devices in the room [14]. Also, automated device-to-device communication (e.g. with sensor networks) might become more common in future mobile scenarios. Cross-platform development frameworks need to consider this additional complexity through device management as well as fast and reliable synchronisation which automatically updates other devices based on the current application state.

3.2   Conceptual UI Mapping

From the current use cases of business apps on smartphones and tablets, some types of user tasks are prevalent. These are mainly related to Create/Read/Update/Delete(CRUD) operations as well as mobile functionalities such as calling a person, receiving notifications, or accessing sensor information (e.g., GPS location). Based on the concepts of *abstract interaction objects* [24] and *presentation units* [5], a mapping is desirable to transform these typical operation components to concrete widget representations of novel smart devices.

In the following, we describe such a conceptual mapping for business app tasks. It is derived from an analysis of the publicly available design guidelines and best practices by several vendors (see Table 1) which provide app-enabled devices for ubiquitous usage (in contrast to specialised devices such as for cycling). Besides identifying suitable patterns complying to these guidelines, we also keep a generalisable appearance in mind (for inclusion in cross-platform frameworks).

Therefore, possible representations are juxtaposed for traditional mobile devices (smartphones, tablets) and novel app-enabled devices (smartwatches, smart glasses, and smart personal agents). However, to allow for concrete visualisations, we chose representative devices of each class, in particular an iPhone smartphone, an Android-based tablet and smartwatch, and head-mounted Google glass.

Table 1. Analysed design guidelines per device class

Device class	OS guidelines	Representative device
Smartphones/Tablets	Android iOS	Samsung Galaxy S8 iPhone X
Smartwatches	Android Wear/Wear OS watchOS Fitbit Tizen	LG Watch Sport Apple Watch Fitbit Ionic Samsung Gear
Smart glasses	Glass OS HoloLens	Google Glass Microsoft HoloLens
Smart personal assistants	Amazon Alexa Actions on Google	Amazon Echo Google Home

Smartphone   Tablet   Smart glasses

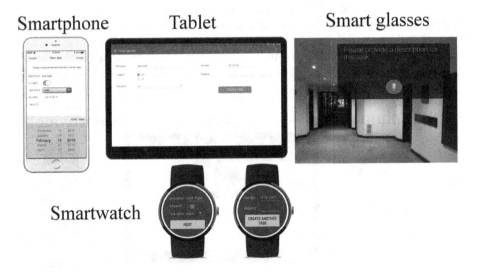

Smartwatch

Fig. 1. Possible interface representations for *Create* and *Update* task types

Create and Update. *Create* and *update* interfaces usually share a similar design and are therefore considered together in Fig. 1. On smartphones, create or update steps are usually represented as a list of input fields with corresponding captions and potentially provide contextual help such as placeholder texts or pop-up hints. To better make use of the available space, tablet apps support a multi-column layout, especially when the input fields can be grouped into multiple categories. Due to screen space limitations, smartwatch input can be either represented using a one-column scrolling layout or by a sequence of views per input field. Smart glasses can display the respective fields one by one and are updated using voice controls similar to voice-based smart personal assistants. To allow for a more flexible order of user inputs, advanced techniques might use the concept of frame-based dialogue managers known from chatbot applications

[9]. Using so-called slots for each attribute to be set, the user can provide the required information in any order and the system can focus on asking for missing information to complete the given task.

Select and Read. The *read* operation needs to be distinguished from another related task type: often the user first needs to *select* an item from a collection of objects, before seeing the object's detailed content as depicted in Fig. 2. Therefore, smartphones often provide a scrollable list of items that can be filtered using search keywords and navigated using jump marks. Smartwatches also provide scrollable lists, for example using curved layouts to exploit the round layout of Android-based watches. After selecting an element, individual objects might further be split into different views (e.g., using logical groups of fields) to avoid scrolling behaviour. The same principles apply to smart glasses which also have a limited virtual screen size. Voice-based interfaces may read the list of potential answers or allow users to provide keywords in order to limit the set of results. However, tablets can combine select and read tasks in a single view using the so-called master-detail pattern: The left column of the view presents the list of objects and upon selection updates the right side displaying its content.

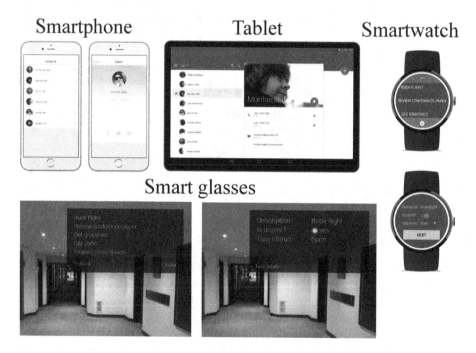

Fig. 2. Possible interface representations for *Select* and *Read* task types

Delete and Modal Pop-Ups. When a *delete* operation is triggered, apps usually require a confirmation to avoid accidental information loss. This confirmation is represented as a modal pop-up view that provides the options to confirm or cancel the current action (in case of deletion) or acknowledge the information prominently displayed on screen. The user must interact with this message in order to continue with his workflow. Therefore, modal views look similar on most screen-based devices and cover the majority of the screen. Voice-based interfaces can instead read out the message and wait for the user to react to it.

Mobile-Specific Tasks. Many mobile-specific tasks have similar representations across screen-based devices. Firstly, *notifications* are present on most devices as unobtrusive information about events when interacting with other apps, either as textual hint at the top or bottom of the screen. In contrast to pop-up messages, notifications disappear automatically or can be closed without blocking the user from performing his actions or waiting for a decision between different options. Voice-based devices can instead read out the message.

Secondly, *phone calls* can be performed not only on smartphones but also on tablets, smartwatches, smart glasses, and smart personal assistants as long as they are equipped with microphone, audio output capabilities, and cellular network connection (potentially indirectly through a connected smartphone). The communication target can usually be chosen by manually dialling a number or selecting someone from a list of contacts (cf. *select* task type) via touch or voice commands.

Finally, *sensor data* may be accessed by specific representations. For example, the GPS location can be visualised by a map on screen-oriented devices. However, this data is commonly contained in attributes of other data objects and therefore already considered in the *read* and *update* task types.

3.3 Modelling Apps Across Device Classes

The model-driven paradigm can provide strong benefits to app development both in terms of development effort regarding the plethora of novel devices as well as the integration and interaction with other applications. Arguably, many concepts from the more established domain of cross-platform development for smartphones can be reused and adapted. To achieve this, the challenges mentioned in Subsect. 3.1 need to be tackled systematically.

Regarding the diversity of input and output characteristics, a high level of abstraction beyond screen-oriented UIs is mandated, for example using declarative notations for representing use tasks. Consequently, arbitrary platforms can be supported by developing respective generators which implement a suitable mapping from descriptive models to platform-specific implementations.

Ideally, a "one model fits all platforms" approach can therefore be achieved by applying two types of transformations that do not modify the content but adapt the task appearance to different supported devices:

1. On the one hand, information can be *layouted* according to the available screen sizes, for example by choosing an appropriate appearance – one could think of tabular vs. graphical representations – or, if necessary, leave out complementary details. In the inventory management example, the round design of a smartwatch can be exploited by the curved list layout such that content readability is improved and screen usage is maximised.
2. On the other hand, the content structure can be *re-formatted* by an adaptive UI according to usual platform interaction patterns, e.g., let the user scroll through large amounts of information, present it in multiple subsequent steps, or as a hierarchical structure providing more details on request [4,5].

A high degree of abstraction can be achieved for user interactions by modelling user inputs in terms of *intended actions* for completing a particular task. An intermediate mapping layer can then transform actual inputs to the respective actions. For instance, a "back" action can be linked to a hardware button, displayed in a navigation bar on screen, bound to the right-swipe gesture (as recommended by the Wear OS guidelines [10]), or recognized by a spoken keyword in smart personal assistants. Another example is the usage of *default actions* to navigate through the app. Whereas in iOS, one possible action can be displayed in the top-right corner of the navigation bar, Wear OS uses so-called *Action-Drawers*[3] which propose one or more possible actions from the bottom edge of the screen.

Business apps are usually designed to support specific goal-oriented workflows which can be decomposed into individual tasks. This perspective of a user task model aligns with the desired high level of abstraction [22]. Subsequently, two task-oriented notations are presented that embody the task-oriented approach. The *ConcurTaskTree (CTT)* notation consists of three main elements [16]:

– the abstract *task* descriptions which together form the use case's functionality,
– temporal *operator*s defining the allowed sequences of executed tasks, representing an abstract notion of navigation actions within a use case, and
– the user *roles* (per task) that are allowed to interact with the system

CTTs have been refined to suit user interface development through decomposition over multiple levels [17]. An exemplary model suited for interface generation is presented in Fig. 3. The example shows an excerpt of a simple inventory management task in which the user (either a warehouse clerk or product manager) first selects an item from a list (with the possibility to filter the list content by title) and gets presented the item details (with data on title, description, pictures, price, product category, and quantity on stock; collapsed in Fig. 3). Depending on the user's role, different modes of editing the inventory are possible before concluding or aborting the process. Warehouse clerks can enter the quantity and position of newly arrived item replenishments. Product managers may instead update the item master data.

---

[3] https://designguidelines.withgoogle.com/wearos/components/action-drawer.html.

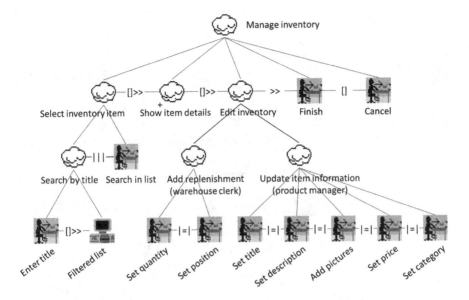

Fig. 3. Sample CTT model for an inventory management use case

As can be seen, the detailed decomposition at operational level creates a tree with user tasks on multiple levels of abstraction which diminishes the overview about the high-level tasks and particular user interactions. In addition, still many aspects such as navigation, item groups, informative labels, or object structures are not explicitly contained in the notation and need to be provided in separate models (e.g., using UML class diagrams for data models) to enable a fully automated generation of user interfaces.

Previously, we have proposed the graphical Müunster App Modeling Language (MAML) for specifying business apps based on five main design goals [18]:

- *Automatic cross-platform app creation* by transforming a graphical model to fully functional source code for multiple platforms.
- *Domain expert focus* to allow non-technical stakeholders to create, alter, or communicate about an app using the actual models.
- *Data-driven process modelling* specifies the application domain but also sets a high level of abstraction by interpreting data manipulation as a process.
- *Modularisation* of activities in distinct use cases helps for maintenance, especially for domain experts.
- *Declarative description* of the complete app, including necessary specifications of data model, business logic, user interactions, and UI views.

Compared to CTTs, the same exemplary scenario is depicted in Fig. 4 as MAML model. In MAML, this task is modelled in a *use case* as depicted in Fig. 4. The model contains a sequence of activities, from a *start event* (labelled with (1) in Fig. 4) towards one or several *end events* (2). In the beginning, a *data source* (3) specifies the data type of the manipulated objects and whether

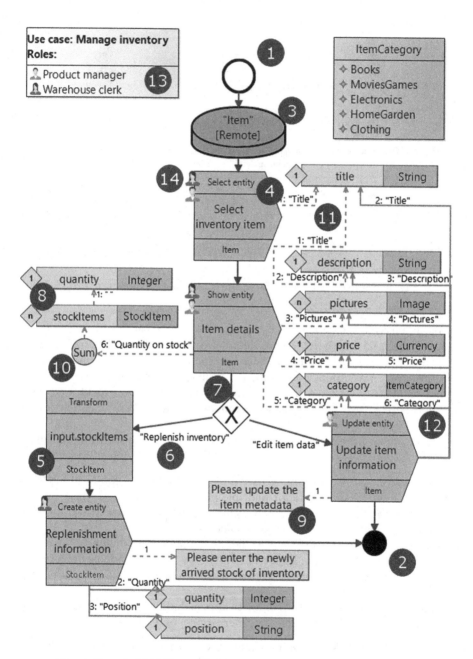

Fig. 4. Sample MAML model for an inventory management use case

they are only saved locally on the device or managed by the remote backend system. Data can then be modified through a pre-defined set of (arrow-shaped) *interaction process elements* (4), for instance to *select/create/update/display/ delete entities*, show *pop-up messages*, or access device functionalities such as the *camera* and starting a phone *call*. This describes the desired user actions on a high level and can be mapped to device-specific UI representations as described in Subsect. 3.2. *Automated process elements* (5) represent invisible processing steps without user interaction, for example *including* other models for process reuse, or navigating through the object graph (*transform*). The navigation between connected process steps happens along the *process connectors* (6) which can be supplied with captions. To account for non-linear workflows, process flows can be branched out using *XOR* elements (7).

In contrast to CTTs, MAML models additionally contain the data objects which are displayed within a respective process step. *Attributes* (8) consist of a cardinality indicator, a name, and the respective data type. Besides pre-defined data types, custom types can be defined and further described through nested attributes. *Labels* (9) provide explanatory text, and *computed attributes* (10) are used to calculate derived values at runtime based on other attributes. In MAML, only those attributes are modelled which will be used in a particular process step, for instance for including it in the graphical user interface.   .

Two types of connectors exist for attaching data to process steps: Dotted arrows represent a *reading relationship* (11) whereas solid arrows signify a *modifying relationship* (12) with regard to the target element. Every connector which is connected to an interaction process element also specifies an order of appearance and a field description. For convenience, multiple connectors may point to the same UI element from different sources (given their data types match). Alternatively, to avoid confusing connections across larger models, UI elements may instead be duplicated to different positions in the model and will automatically be matched at runtime.

Finally, MAML supports a multi-role concept to define (13) and annotate (14) arbitrary role names to the respective interaction process elements because many business processes such as approval workflows involve different people or departments.

It can be observed that the domain-specific MAML notation allows for a more concise and clearly arranged representation of the app content, for example by offering different task types which encapsulate the respective semantics as opposed to the more general CTT models. At the same time, MAML models contain precise technical details on the resulting app, such that fully functional apps can be generated from the notation. Using the presented mapping approach, apps can be flexibly generated from the same MAML models both for smartphones (Android and iOS) as well as Wear OS smartwatches.

4 Discussion

To put the presented approach in a broader context, we discuss two scenarios that underline the aforementioned issues and potential solution.

The first scenario in the *logistics* domain with an inventory management app was already depicted in Figs. 3 and 4. It represents a typical business process that can be performed by a single user when interacting with a centralised back-end system. However, it proves the potential for MDSD in generating apps for very different devices simultaneously from a common model: Firstly, a warehouse clerk might want to use smart glasses in order to have hands-free interaction with the inventory system when replenishing items. A product manager might instead use a smartphone to update erroneous information while inspecting shelves. Achieving business app development using model-driven techniques therefore seems particularly beneficial with regard to the flexibility it provides towards the future end user. This freedom to choose an appropriate device given the current usage context or personal preferences can not only propel technology acceptance but also allows for more experimentation with different modes of work.

As a second scenario, consider a *health app* which is integrated with a patient information system. Before making an appointment, patients can be asked to give more details about the health issue they are experiencing, for example through standardised questionnaires. This information is passed to the doctor to support his diagnosis. In order to follow-up on the medical treatment, sensors can regularly monitor vital parameters over a specified time interval and report the results back to the medical office such that doctor's assistants can take action when observing abnormal values.

This complex workflow involves multiple actors who need to share information over a longer period of time. In addition, different devices are combined according to their capabilities (e.g., wearable devices for sensing heart rate). However, tasks related to data manipulation might be limited on some devices, e.g., entering lots of data on a smartwatch is tedious. Using automated transformations of user interfaces can alleviate the problem only to a certain degree. Most probably, a co-existence of apps for multiple devices in parallel will be more useful than forcing all tasks to be performed on the same device. Again, the model-driven paradigm can provide significant benefits when offering a broad range of devices without linear increase of development efforts. However, to achieve the sketched multi-device usage, the potentially concurrent interaction between multiple devices requires a reliable and fast synchronisation of data among the respective devices. Different techniques such as Operational Transformation (OT) and Conflict-Free Replicated Data Types (CRDT) have been proposed for mobile data synchronisation but further research is necessary to apply them to the context of business apps [7,20]. In both scenarios, the diversity of user interfaces is best tackled by transforming a high-level and platform-agnostic model that relies on abstract *presentation units* which are later mapped to *concrete interaction objects*, i.e. suitable widget representations for platform-specific look-and-feel [5,24].

When putting the presented mapping into practice, the CTT representation as a general purpose notation for user tasks is not sufficient. Additional notations are required to specify the data model and possible interaction and navigation flows within an app. Other cross-platform approaches targeted to smartphones such as BiznessApps [2] and Bubble [3] provide graphical configurators for simplified app modelling, however, their screen-oriented approach falls short of covering wearable UIs. Similarly, user interaction standards such as the Interaction Flow Modeling Language (IFML) are implicitly tied to screen-based output [15]. In contrast, domain-specific languages such as MAML can provide components on a high level of abstraction while at the same time integrating UI and interaction aspects. Apart from being useful for holistically modelling apps, the MAML framework also includes code generators that output fully functioning smartphone apps. To demonstrate the feasibility of deriving a suitable representation from the same input models, the framework was extended by implementing a generator for Android Wear 2.0 smartwatches (Figs. 1 and 2 contain actual app screenshots).

The proposed high-level modelling approach for wearable app specifications also caters for the limitations of this paper regarding the future evolution of the field. Whereas differences in smartphone UIs have assimilated over time to a large degree (at least with regard the main input and output components), the chosen representations in Subsect. 3.2 can only represent a small subset of the various UIs and interaction patterns which already exist or maybe emerge in the future for wearable devices. The novelty of this highly dynamic field of wearables will certainly entail several changes to typical platform characteristics regarding both hardware and software. Vendors continuously explore interfaces and interaction possibilities, heavily modifying their best practice guidelines when presenting new versions of their platform. At the same time, this paper only scratches the surface of cross-platform development complexities across multiple device classes. In-depth research needs to address each device class individually which still exhibits a high variability of devices capabilities – future consolidation across vendors is possible but not foreseeable anytime soon.

5   Conclusion and Outlook

In this paper, we have investigated the challenges and potential solutions for applying model-driven techniques to the development of business apps for novel app-enabled devices. In particular, user interface related challenges currently limit the extension of established cross-platform techniques to these new classes of heterogeneous devices. We exemplify how the typical building blocks of business apps might be generically mapped to smartphones, tablets, smartwatches, and smart glasses.

In order to incorporate these in a model-driven approach, task-oriented modelling – without actually specifying the concrete user interface – allows for a suitably high level of abstraction. We deem this approach promising to bridge the heterogeneity of devices and enable fast development of apps that are flexibly targeted to a broader range of devices through adaptive layouts as well as device class specific reformatting of contents. Although both the MAML notation and CTT utilise a task-oriented approach, we argue that domain-specific languages such as MAML might be more suitable to modelling user interfaces than general purpose modelling notations due to the alignment with the target domain, thus condensing domain concepts more clearly to a high level of abstraction.

However, the current situation leaves room for further research in different directions such as observing emerging commonalities in user interfaces of the individual device classes that are subsumed by the umbrella term "wearables", and technical hurdles to synchronise content and application state in the dynamic interplay of mobile devices. Furthermore, the implementation of the presented concepts in an actual model-driven framework constitutes ongoing work of the authors by extending the MAML cross-platform framework with support for further novel device classes using the presented mapping approach.

References

1. Alulema, D., Iribarne, L., Criado, J.: A DSL for the development of heterogeneous applications. In: FiCloudW, pp. 251–257 (2017)
2. Bizness Apps: Mobile app maker – bizness apps (2018). http://biznessapps.com/
3. Bubble Group: Bubble - visual programming (2018). https://bubble.is/
4. Eisenstein, J., Vanderdonckt, J., Puerta, A.: Applying model-based techniques to the development of UIs for mobile computers. In: IUI (2001)
5. Eisenstein, J., Vanderdonckt, J., Puerta, A.: Applying model-based techniques to the development of UIs for mobile computers. In: Proceedings of the 6th International Conference on Intelligent User Interfaces, pp. 69–76. ACM (2001)
6. El-Kassas, W.S., Abdullah, B.A., Yousef, A.H., Wahba, A.: ICPMD: integrated cross-platform mobile development solution. In: ICCES (2014)
7. Ellis, C.A., Gibbs, S.J.: Concurrency control in groupware systems. In: SIGMOD, pp. 399–407. ACM (1989)
8. Esakia, A., Niu, S., McCrickard, D.S.: Augmenting undergraduate computer science education with programmable smartwatches. In: Decker, A., Eiselt, K., Alphonce, C., Tims, J. (eds.) SIGCSE, pp. 66–71. ACM (2015)
9. Goddeau, D., Meng, H., Polifroni, J., Seneff, S., Busayapongchai, S.: A form-based dialogue manager for spoken language applications. In: ICSLP, pp. 701–704 (1996)
10. Google LLC: Google developers. https://developers.google.com/
11. Jesdabodi, C., Maalej, W.: Understanding usage states on mobile devices. In: International Joint Conference on Pervasive and Ubiquitous Computing, pp. 1221–1225. ACM (2015)
12. Koren, I., Klamma, R.: The direwolf inside you: end user development for heterogeneous web of things appliances. In: Bozzon, A., Cudre-Maroux, P., Pautasso, C. (eds.) ICWE 2016. LNCS, vol. 9671, pp. 484–491. Springer, Cham (2016). https://doi.org/10.1007/978-3-319-38791-8_35
13. Majchrzak, T.A., Ernsting, J., Kuchen, H.: Achieving business practicability of model-driven cross-platform apps. OJIS 2(2), 3–14 (2015)
14. Neate, T., Jones, M., Evans, M.: Cross-device media: a review of second screening and multi-device television. Pers. Ubiquit. Comput. 21(2), 391–405 (2017)
15. Object Management Group: Interaction flow modeling language (2015). http://www.omg.org/spec/IFML/1.0
16. Paternò, F.: Model-Based Design and Evaluation of Interactive Applications. Springer, London (2000). https://doi.org/10.1007/978-1-4471-0445-2

17. Pribeanu, C.: An approach to task modeling for user interface design. In: Proceedings of the 3rd World Enformatika Conference, vol. 5, pp. 5–8 (2005)
18. Rieger, C., Kuchen, H.: A process-oriented modeling approach for graphical development of mobile business apps. Comput. Lang. Syst. Struct. **53**, 43–58 (2018)
19. Rieger, C., Majchrzak, T.A.: Conquering the mobile device jungle: towards a taxonomy for app-enabled devices. In: WEBIST, pp. 332–339 (2017)
20. Shapiro, M., Preguiça, N., Baquero, C., Zawirski, M.: Conflict-free replicated data types. In: Défago, X., Petit, F., Villain, V. (eds.) SSS 2011. LNCS, vol. 6976, pp. 386–400. Springer, Heidelberg (2011). https://doi.org/10.1007/978-3-642-24550-3_29
21. Singh, K., Buford, J.: Developing WebRTC-based team apps with a cross-platform mobile framework. In: Consumer Communications and Networking Conference (2016)
22. Sinnig, D., Chalin, P., Khendek, F.: Common semantics for use cases and task models. In: Davies, J., Gibbons, J. (eds.) IFM 2007. LNCS, vol. 4591, pp. 579–598. Springer, Heidelberg (2007). https://doi.org/10.1007/978-3-540-73210-5_30
23. van der Meulen, R., Forni, A.: Gartner says worldwide wearable device sales to grow 17 percent in 2017 (2017). https://www.gartner.com/newsroom/id/3790965
24. Vanderdonckt, J.M., Bodart, F.: Encapsulating knowledge for intelligent automatic interaction objects selection. In: Proceedings of the INTERACT '93 and CHI '93 Conference on Human Factors in Computing Systems, pp. 424–429. ACM (1993)

Development of a Mobile News Reader Application Compatible with In-Vehicle Infotainment

Başak Kurt and Sezer Gören

Department of Computer Engineering, Yeditepe University,
Kayışdağı, Ataşehir, Istanbul, Turkey
basak.kurt1@std.yeditepe.edu.tr, sgoren@cse.yeditepe.edu.tr
https://cse.yeditepe.edu.tr

Abstract. People spend a lot of time behind the wheel every day. Reading newspapers while driving a car is almost impossible. In this work, a mobile news reader application is developed to deliver the latest news from various sources to the drivers. The major difference from other news reader applications is that it is developed in accordance with the Ford SYNC technology. The user will be able to view the latest news on the SYNC screen while driving and listening to the selected news. In addition, drivers can select the desired news source and the desired news with the voice commands. Therefore, our proposed news reader application is an enabler for the drivers to follow the news in a safe way without distraction while keeping their hands on the wheel and their eyes on the road.

Keywords: In-Vehicle-Infotainment · Smart Device Link · SYNC · JSON · RSS
Ford Applink®

1 Introduction

1.1 Motivation

Limited time causes people to do multiple tasks at the same time and this results in distraction. Distraction affects some of the tasks that require significant attention for human life such as driving, and it causes traffic accidents which have become a major social problem with the increasing of vehicle usage in cities. According to World Health Organization [1], each year, around 1.3 million people were killed and 50 million were injured because of traffic accidents.

The focus of many researches in this area is the driver distraction caused by the widespread use of mobile phones [2] and other technological products among the drivers. The usage of a mobile phone while driving means taking the driver's eye away from the road and pulling the hand from the steering wheel. The numbers of scientific researches and evidences which show that distraction caused using mobile phones negatively affects the performance of the driver in many ways such as prolongation of reaction time, reduction in the ability to follow the tape correctly, unable to adjust tracking distance or loss of seriousness of driving a car, are increasing. While it is difficult to pinpoint the impact of mobile phone usage on the risk of an accident, according to

© Springer International Publishing AG, part of Springer Nature 2018
M. Younas et al. (Eds.): MobiWIS 2018, LNCS 10995, pp. 18–29, 2018.
https://doi.org/10.1007/978-3-319-97163-6_2

studies, drivers who use mobile phones on board are four times more likely to be involved in an accident. Especially with the spread of smartphones and mobile Internet, people spent a significant amount of their time with their smartphones.

To solve these problems, car manufacturers first added the ability to make phone calls via Bluetooth technology to their cars. With the advancement of automotive technology, touch screens and infotainment technologies which allow drivers to interact with their phones without using it, are added to the cars. Nokia, Apple, and Google have started to work on device interoperability technologies that integrate a smartphone and a car's infotainment system such as MirrorLink [3] by Nokia Research, Apple CarPlay [4] by Apple, and Android Auto [5] by Google. These products offer users the ability to give voice commands and do many things such as listening music, responding incoming messages, making phone calls even controlling their smart home devices without touching their phones. Basically, the idea is to transform smartphones into automotive application platforms where applications are hosted and run on the smartphone while drivers and passengers interact with them via steering wheel controls, dashboard buttons, and touch screens of the car's In-Vehicle Infotainment (IVI) system.

These projects are not the exact solution for this problem, but the main purpose is to decrease the risk of the car accidents by keeping drivers' eyes on the road and hands on the steering wheel. Also, they solve the problem of limited time as serving an assistant. Some of the firms such as Spotify are started to support these technologies with making their applications compatible with it.

The new generation is now choosing products that respond to their desire rather than being offered. The significant proof is increasing the number of users of Spotify and Apple Music. In recent years, the numbers of radio listeners are decreased because of the freedom those applications offer. Users can now listen whatever they want without any advertisements thanks to these applications. On the other hand, people still need to use the radio stations to listen to the news on the road.

The proposed News Reader application aims to provide drivers listen to the news that they want to read on the road with controlling it by voice commands without distraction. The application is developed for Ford vehicles that have SYNC 3 and it uses Ford AppLink® technology to read the news to the users with the motto of "Keep eyes on the road, hands on the wheel".

1.2 Background

Basic concepts of RSS and how to develop a news reader based on it is given in [6]. In [6] an RSS reader as a desktop application is developed with Eclipse IDE and Java in model-view-controller (MVC) structure. The purpose of this desktop application is that users can reach the information without logging in many websites on a single platform by using the advantages of the RSS technology. The application is user-friendly and efficient such that subscribing/canceling RSS sources is very simple.

RSS Reader [7] is an Android application. It enables users to import and export feed as an OPML format. OPML format is a kind of XML format that is developed by Microsoft. It is usually used to transfer data. It provides offline reading with pictures and full text. Users can prefer automatic or scheduled synchronization to refresh the feeds. It clears old news automatically and shows notifications for the new news.

Fast News [8] is another Android RSS Reader application. It provides comparison of the news from different resources and supports many countries.

The n-tv.de news application [9] is an Android-based application for Ford SYNC© AppLink™. It is one of the most popular news applications in Germany and provides users news in the car quickly and informative with audio messages from business, politics, entertainment, travel, and sports. The app offers a comprehensive audio offering: full-hour hourly news, compact news from the world and business on demand. Breaking News also informs users in the car about what's going on around the world. The specially narrated article of n-tv.de from economy, politics, entertainment, and sport of our professional speakers. This application informs users about the economy in Germany and abroad within two minutes.

The wetter.de application [10] is an Android-based application for Ford SYNC© AppLink™. It informs users quickly and reliably about weather conditions at any time and in any place. Users need to add a place to their favorites on the smartphones to get all desired weather data directly on the SYNC screen of the vehicle. It also includes alert functions that inform users with the help of acoustic and optical signals as soon as there is a weather change or driver approaches a region with severe weather warnings.

Ford+Alexa [11] is developed by Ford and Alexa collaboration to implement the Alexa (Amazon's cloud-based voice service) to SYNC 3 AppLink™. Ford SYNC technology is an advanced in-car multimedia system. Drivers can make phone calls, listen to music or even manage their banking application with very simple voice commands without removing their hands from the wheel. It is designed to keep driver's hands on the wheel and their eyes on the road. Ford+Alexa provides access to voice commands to voice navigation, traffic information, Amazon Prime shopping and control their supported smart home devices from the car. It has over 30,000 skills such as playing music, delivering news, reading audiobooks and controlling lighting, security systems, garage doors etc.

MirrorLink [3] is the first IVI which is originally developed by Nokia for use with Nokia phones. This technology was later acquired by the Car Connectivity Consortium and is becoming increasingly common. MirrorLink offers more practical and functional operation than others because it provides access to all the applications and features by transferring the screen of the phone. The major difference of MirrorLink is that the other infotainment systems such as CarPlay [4] or Android Auto [5], are proprietary. But, MirrorLink is completely open source. Unlike other systems, this technology allows users to connect to their phones in a much more comprehensive way.

Apple CarPlay [4] is an advanced multimedia technology that is designed by Apple for passenger cars and serves as co-pilot. With the Siri features, users can perform the desired operations without using the phone in the car. Users can use the navigation feature, answer calls, read and reply to incoming messages, and listen to music without distracting their drive attention. The user can press and hold the voice control button on the steering wheel to enable synchronization between CarPlay compatible multimedia devices and iPhone to activate the voice control feature. It can be used by touches in the touchscreen vehicles.

Android Auto [5] is a smartphone projection standard developed by Google to control the smartphones from vehicles. Android Auto uses the USB interface to display the Google Now interface on the car's info screen. Users can continue to use the car's touch screen, steering controls, knobs, and other control arms while using Android Auto. Considering the risk posed using a mobile phone while driving a car, manual use of mobile phone is not allowed while the phone is connected to the car. The Android Auto interface can only support the approved applications that meet Google's security requirements.

The organization of this paper is as follows: Next section analyzes the requirements of the application and presents the development stages. Section 3 presents the design and implementation which is then followed by the tests and results. Finally, Sect. 5 concludes the paper.

2 Requirements Analysis

In this paper, we present the development of a news reader application for IVI. The hardware and software requirements for the application are given as follows:

- SYNC 3 AppLink compatible car: An AppLink compatible Ford vehicle is required to run the application, because SYNC 3 is a Ford product and it is designed especially for Ford's vehicles.
- AppLink Emulator: To test the application on the computer AppLink Emulator is needed.
- Android based mobile device: A mobile device such as tablet or smart phone with Android OS is needed to run the application, because the application is designed on Android Studio for Android operating systems.
- Internet connection: An Internet connection must be activated to take a news feeds, weather and location information. The application coonects to the news sources online to provide the news to the end user.
- Bluetooth: Bluetooth must be activated on mobile device and SYNC 3 to make the connection between them.
- API Connection: API connection is essential to get the information in real-time from the sources. To get information by API, an API Key needs to be acquired from the source.
- SDL Library: To integrate the application with AppLink, SDL Library is required. SDL Library can be downloaded from SDL's official GitHub account.

In the next subsections, we will briefly describe and analyze their usage in our development.

2.1 Web APIs

Web APIs are defined interfaces where interactions occur between the organization and applications. An API approach is an architectural approach that provides services with different applications that serve different types of consumer communities by providing a programmable interface.

2.2 JSON vs XML

In the Web development context, an API is typically a description of Hypertext Transfer Protocol (HTTP) request messages and response messages in Extensible Markup Language (XML) or JavaScript Object Notation (JSON) format. XML is a markup language that is designed to store and carry the data. It is intended to be human-readable and machine readable. RSS (Rich Site Summary) is an XML-based format for content distribution that allows users to access to online content. It is used by news provider, blog sites and podcast to share new content with the users. Users can subscribe to websites that use RSS feeds to take updated information. Both RSS and JSON are the program-readable formats of data. Web publishers make these feeds, so their content will be easily accessible for re-use. The difference between RSS and JSON really lie in how they are parsed. Although they are both strings (RSS is essentially just plain-text XML), JSON is far lighter-weight than RSS. In this work, JSON format is preferred to take the information from API's. JSON has been developed on the fact that the XML is large and slow when exchanging data. The structure of JSON, which is very similar to XML, is that the main purpose is to send and receive data in smaller sizes while exchanging data. JSON is even faster and more practical than XML. It can be used effectively in all programming languages like XML. JSON is lightweight and takes up less space than XML files.

2.3 tPacketCapture Pro and Wireshark

tPacketCapture Pro [12] and Wireshark [13] programs are used to finding a news source that supplies the news feeds in JSON format. tPacketCapture allows users to collect data packets without root authority. tPacketCapture uses the VPN Service supported by Android. The collected data is saved in external storage in pcap format.

Wireshark is the world's leading network protocol analysis program. It allows you to see what is on your network at the microscopic level. It is the legal standard in many institutional and educational institutions. The development of Wireshark is made possible by network experts from around the world.

2.4 Smart Device Link and Ford Applink

SmartDeviceLink (SDL) [14] is a standard protocol and message set for connecting smartphones to in-vehicle infotainments systems. First, AppLink was developed by a team at Ford Motor Company to interface telephony applications with the tools. Later, Ford released this software as an open source and was born this way.

AppLink is the Ford brand that uses the SDL technology. It is set of APIs that supply the ability for mobile application developers to extend the command and control of an application to the in-vehicle Human Machine Interface (HMI).

SDL uses a common language to allow the two devices to talk to each other. It enables that the user interacts with the in-vehicle interfaces like the touch screen, voice recognition, steering controls, and various vehicle buttons.

The SDL ecosystem consists of three main components:

- Core Component: A core component is a software that vehicle manufacturers install in their vehicle head units. This software enables their head units to have access to various smartphone applications.
- SDL Server: Optional SDL Server is used by vehicle OEMs to collect usage information from connected applications and to update the application policies.
- Libraries: The iOS and Android libraries are implemented by app developers into their applications to enable command and control via the connected head unit.

SDL is an open-source library and allows everyone to access and contribute to it. SDL Consortium, Inc. (SDLC) was established for this. SDLC membership is open to developers, OEMs, and suppliers that want to work with SDL.

2.5 SYNC Technology

Ford SYNC is an integrated in-car communication and entertainment system that allows users to make hands-free phone calls, control music, and perform voice commands and other functions. It is composed of both Ford and other third-party applications and user interfaces.

Ford SYNC's first two versions was running on WEA (Windows Embedded Automotive) operating system which is developed by Microsoft. Ford SYNC 3, the latest version is running on QNX operating system designed by BlackBerry Ltd.

The SYNC computer is called as Accessory Protocol Interface Module (APIM) by Ford. It is hosted separately from the head unit that is named as the Audio Control Module (ACM). Also, it interfaces with all vehicle audio sources as well as the high-speed and medium-speed vehicle CAN-buses.

SYNC 1.0 is a system that is activated with voice and works via Bluetooth with mobile phones or portable media players. The users must give permission to SYNC 1.0 to reach the contacts to make phone calls and answer the incoming calls. After the required connections set, users can call someone who is on their contact list with a simple voice command. Also, SYNC alerts the driver with a special tone, when a text message received by mobile phone. A notification appears on the screen such as "New Messages from <Name>". To listen to the message, users can click the "Listen" button on the screen.

SYNC 1.1 is the updated version of SYNC 1.0. AppLink feature is added. Applink offers the ability to access and control the favorite applications on smartphones via using voice commands, buttons on the steering wheel, or the center console display. The applications must be compatible with AppLink to be used on SYNC. Android devices can connect to SYNC via Bluetooth, for IOS devices USB cable is required.

SYNC 2 is the second version of Ford SYNC. In this version, the touchscreen feature is introduced. Users can make phone calls, control the music or change climate settings with voice command or by using the touchscreen. It also contains voice navigation. In navigation, users can add a destination point with one touch or call POI with voice command. It can show the most efficient route in terms of fuel.

SYNC 3 is the latest version of Ford SYNC technology shown in Fig. 1. It has 8″ touchscreen which is supporting zoom in and zoom out movements. Apart from being compatible with AppLink, it has a feature to connect to Apple CarPlay. It is 10 times faster than SYNC 2. Another significant feature of SYNC 3 is that it has more powerful sound detection than the old versions. Users can access the catalog of the mobile applications which can access Ford SYNC with AppLink on Ford's websites.

In the next section, the implementation of the news reader is given based on the development phases shown in Fig. 2.

Fig. 1. SYNC 3

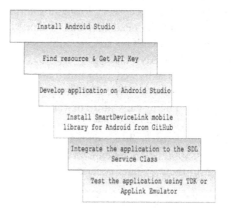

Fig. 2. Development phases.

3   Design and Implementation

Figure 3 presents the use cases of the proposed news reader application where weather and location information together with the news from different sources can be retrieved on both Android smartphone and SYNC.

The most popular news sources in Turkey are Milliyet and Hürriyet. To reach Hürriyet's news, its public API can be found. While examining the API, it is observed that the responses of API are in JSON Object format and desired news can be returned. It also observed that Hürriyet rarely sends some news that has no description. At the development part, with a filtering operation is implemented to hide such news.

On the other hand, the source of Milliyet news is provided as RSS feeds and does not have an API. A different approach has been tried to reach Milliyet news. Milliyet has RSS feeds on her site. However, in order to access these resources in JSON format, tPacketCapture Pro application is installed on an Android-based phone, where Milliyet's mobile application is listened to. The resulting capture file has been transferred to the computer. This file is then opened using the Wireshark program and filtered using the HTTP GET method. A link is found after the filtering. This link provides Milliyet's news in JSON format. Lastly, to hide the news that has no details, implementing same filtering operation here is also implemented.

The application is developed in two stages. As the first stage, a mobile application is developed in Android Studio IDE. Secondly, it is then integrated into AppLink and made compatible with SYNC 3. SDL Android library is imported to code and SDL Service class is modified.

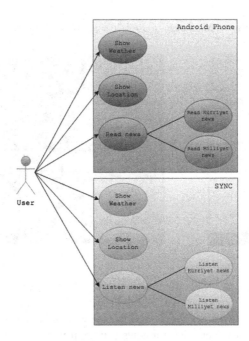

Fig. 3. Use case diagram

On the main page, the user is provided with current weather and location information. On the rear panel, the current information of the exact longitude and latitude is checked without stopping. Every 10 s an OpenWeatherMap API query is being thrown. In this way, when the driver changes position while driving, current weather information will be available on this main screen.

In Fig. 4a, mobile side of the application is shown, where as "TEXT_AND_SOFT-BUTTONS_WITH_GRAPHIC" layout is used on the main page of the SYNC Screen and it is shown in Fig. 4b. Note that there are fifteen different available SYNC layouts.

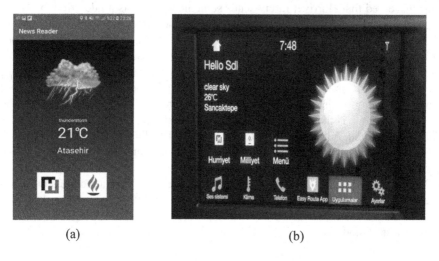

(a)   (b)

Fig. 4. Main page (a) Mobile side, (b) SYNC side.

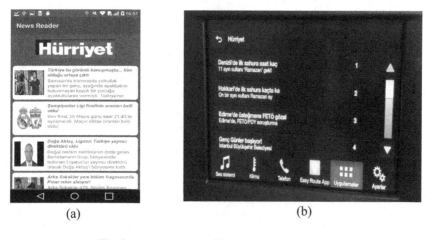

(a)   (b)

Fig. 5. News list (a) Mobile side, (b) SYNC side.

The user is offered two news source options. News sources are shown as buttons on the main screen. When a user selects a news source, it is presented as a list of the 10 news to users. These lists contain up-to-date news from all categories. The news list pages of mobile side and SYNC side are shown in Fig. 5a and b.

After a news is selected from the list, user can read the news from mobile side. On the SYNC side, if the news is selected by clicking or voice commands, SYNC narrator starts to read the details of the news. The full content of the news is shown only in the mobile side, not in SYNC side. Because the purpose of the application is not to let the driver read the news while driving, but to listen. The mobile side news details page is shown in Fig. 6a. The news detail page on SYNC is shown in Fig. 6b and the news is delivered via narrator. The pseudocode of retrieving news from a source is presented in Fig. 7.

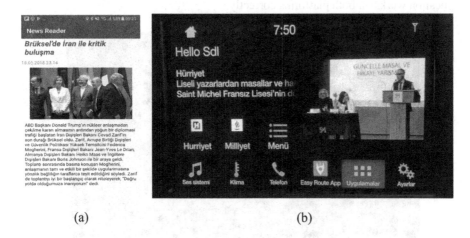

(a)   (b)

Fig. 6. News details (a) Mobile side, (b) SYNC side.

```
set counter to zero
start timer
for every 30 seconds
     request to NewspaperAPI
     for k=1 to (10+counter)
          extract pictureURL from response
          extract title from response
          extract description from response
          extract createdDate from response
          if length of description == 0
               counter ++
          else
               create news item
```

Fig. 7. Pseudocode for news retrieval.

4 Tests and Results

To evaluate the performance of the news reader application, the arrival time of the news after the news publication is measured for 10 different times. The average arrival time of the news after its publication is measured between 3 to 5 s. Secondly, the voice command recognition test has been successfully done where a voice command is recognized in less than 3 s. In addition, a voice command execution is usually realized in about 2.5 s.

As shown in Fig. 8, the weather, location, and news have been transferred properly to both SYNC screen and the smartphone successfully and our proposed news reader application works on both platforms correctly.

Fig. 8. News reader application running on both SYNCH and phone.

5 Conclusion

In this work, an Android-based mobile application has been developed. This application uses JSON feed of many websites of national newspapers. Therefore, users can access updates from various newspapers in one place instead of visiting them separately. It provides saving on time to users.

The significant difference of this application is that it allows users to listen to news from the SYNC Screen while driving without distraction. Ford AppLink is a product that is built by the SmartDeviceLink platform to communicate between applications running on a smartphone and SYNC in-vehicle software. Our news reader application is AppLink compliant so that it can be connected to a SYNC 3 AppLink compatible car and it recognizes and executes the saved commands that exist in the implementation.

In the future, new news sources or blog sites that provide RSS or JSON feeds may be added to this application, according to the user's interest. Thus, the driver can listen to the desired content on the road at any time.

References

1. Mobile Phone Use: A growing problem of driver distraction. http://www.who.int/violence_injury_prevention/publications/road_traffic/distracted_driving_summary.pdf. Accessed 19 May 2018
2. Oviedo-Trespalacios, O., Haqueb, M., King, M., Washington, S.: Understanding the impacts of mobile phone distraction on driving performance: a systematic review. Transp. Res. Part C Emerg. Technol. **72**, 360–380 (2016)
3. MirrorLink Homepage. https://mirrorlink.com/. Accessed 20 May 2018
4. Apple CarPlay. https://www.apple.com/ios/carplay/. Accessed 20 May 2018
5. Android Auto. https://www.android.com/auto/. Accessed 20 May 2018
6. Xin, Z., Yan, C., Taoying, L.: The design and implementation of news reader based on RSS technology. In: Proceedings of the 7th IEEE Software Engineering and Service Science (ICSESS), pp. 576–579, Beijing (2016)
7. Svyatoslav, V.: RSS Reader. Google Play (2017). https://play.google.com/store/apps/details?id=com.madsvyat.simplerssreader. Accessed 20 May 2018
8. Pinenuts Android Developers: Fast News. Google Play (2018). https://play.google.com/store/apps/details?id=it.pinenuts.rassegnastampa&hl=en. Accessed 20 May 2018
9. Ford Motor Company: n-tv.de. Der Ford App Katalog (2018). https://secure.ford.de/Rund-um-den-Service/Ford-SYNC/App-Katalog/. Accessed 20 May 2018
10. Ford Motor Company: wetter.de. Der Ford App Katalog (2018). https://secure.ford.de/Rund-um-den-Service/Ford-SYNC/App-Katalog/. Accessed 20 May 2018
11. Ford Motor Company: Ford+Alexa. Google Play (2018). https://play.google.com/store/apps/details?id=com.ford.fordalexa&hl=en. Accessed 20 May 2018
12. tPacketCapture Pro: Google Play. https://play.google.com/store/apps/details?id=jp.co.taosoftware.android.packetcapturepro&hl=en. Accessed 20 May 2018
13. Wireshark. https://www.wireshark.org/. Accessed 20 May 2018
14. SDL. https://www.smartdevicelink.com/. Accessed 20 May 2018

Mobile Applications Used in Multiple Sclerosis

Blanka Klimova[✉]

University of Hradec Kralove, Rokitanskeho 62, Hradec Kralove, Czech Republic
blanka.klimova@uhk.cz

Abstract. Multiple sclerosis (MS) is a chronic neurological disease. It is characterized by inflammatory damage to central nervous system structures and neurodegenerative brain changes. Although early diagnostics and consequent pharmacological treatment can slow down MS progression, maintain long-term functionality of patients, and prevent permanent damage to their nerve structures, the disease itself cannot be fully cured. Therefore, apart from the traditional pharmacological therapies, alternative strategies to the improvement of MS symptoms are applied. Most recently, with the emergences of modern technologies, mobile devices and applications started to be used by MS patients. The purpose of this article is to discuss the mobile applications (apps) used in MS and summarize their benefits and limitations for MS patients. The methods used in this study include a literature review of available sources found in the world's acknowledged databases Web of Science, Scopus, and PubMed, as well as the methods of comparison and evaluation of the findings from the selected studies. The results indicate that mobile apps can serve as appropriate self-management tools for MS patients. Their benefits, such as reliability, cost-effectiveness, or improvement of symptoms, as well as patients' awareness of these advantages make mobile apps useful and motivating tools in the fight with MS. However, more research should be conducted in the area of the efficacy on the use of mobile apps by people with MS. Currently, there are no evidence-based studies on this topic.

Keywords: Mobile apps · Multiple sclerosis · Benefits · Limitations

1   Introduction

Multiple sclerosis (MS) is an immunopathological disease characterized by inflammatory damage to central nervous system structures and neurodegenerative brain changes [1]. It is a serious illness whose prevalence is rising globally and affects especially younger people at the age of 20–40 years. Currently, about 2.3 million people worldwide suffer from this disease [2].

The disease usually occurs with sensory (46%), visual (33%), cerebral (30%) and motor (26%) symptoms [3]. Common MS symptoms include sensitivity disorders, visual disturbances, weakness of limbs, vertigo, fatigue, sexual and sphincter problems, pain, mood disorders, cognitive decline, or walking disorder [4]. Although early diagnostics and consequent pharmacological treatment can slow down MS progression, maintain long-term functionality of patients, and prevent permanent damage to their nerve structures, the disease itself cannot be fully cured. MS is a long-term and debilitating disease

© Springer International Publishing AG, part of Springer Nature 2018
M. Younas et al. (Eds.): MobiWIS 2018, LNCS 10995, pp. 30–37, 2018.
https://doi.org/10.1007/978-3-319-97163-6_3

associated with a reduced quality of life and a very high socio-economic impact. Economic costs are not only associated with basic treatment, but they are also indirect costs associated with early and high unemployment rates. [5].

Therefore, to reduce economic and social burden of both patients and, in more severe cases, their caregivers, there are certain recommended supporting therapies, which can maintain patients' quality of life, such as a diet. Most recently, with the emergence of modern technologies, mobile devices and applications started to be used by MS patients, as well as by their caregivers. For example, smartphones with appropriate MS patient applications can support patient adherence to treatment.

The purpose of this article is to discuss the mobile applications (apps) used in MS and summarize their benefits and limitations for MS patients.

2   Methods

The methods include a literature review of available sources found on the research topic in Web of Science, Scopus, and PubMed. The searched keyword collocations were *mobile technologies* AND *multiple sclerosis*; *mobile apps* AND *multiple sclerosis*. In addition, websites on the use of mobile apps by MS patients were also checked. The search was not limited by any period because there were not many findings on the research topic. The author of this article has discovered that most of the mobile apps are now available for patients with diabetes (cf. [6]). For example, the keyword search in PubMed generated 375 studies on the use of mobile apps for diabetes [6] and only 10 studies on the use of mobile apps for multiple sclerosis [7]. As Giunti, Guisado-Fernandez, and Caulfield [8] state, their review, published in 2017, on the commercially available mobile apps for people with MS was the first one.

The author also used methods of comparison and evaluation of the findings from the selected relevant studies.

3   Results and Their Discussion

As it has been stated above, there have not been many studies on the research topic. Nevertheless, the findings from these rare research studies can be grouped into three main areas, which describe:

1. commercially available mobile apps;
2. pilot studies on the real use of mobile apps by MS patients;
3. attitude of MS patients to mobile technologies and apps.

3.1 Commercially Available Apps

Recent surveys [8, 9] state that there are about 25 mobile apps suitable for MS patients. Most of them uses the Android MS operating system and is accessible through iTunes and Google Play stores. These detected mobile apps can be divided according to their functionality. The most numerous apps are the mobile apps dealing with disease and treatment (70%). These are then followed by disease management apps (25%) and the least numerous group contains the apps aimed at awareness raising and support (5%) [8].

Probably the most popular mobile app out of these commercially available apps seems to be SymTrac™ MS (Fig. 1). This smartphone app allows to record anytime, anywhere patient symptoms, troubles, feelings with MS, their intensity and frequency. It enables to keep an overview of the medications the patient uses, and the patient's application indicates when to take the medicine. It also brings graphically illustrated exercises for different groups of difficulty with MS. The recorded data can be viewed at any time and then consulted with a physician at the MS center [10].

Fig. 1. Mobile app SymTrac™ MS [11]

There are also very specialized mobile apps. One of such mobile apps is called MS Compass+ (Fig. 2). This app is intended for the MS patients treated with copaxone. It recalls the use of the drug and provides advice on the place of injection. The mobile phone can therefore teach a patient with MS how to apply a drug injection and reminds him or her when it is time to administer the drug. In addition, it shows the most appropriate places on the body to apply the drug, and allows the patient to run an application diary. This application was produced by the company Pears Health Cyber and it is marketed by TEVA [12].

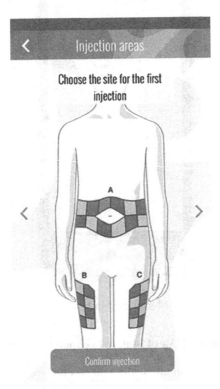

Fig. 2. Mobile app MS Compass+ [12]

One of the most common symptoms of MS is fatigue. It is typical of 90% of MS patients [13, 14]. Therefore, there are also specialized mobile apps, which help alleviate this symptom. One of them MS Energise app (Fig. 3), developed by a New Zealander team (cf. [14]), uses cognitive behavioral therapy (CBT) principles to help patients self-manage the fatigue they experience as a result of their condition. It consists of seven modules that patient work their way through over time, with a focus on learning new information, and interacting with the app to gain new tools to apply in day-to-day life. The app also allows patients to track their progress and record future plans [15].

Fig. 3. Mobile app MS Energise [16]

3.2 Pilot Studies on the Real Use of Mobile Technologies and Apps by MS Patients

Although there is a number of commercially available mobile apps on the current market [17], the author of this article detected only two pilot studies, which were targeted at testing these apps among MS patients. Greiner et al. [18] in their study conducted an experiment with 42 MS patients who in the course of six weeks completed weekly health reports via MSdialog. Majority of patients considered this electronic record of MSdialog very useful and they were very satisfied with it. In addition, they were highly motivated to use MSdialog because it helped them remember what to mention to their doctor.

The second pilot study by Tacchino et al. [19] focused on the use of COGNI-TRAcK app, which promotes intensive and personalized cognitive rehabilitation, based on working memory exercises, and should contribute to the improvement of cognitive status among MS patients. This app was tested with 16 cognitively impaired MS patients during an 8-week at-home intervention. The intervention consisted of five daily scheduled 30-min sessions per week. The adherence to the treatment was 84%. Out of the patients with MS, 94% comprehended the provided instructions, 100% were able to use it on their own at home, 75% liked the exercises, and 81% found the exercises useful and were motivated to use the app again. Moreover, during the exercises, patients with MS were highly motivated to perform well, experienced rather low levels of stress, were not bored, and felt amusement.

3.3 Attitude of MS Patients to Mobile Technologies and Apps

A few detected studies also explored the attitude of MS patients towards the use of mobile technologies and apps. As the study by Haase et al. [20] shows, MS patients use modern technologies. About 90% of all surveyed MS patients used a personal computer and the Internet at least once a week, 87% used email, and 85.6% communicated by mobile phone. When they were asked about their comfort with using electronic communication methods for communication with healthcare providers, 20.5% accepted communication by mobile Internet application or short message service via mobile phone, 41.0% by websites, 54.3% by email service, and 67.8% by at least one type of electronic communication. Furthermore, those, who scheduled appointments with their mobile phones, would also use a mobile app in future.

Another study by Winberg et al. [21] reports that their subjects used mobile apps in the same way as persons without disabilities. The main disadvantages in the exploitation of mobile apps were patients' impairments and trustworthiness. As they suggest, both these aspects could be diminished by a tailored-made design of the mobile app as well as relevant training. Nevertheless, all participants found the use of mobile apps supportive and motivating.

The numerous usability problems with current mobile touchscreen interfaces were also confirmed in the study by Ruzic and Sanford [9].

Figure 4 below then summarizes the main benefits and limitations of the use of mobile apps by MS patients.

Benefits	Limitations
• increased motivation and awareness • reduced treatment costs • reduction of stress • improvement of symptoms • improved disease self-management • reliability • no side efffects	• patients' impairments • trustworthiness • usability problems • a lack of training

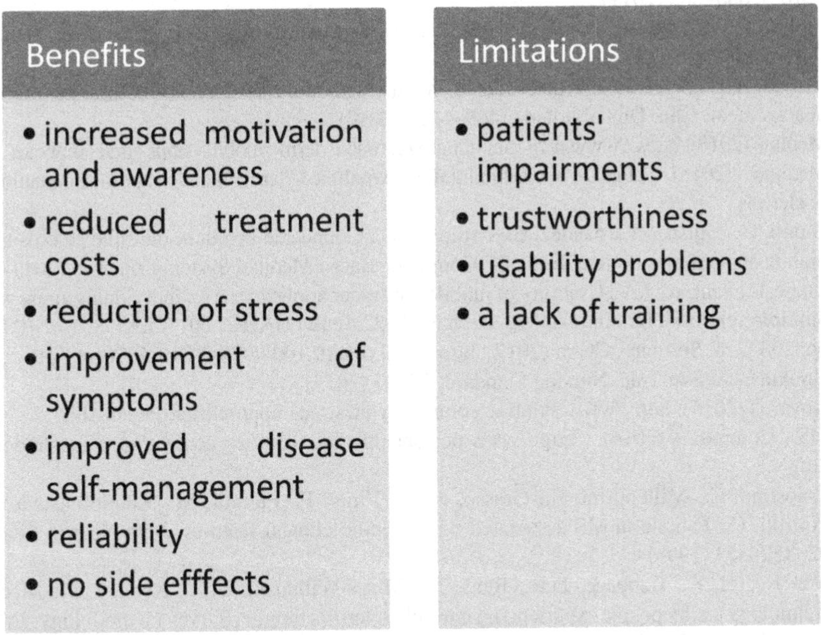

Fig. 4. Key benefits and limitations of the use of mobile apps by MS patients (author's own processing)

4   Conclusion

In conclusion, mobile apps can serve as appropriate self-management tools for MS patients. Their benefits, such as reliability, cost-effectiveness, or improvement of symptoms, as well as patients' awareness of these advantages make mobile apps a useful and motivating tool in the fight with MS.

However, more research should be conducted in the area of the efficacy on the use of mobile apps by people with MS. Currently, there are no evidence-based studies on this topic.

Acknowledgments. This article is supported by the SPEV project 2104/2018, run at the Faculty of Informatics and Management, University of Hradec Kralove, Czech Republic. The author thanks Josef Toman for his help with the data collection.

References

1. Krejsek, J.: Novinky v patogenezi roztroušené sklerózy. Co je skryto za disabilitou pacientů s RS, Remedia, S2-4 (2014)
2. National Multiple Sclerosis Society (2017). https://www.nationalmssociety.org/What-is-MS/Who-Gets-MS
3. Santos, E.C., Yokota, M., Dias, N.F.: Multiple sclerosis: study of patients with relapsing-remitting form registered at minas gerais secretary of state for health. Arq. Neuropsiquiatr. **3B**(65), 885–888 (2011)
4. Frohman, T.C., Castro, W.: Symptomatic therapy in multiple sclerosis. Ther. Adv. Neurol. Disord. **4**, 83–98 (2011)
5. Graves, J., Balcer, L.J.: Eye disorders in patients with multiple sclerosis: natural history and management. Clin. Opthalmol. **4**, 1409–1422 (2010)
6. Medline (2018). https://www.ncbi.nlm.nih.gov/pubmed/?term=mobile+apps+and+diabetes
7. Medline (2018). https://www.ncbi.nlm.nih.gov/pubmed/?term=mobile+apps+and+multiple+sclerosis
8. Giunti, G., Guisado-Fernandez, E., Caulfield, B.: Connected health in multiple sclerosis: A mobile applications review. In: IEEE Computer-Based Medical Systems, pp. 1–6 (2017)
9. Ruzic, L., Sanford, J.A.: Usability of mobile consumer applications for individuals aging with multiple sclerosis. In: Antona, M., Stephanidis, C. (eds.) UAHCI 2017. LNCS, vol. 10277, pp. 258–276. Springer, Cham (2017). https://doi.org/10.1007/978-3-319-58706-6_21
10. Hopkins, G.: SymTrac, Nursing Standard, **29**, 33 (2015)
11. Novartis (2015). http://www.symtrac.com/ms/symtrac-ms-app/multiple_sclerosis1/
12. MS Compass + (2016). http://www.pearshealthcyber.com/wp-content/rskompas/index2.html
13. Colosimo, C., Millefiorini, E., Grasso, M.G., Vinci, F., Fiorelli, M., Koudriavtseva, T., Pozzilli, C.: Fatigue in MS associated with specific clinical features. Acta Neurol. Scand. **92**, 352–353 (1995)
14. Van Kessel, K., Babbage, D.R., Reay, N., Miner-Williams, W.M., Kersten, P.: Mobile technology use by people experiencing multiple sclerosis fatigue: Survey methodology. JMIR Mhealth Uhealth **5**(2), e6 (2017)
15. New fatigue fighting tool offers MS patients hope (2018). http://www.news.aut.ac.nz/news/2017/september/new-fatigue-fighting-tool-offers-ms-patients-hope

16. MS Energise (2018). https://msenergise.com/
17. The best multiple sclerosis apps of the year (2018). https://www.healthline.com/health/multiple-sclerosis/top-iphone-android-apps
18. Greiner, P., Sawka, A., Imison, E.: Patient and physician perspectives on MSdialog, an electronic PRO diary in multiple sclerosis. Patient **8**(6), 541–550 (2015)
19. Tacchino, A., Pedullà, L., Bonzano, L., Vassallo, C., Battaglia, M.A., Mancardi, G., Bove, M., Brichetto, G.: A new app for at-home cognitive training: Description and pilot testing on patients with multiple sclerosis. JMIR Mhealth Uhealth **3**(3), e85 (2015)
20. Haase, R., Schultheiss, T., Kempcke, R., Thomas, K., Ziemssen, T.: Use and acceptance of electronic communication by patients with multiple sclerosis: a multicenter questionnaire study. J. Med. Internet Res. **14**(5), e135 (2012)
21. Winberg, C., Kylberg, M., Pettersson, C., Harnett, T., Hedvall, P.O., Mattsson, T.: Månsson, Lexell, E.: The use of apps for health in persons with multiple sclerosis, Parkinson's disease and stroke - barriers and facilitators. Stud. Health Technol. Inform. **242**, 638–641 (2017)

Prototype of a Smart Google Glass Solution for Deaf (and Hearing Impaired) People

Ales Berger[(✉)] and Filip Maly

Faculty of Informatics and Management, University of Hradec Kralove,
Hradec Kralove, Czech Republic
{ales.berger,filip.maly}@uhk.cz

Abstract. Nowadays (in 2018), we are facing an accelerated development of smart devices. This technological boom is based on rapidly growing software and hardware requirements not only from the users, but also from producers. Statistic results show that every second person in the world will pose a smart phone (i.e., smart mobile device) in 2018. The majority of our society uses these devices for daily purposes, such as communications, work, but there are many other capabilities of these devices to be discovered. One of their best potential represents their utilization for handicapped or sensually impaired people. In this article, the authors present a specialized smart solution developed especially to help people with hearing impairment. Compared to conventional compensating aids, the developed solution connect modern technologies and originality. The aim of the solution is to digitally capture the ambient sound and based on its evaluation using neural networks, to present users needed information in a text form. To accomplish this smart solution, are used modern cloud services and a special smart device – Google Glass (abbreviated GG). These smart goggles offer sensors with the ability to compensate user's disadvantages. In the direction of facilitating the work for hearing impaired people, authors intend to further develop this technology and offer solutions in the following research to make daily life easier for people with hearing impairment.

Keywords: Smart device · Smart solution · Mobile device · Smart phone
Android · Deafness · Google Glass

1 Introduction

The first chapter describes the basic definition of the key words and terms necessary for this research. Firstly, the background and predictions for further development of the Smartphone trends and technologies such Google Glass, are presented. For the year 2017, the number of mobile phone users was forecasted to reach 4.77 billion. The number of mobile phone users in the world, is expected to pass the five billion mark by 2019. Most of the mobile market growth can be attributed to the increasing popularity of smartphones. By 2014, around 38% of all mobile users were smartphone users. By 2018, this number is expected to reach over 50% [1]. Therefore, end users are regularly shifting towards choosing a smart phone as their preferred device. The first term to explain, are

© Springer International Publishing AG, part of Springer Nature 2018
M. Younas et al. (Eds.): MobiWIS 2018, LNCS 10995, pp. 38–47, 2018.
https://doi.org/10.1007/978-3-319-97163-6_4

smart devices. Smart devices are interactive electronic gadgets that understand simple commands sent by users and help in daily activities. Some of the most commonly used smart devices are Smartphones, tablets, smart watches, smart glasses and other personal electronics. While many smart devices are small, portable personal electronics, they are in fact defined by their ability to connect to a network to share and interact remotely. Many TV sets and refrigerators are also therefore considered smart devices [2].

1.1   Google Glass

Project Google Glass represents a futuristic gadget, which can be personalized by using different smartphone's' options and an Internet connection. Glass is a new first-party hardware product designed by Google. Google Glass is a head-mounted computer that sits on a human face very similar to a pair of glasses (resting on the ears and nose). It has a camera, a display, a touchpad (along the right arm), a speaker, and a microphone. The display is projected into a right eye using a prism, and sound is played into an eardrum from above the ear via bone conduction. While Glass looks very different from any other device, it runs an operating system that is now very common: Android OS. We can use this technology of your Smartphone, while not use of your hands. It is a bit like alternative device having software package and every other option that offered in a smartphone. However, the main issue is that it is quicker, wearable and you will be able to use it whereas doing day-to-day activities [3]. Google Glass provides many useful advantages, but the most important is that the GG communicates the request from the user to the computer, then evaluate this request and give back the estimated answer or result. From the users' point of view, the advantage of wearing means that the GG is easily wearable as well as easy to handle and there is a natural voice command language for communication. This smart device also provides quick access to the documents, pictures, photos, videos or maps. The best activities to do with GG are navigation, communication and social media or application tools [4]. The operating system Android, Bluetooth and Wi-Fi technology provide wide range for further development and inter-connection with Smartphone. However, to buy the Google Glass device nowadays is not possible, because the company stopped with their mass production.

Google Glass is widely used by many institutions and companies. Google Glass is currently used by: DHL, Volkswagen, GE, Opel, NSF, Penny Market, KONI, WSC, etc. These companies have found this smart device useful to meet all their recommendations and advantages. These now organize further development in practice and cooperate with other organizations unified in a platform called "GLASS" [5] Thank to this source, the authors found useful application, experience and interesting technical upgrades.

Florida Institute for Human & Machine Cognition
Thanks to the Florida Institute for Human & Machine Cognition (abbreviated IHMC, https://www.ihmc.us/ [6]), the authors have this rare opportunity to explore, evaluate and develop application for this smart device according to their research. University of Hradec Kralove is collaborating with the IHMC; their students can travel to the United States and participate in various projects. In 2015, the first author got into a project where he could use the modern or smart equipment. He got into Google Glass and IHMC

offered him the chance to use this device for his own research. Because of the author's interests in helping people, they have designed a smart solution to help people with hearing impairment (especially for elderly people, who are often struggling with deafness or hearing loss). The Google's Glass used in presenting research was kindly provided for free by IHMC.

2 Deafness and Hearing Loss

Over 5% of the world's population – 360 million people – has disabling hearing loss (328 million adults and 32 million children). Disabling hearing loss refers to hearing loss greater than 40 decibels (dB) in the better hearing ear in adults and a hearing loss greater than 30 dB in the better hearing ear in children. Most people with disabling hearing loss live in low- and middle-income countries. As for elderly people, approximately one third of people over 65 years of age are affected by disabling hearing loss.

The prevalence in this age group is greatest in South Asia, Asia Pacific and sub-Saharan Africa. A person who is not able to hear as well as someone with normal hearing – hearing thresholds of 25 dB or better in both ears – is said to have hearing loss [7]. In 1980, the World Health Organization (abbreviated WHO) published a classification of degrees of hearing impairment. The hearing state is calculated as the average of the audiogram values as frequencies of 500 Hz, 1 000 Hz and 2 000 Hz on a better ear. The resulting average hearing loss is expressed in decibels (dB). The amount of hearing loss, according to the classification from WHO is:

1. Normal hearing (0–25 dB),
2. Light hearing loss (26–40 dB),
3. Moderate hearing impairment (41–60 dB),
4. Heavily damaged hearing (61–80 dB),
5. Very heavy hearing damage to deafness (81 dB and more).

It can affect one ear or both ears and leads to difficulty in hearing conversational speech or loud sounds. 'Hard of hearing' refers to people with hearing loss ranging from mild to severe. People who are hard of hearing usually communicate through spoken language and can benefit from hearing aids, cochlear implants, and other assistive devices as well as captioning. People with more significant hearing losses may benefit from cochlear implants. 'Deaf' people mostly have profound hearing loss, which implies very little or no hearing. They often use sign language for communication [8].

2.1 Impacts of Deafness and Hearing Loss

The physical and psychological impacts of deafness are quite different for every individual impaired person. Deaf people who are without hearing from birth has other problems, then the elderly who struggle with hearing loss in the last phase of their life. These elderlies have spent the whole life with normal hearing, so the loss of hearing can be much more stressful and because of it, they must change their daily living. Because of hearing impairment, impaired person is not able to fully understand the sounds of speech and to hear other sounds from his surroundings [9].

Authors' solution compensates for the complex tool of nature - the human ear. The authors only come closer to the human ear to compensate for the lack of hearing necessary for communication with other people. To further and following research, authors will try to get closer to community of deaf and hearing-impaired people. The secondary output of the research aims at informing and active work with another organization, where authors can already test developed solutions with a specific group of affected (i.e., hearing impaired or deaf) people.

3 Problem Definition

People with hearing impairment cannot live in a standard way because of their problem and communication barriers, but many daily problems must be solved in a quite different way. Hearing impairment can be compensated by various aids that help people to communicate in a great extent. Not all people want to use it, however, due to their feelings by showing their impairment to healthy around them. Elderly people do not recognize their hearing loss in the time that is why they often think that their family members (or other people surrounding them) are whispering or slandering behind their back on purpose. These people are emotionally more frustrated or stressed because they cannot recognize the hearing-loss and feel isolated from a society [10].

Because some people with hearing impairment have a hearing debris, they can use it and then to that use different compensating aids to improve their reception of sounds. Hard-of-hearing have useful hearing debris and they often use different compensating aids, such as hearing aids, to improve the reception of sounds. This group of hearing impaired people is, however, considerably inconsistent, as the amount of hearing loss may vary considerably from person to person. One hearing impaired person can understand the spoken word even in a busy environment, another one has a tiny noise in the environment and he cannot understand anything at all. Some of them often, hear the spoken word and they receive the information from a combination of tapping and reading. With hearing impaired people, it is possible to communicate without troubles in a written form. Hearing impaired people often use paper or smartphone to tape the communication flow to a hearing person [11]. In addition, communication is likely to be a particularly important issue for deaf or blind people, due to the significance of hearing for communication by non-disabled people, leading to possible barriers, exclusion, and isolation. The fact that many deaf people need support with communication, access to information, and mobility gives rise to the risk that other people may with the best of intentions act as gatekeepers and reduce the control deafblind people have over their own lives, making independence an important issue for them [12].

3.1 Current State and Solution – Simultaneous Speech Transcription of Spoken Czech

Nowadays, there are several companies that offer simultaneous speech transcription. Compared to English, the Czech language is quite demanding and hard to recognize. Simultaneous speech transcription of spoken Czech is provided with a help of trained transcriber, who is writing everything on the computer or notebook [13]. The text appears on the screen or on a board or tablet. By reading the transcribed text, a person with hearing impairment acquires needed information by sight, a sense more accessible to people than listening to spoken speech. This solution is almost immediate, it is only dependent on the speed of the transcriber and the second disadvantage is that you need a normal hearing person (i.e., transcriber). The authors' research aims on the effective use of the GG, as it is an innovative device and it is very promising for further development (thanks to the fact that is quite new, full of technology and not entirely explored).

3.2 Evaluation of Google Glass Technology

The first phase of the article is to analyze and evaluate main technical possibilities of Google Glass (such as memory, processor and operating system). This process is crucial to find all positive as well as negative characteristics of GG and work with them in author's research. The analysis can help us to find the best solution for deaf people. The second output of the evaluation is to decide about the utilization of GG or find another way (device or architecture). The results of the evaluation can be usable, not usable or usable with limits.

The second part of the analysis is based on development experience with GG device. Here is the main aim to find out more data to decide the best GG usability for deaf (or hearing impaired) people. Further development of this version GG is quite limited and very dependent on a connection with a smart phone. Controlling the whole Google Glass is based on a voice response from the user, where the main controlling word is "OK, Glass...". This short command sentence starts up next voice menu. Google Glass has also a touchpad on the side, which controls other gestures, such as: tap, swipe down (BACK), swipe right, swipe left etc. All these gestures are available for developers to use it (see Table 1). Compared to common Android development it is possible to change a lifecycle of the whole page (Activity). As for GPS module, it is necessary to have your smart phone connected with Google Glass. Otherwise, there is no module for GPS in Glass (or through the Internet) and it is the same case with API, so these are negative characteristics of GG. Internet connection is based on Wi-Fi connection with a smart phone, so this leads to questions about the battery capacity and its limitations. All capacity demanding processes and applications, such as camera control or other actions, are discharging the battery. This feature of the GG is also important for testing. Also, all sensors are working properly without any problem. On the other hand, the most important cons of GG are: noisy environment for utilization, foreign languages and pronunciation problems. Thank to these cons the Google Glass device is marked as usable with limits. Because the GG device can be easily replaced by a smart phone connected to the Internet and smart phones are quite common for most in a today's society.

Table 1. Technical specification (Hard Data conducted by Authors) of used Google Glass

Processor	OMAP 4430 SoC
Memory	1 GB RAM (682 MB available for developers)
Video modes	Mini-projector that uses a semi-transparent prism, 640 × 360 pixels (equivalent to the 25″ screen from a distance of eight feet)
External Memory	16 GB Flash total (12 GB usable memory)
Operating System	Android OS, ver. 4.0.4. (API 19)
Connectivity	Wi-Fi 802.11 b/g & Bluetooth
Sensors	3 axis gyroscopes, accelerometer & magnetometer (compass), ambient world (surrounding) shooting/camera & proximity sensor
Start of mass production	1. For developers (US): February 2013 2. For consumers: 2014

4 Developed Smart Solution

Nowadays, sound recognition offers also public services built on robust neural networks that can instantly convert a recorded audio track of different quality to the text. Therefore, it is not necessary to implement a solution that would not produce such high-quality results. The key element is to prepare a client who can capture the ambient sound, process the acquired data and make it clear to the user again in the form of specific information. Compared to conventional compensation aids, this solution works with modern technology and opens opportunities for improvement and customization. The Cloud Speech API was selected for this research from the Google Cloud Platform. The service offers up to 110 different languages to translate and offers real-time high-quality results [14].

The next figure shows the prototype of designed architecture, which is used for effective communicating between three environments. GG, mobile device as a smart mediator, and neural network server.

Authors's architecture consists of two client parts and one server part (see Fig. 1). Client's parts consist:

1. **Google Glass** device performs as little work as possible and
2. let all **Mobile computing** and complex logic work together.

Due to the low volume of scanned sound data, it is possible to capture sound on Google Glass and stream it through Bluetooth to a connected mobile device. The mobile device communicates with the cloud and receives a response in the form of JSON objects. For every short recording, we get the words that are contained in the recording and the percentage estimate of how much the neural network is certain to be true words. In Google Glass, users only see translated words that they can respond to. Mobile client development for both Google Glass and other mobile devices running Android was in Java.

In addition to new information about current events, it also opens the possibility of storing the history of individual discussions. This path would allow users with memory failures to recall the information they learned during an interview with someone else. The second benefit is data stored of all conversations and discussions. The end user can easily find in his smart phone, what he did not hear or forgot. This feature can significantly help elderly people, who must deal with memory loss in a daily basis.

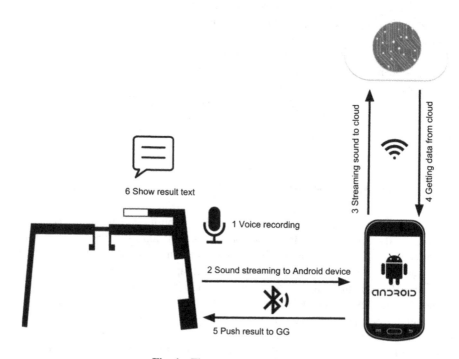

Fig. 1. The prototype architecture

5   Testing the Prototype Architecture

Firstly, authors must design the prototype architecture according to the scheme on Fig. 2. This part was fulfilled during the first pre-testing stage in a functional solution (i.e., prototype architecture is communicating with a server and the information are presented to a user in a satisfactory amount of time. After this goal, authors continued to the key (2nd) phase of the research, which is another real-use testing by deaf or hearing-impaired people. Finishing 2nd phase of research showed quite interesting results. These results are based on the experience, tracking and interviewing about 10 deaf (or hearing impaired) people from the Czech Republic. The majority of these people were satisfied with the results, functioning and the whole idea leading towards their higher independence in communication with a normal hearing people without needing of transcriber or assistant. Data were obtained from the interviews and practical experiment that were carried out as part of a larger research project. The first phase of testing proved that the prototype architecture designed by the authors is functional; however, there are still some aspects to be improved. The most significant pro is that authors' solution can recognize the voice (even with a different pronunciation or accent in a common, noisy environment) and with the help of neural network, this speech is converted into a text.

This transcribed text is then displayed on the GG's display. This means the communication is not interrupted by a transcriber or an assistant, the responses are faster than with a help of another person or paper, etc. Testing was conducted on a smart phone interconnected with a smart phone through Wi-Fi.

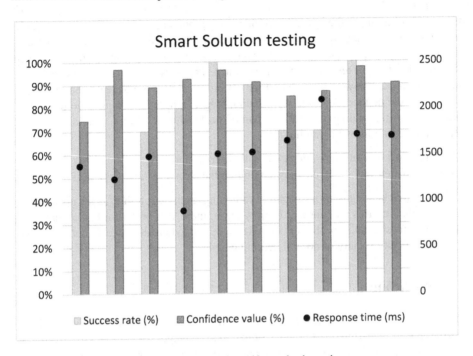

Fig. 2. Results conducted by author's testing

This testing is based on the 10 randomly selected English phrases that, can anyone use in a daily communication in English, such as: "Never mind. Don't give up. You are improving a lot. Let me check. Enjoy your stay with us. What is your key to success?, etc." These sentences were pronounced by a 10 different people with a normal level of hearing (with a different pronunciation and accents) and the correct translation as well as displaying the output of the neural network was tested. The total number of conducted tests proving the level of successful voice recognition and translation is 100 test cases. The level of successful recognition and translation is expressed in percentage terms. On the other hand, authors were also measuring a time in milliseconds (abbr. ms). This time shows the response, i.e. for how long it takes to get a result from the server. During this 100 test cases, authors were also testing a confidence value. The confidence value is an estimate between 0.0 and 1.0. A higher number indicates an estimated greater likelihood that the recognized words are correct. For example, you may use the confidence value to decide whether to show alternative results to the user or ask for confirmation from the user. If the confidence for the top value is high, it's likely correct. Whereas if the confidence in the top value is lower, there is a greater chance that one of the other alternatives is more accurate. Your code should not require the confidence field as it is not guaranteed to be accurate, or even set, in any of the results [15].

For detailed results, please see the Fig. 2. below. The most significant result is that in 85% (85 test cases) the designed solution was successful. Only 15% of cases are wrong, it means that the solution is incorrect in 15 test cases from 100. This success rate of developed solution is quite high and provides very promising results for further research (after a few small improvements). Indicator called "Confidence value" reached a mark 90% that are quite high number for this phase of testing. The average response time is 1515 ms (1st phase of testing), which is not ideal. That is why, the authors are working on improvements (how to save some time) in order to get close to real-time response. The only disadvantage the users were mentioning is a little bit longer time to get the output, so it is important to work on this part of the developed solution. Another possible disadvantage to improve by authors is:

1. Changing a way of communication with a server and,
2. decide which way is the best for passing on the output results to the user.

These two challenges are a key part of following research activities in the near future. After eliminating this and another testing phase, there will be no further obstacles to offer this solution to non-profit deaf organizations and to help deaf people communicate with the majority society of normal hearing people.

6 Conclusion

In this article, the authors present a specialized smart solution developed specially to help people with hearing impairment. Compared to conventional compensating aids, the developed solution connects modern technologies and originality. The aim of the solution is to digitally capture the ambient sound and based on its evaluation using neural networks, to present users needed information in a text form. This aim was successfully accomplished, and smartphone/GG was a well-chosen device for this purpose. However, because GG is no longer produced (and was very expensive) and there is no support for it, it will be necessary to choose another device (e.g., smart phone or other "smart glasses") or makes author's own smart glasses. Today, there are other glasses than GG, for example, Intel provides its own as well as other technological companies. The next step is to take advantage of virtual reality.

Technical evaluation also showed that the Glass technology can be excluded from the prototype architecture and it is possible to replace it with a common smart phone. Therefore, the used version of GG is out of date and works in a very energy-intensive way, has an inefficient microphone and is transferring more data than necessary. The testing success rate of developed solution is quite high and provides very promising results for further research (after a few small improvements). Indicator called "Confidence value" reached a mark 90% that are quite high number for this phase of testing. The average response time is 1515 ms.

Firstly, the next step in this research is the optimization of the developed solution. Secondly, the authors will focus on distinguishing the color of the voice, so that the user can recognize who is speaking and what (during the talk of more than two people). Unexpected utilization of the author's solution is that it can serve the deaf, but also for normal "hearing" people travelling or working abroad who do not understand the foreign language (in the future).

Acknowledgement. This work and the contribution were supported by the project of Students Grant Agency – FIM, University of Hradec Kralove, Czech Republic, no. 2108 "Spatial positioning and visualization". Ales Berger is a student member of the research team.

Thanks to IHMC in Florida and mainly to Niranjan Suri for providing Google Glass device for free, which was very important for our research. The Google Glass device will be also used in the next step of authors' research.

References

1. Statista. Forecast of mobile phone users worldwide. https://www.statista.com/statistics/274774/forecast-of-mobile-phone-users-worldwide/
2. Technopedia. Smart Device. https://www.techopedia.com/definition/31463/smart-device/
3. Holey, P.N., Gaikwad, V.T.: Google glass technology. Int. J. **2**(3) (2014)
4. Berger, A., Vokalova, A., Maly, F., Poulova, P.: Google glass used as assistive technology its utilization for blind and visually impaired people. In: Younas, M., Awan, I., Holubova, I. (eds.) MobiWIS 2017. LNCS, vol. 10486, pp. 70–82. Springer, Cham (2017). https://doi.org/10.1007/978-3-319-65515-4_6
5. Google Developers. Glass Explorer Edition. https://developers.google.com/glass/develop/gdk/quick-start/
6. IHMC. Institute of Human and Machine Cognition Story. https://www.ihmc.us/about/aboutihmc/
7. Shearer, A.E., Hildebrand, M.S., Smith, R.J.H.: Hereditary hearing loss and deafness overview (2017)
8. World Health Organization. Deafness and hearing loss. http://www.who.int/mediacentre/factsheets/fs300/en/
9. Kyle, J.G., Woll, B.: Sign Language: The Study of Deaf People and Their Language. Cambridge University Press, Cambridge (1988)
10. Correia, S., et al.: A stress "deafness" effect in European Portuguese. Lang. Speech **58**(1), 48–67 (2015)
11. Shearer, A.E., et al.: Utilizing ethnic-specific differences in minor allele frequency to recategorize reported pathogenic deafness variants. Am. J. Hum. Genet. **95**(4), 445–453 (2014)
12. Bodsworth, S.M., et al.: Deafblindness and mental health: psychological distress and unmet need among adults with dual sensory impairment. Br. J. Vis. Impair. **29**(1), 6–26 (2011)
13. Berger, A., Maly, F.: Smart solution in social relationships graphs. In: Younas, M., Awan, I., Kryvinska, N., Strauss, C., van Thanh, D. (eds.) MobiWIS 2016. LNCS, vol. 9847, pp. 393–405. Springer, Cham (2016). https://doi.org/10.1007/978-3-319-44215-0_33
14. Google Developers. Cloud Speech API Documentation. https://cloud.google.com/speech/docs/
15. Manzi, A., et al.: Design of a cloud robotic system to support senior citizens: the KuBo experience. Auton. Robot. **41**(3), 699–709 (2017)

Wireless Sensor Networks

Finding Degree Constrained
k-Cardinality Minimum Spanning Trees
for Wireless Sensor Networks

Pablo Adasme$^{(\boxtimes)}$, Ismael Soto, and Fabian Seguel

Departamento de Ingeniería Eléctrica, Universidad de Santiago de Chile,
Avenida Ecuador 3519, Santiago, Chile
{pablo.adasme,ismael.soto,fabian.seguelg}@usach.cl

Abstract. In this paper, we consider the degree constrained k-cardinality minimum spanning tree network problem (k-DCMST). This problem arises as a combination of two classical optimization problems, namely the degree constrained and k-minimum spanning tree problems (Resp. DCMST and k-MST). Let $G(V, E)$ be a connected undirected graph formed with vertex and edge sets V and E, respectively. The DCMST problem asks for a minimum spanning tree where each maximum vertex degree is limited to a certain constant d lower than the cardinality of V minus one whilst the k-MST asks for a minimum spanning sub-tree formed with k nodes chosen from set V. Consequently, the k-DCMST asks for a sub-tree formed with k vertices where each vertex has degree lower than or equal to d. This problem is mainly motivated from the domain of wireless sensor networks where connected backbone sub-tree topologies will be mandatorily required for future technologies in order to connect any network under the internet of things paradigm. Vertex degree constraints arise naturally in order to avoid overloaded nodes in the network. We propose two compact formulations for this problem. More precisely, a Miller-Tucker-Zemlin constrained version and a single flow based formulation that we further strengthen by using the Handshaking lemma and with valid inequalities adapted from the DCMST and dominating tree problems. Numerical results are given for complete and disk graph instances for different degree values. Our preliminary numerical results indicate that the flow based model allows one to obtain optimal solutions in less CPU time for most of the instances.

1 Introduction

Wireless sensor networks have become an important subject of research within last decades and play a key role when designing intelligent systems for real-life applications related with military communications, emergency, medicine, transportation, agriculture, industrial processes, environmental and health monitoring systems, smart buildings and cities, to name a few [25].

In a wireless sensor network, minimizing power consumption is a major challenge and a hot topic research field. This is due to the fact that power is strongly

© Springer International Publishing AG, part of Springer Nature 2018
M. Younas et al. (Eds.): MobiWIS 2018, LNCS 10995, pp. 51–62, 2018.
https://doi.org/10.1007/978-3-319-97163-6_5

related with network lifetime. The lower the power consumed by the network, the larger the network lifetime. Consequently, in the literature several mathematical formulations have been proposed in order to connect optimally a sensor network by means of a tree graph.

Let $G(V, E)$ represent a connected simple undirected graph with set of nodes $V = \{1, \ldots, n\}$ and set of links (edges) $E = \{1, \ldots, m\}$. A tree graph T is an induced subgraph obtained from G where no cycles (loops) do exist and where all nodes are connected with exactly $n - 1$ edges. Two classical tree based optimization problems have been studied in the literature. The degree constrained and the k-minimum spanning tree problems (Resp. DCMST and k-MST). Both have proved to be NP-Hard. The DCMST problem asks for a minimum spanning tree where the maximum vertex degree is limited to a certain constant $d \in \{2, \ldots, n-2\}$ whilst the k-MST asks for a minimum spanning sub-tree formed with at least k nodes out of n. In this paper, mainly motivated by the domain of wireless sensor networks, we consider the degree constrained k-cardinality minimum spanning tree problem (k-DCMST) which arises as a combination of both the DCMST and k-MST problems where a connected sub-tree topology is required from a larger set of nodes. Vertex degree constraints are imposed in order to avoid overloaded nodes in the network. Consequently, the k-DCMST asks for a sub-tree formed with k vertices where each vertex has degree lower than or equal to d. As far as we know, this problem has not been studied in depth in the literature so far. We have recently found only one paper [26] where the authors introduce this problem in order to determine the least weighted spanning tree with exactly k vertices such that except the root vertex, no other vertex in the resulting spanning tree exceeds the specified degree limit in each vertex. In this paper, we consider the more general case of the k-DCMST where all vertices in the resulting subgraph must respect the degree vertex constraint. Without loss of generality, we assume that the cardinality number k is fixed. Notice that the k-DCMST problem can be seen as a generalization of both DCMST and k-MST problems. When $k = n$, k-DCMST reduces to DCMST. Similarly, when $d = n - 1$, k-DCMST reduces to k-MST. Finally, when $k = n$ and $d = n - 1$, k-DCMST reduces to the classical minimum spanning tree problem which can be solved in polynomial time by a greedy algorithm such as Kruskal and/or Prims algorithms [19, 23]. Example applications of wireless sensor networks that can be handled with the k-DCMST problem are directly related for example, with sleep scheduling or density control methods [11, 29]. This is a common strategy that allows to reduce energy consumption in a wireless sensor network and consists of activating or putting into sleep mode some of the nodes of the network while ensuring simultaneously sensing operations, communication and connectivity of active nodes. Sleep scheduling protocols does also allow to handle more efficiently redundant network traffic, packet collisions, and dense network problems together with many other network management problems. For a deeper understanding on sleep scheduling protocols, the reader is referred to the works by [9, 16, 28, 29] and references therein. Notice that all these protocols will be mandatorily required in order to develop future wireless technologies and to connect any sensor network used in any application under the internet of things paradigm [7,10].

In the literature, the DCMST problem has been studied more in depth than the k-MST problem. Intractability of the DCMST problem is proved in [14]. The proof consists of reducing the problem to an equivalent symmetric traveling salesman problem. If the degree of every node is at most $d = 2$, then the problem reduces to a Hamiltonian path problem [14]. Several heuristic and exact methods have been proposed in the literature to solve the DCMST problem including lagrangean relaxations, branch and bound and Branch and cut methods, and meta-heuristics based approaches too [5,8,18,21,27].

On the other side, the k-MST problem was first formulated by Lozovanu and Zelikovsky in 1993 and by Ravi et al. in 1996 [20,24]. In [24], the authors also consider a geometric version of the problem where the input set of vertex points are drawn in a plane. For the particular case where k is fixed, the k-MST problem can be solved in polynomial time by a brute force search algorithm while evaluating all possible k-tuples of vertices. However, for the general case where k is variable, the problem is also NP-hard. The proof consists of a reduction from the Steiner tree problem [20,24]. The best approximation algorithm proposed so far has an approximation ratio of 2 [22]. In particular, if the vertex set is drawn in an Euclidean plane there exists a polynomial time approximation method [6]. Further applications related with the k-MST problem are given in [26].

In this paper, we propose two compact polynomial formulations for the k-DCMST problem. A Miller-Tucker-Zemlin constrained version and a single flow based formulation that we further strengthen by using the Handshaking lemma and with valid inequalities adapted from the DCMST and dominating tree problems [1–3,8,13]. All the proposed models are formulated as mixed integer linear programming (MILP) problems.

The remaining of the paper is organized as follows. In Sect. 2, we present the new compact formulations with and without valid inequalities. Subsequently, in Sect. 3, we conduct preliminary numerical results in order to compare all the proposed models. Finally, in Sect. 4 we give the main conclusions of the paper.

2   Problem Formulation

In this section, we present two compact formulations for the k-DCMST problem in the form of MILPs. Subsequently, we reformulate the initial compact models while using the Handshaking lemma and adding valid inequalities adapted from the DCMST and dominating tree problems [2,3,8,13].

2.1   MILP Models

In order to present a first MILP model, let $H(V, A)$ represent a directed graph obtained from $G(V, E)$ where each element $(i, j) \in E$ is replaced by the two arcs

(i, j) and $(j, i) \in A$. Our first MILP model can thus be written as

$$P_1: \quad \min_{\{x,u,z\}} \sum_{(i,j)\in A} P_{ij} z_{ij} \tag{1}$$

$$\text{s.t.} \quad \sum_{j\in V} x_j = k \tag{2}$$

$$\sum_{(i,j)\in A} z_{ij} = k - 1 \tag{3}$$

$$u_i \leq k, \quad \forall i \in V \tag{4}$$

$$u_i \geq 1, \quad \forall i \in V \tag{5}$$

$$\sum_{l|(l,j)\in A} z_{lj} \leq x_j, \quad \forall j \in V \tag{6}$$

$$u_i - u_j \geq 1 - k(1 - z_{ji}), \quad \forall (i,j) \in A \tag{7}$$

$$\sum_{l|(l,j)\in A} z_{lj} + \sum_{l|(j,l)\in A} z_{jl} \leq dx_j, \quad \forall j \in V \tag{8}$$

$$\sum_{l|(l,j)\in A} z_{lj} + \sum_{l|(j,l)\in A} z_{jl} \geq x_j, \quad \forall j \in V \tag{9}$$

$$x \in \{0,1\}^n, z \in \{0,1\}^{n^2}, u \in [0,\infty]^n \tag{10}$$

where the total power consumption of the network is minimized in (1). For this purpose, we define the input symmetric matrix $P = (P_{ij})$ for each $(i,j) \in A$ where P_{ij} denotes the amount of power to be consumed between nodes $i, j \in V$. Similarly, we define the binary variable z_{ij} to be equal to one if the arc $(i,j) \in A$ is in the solution of the resulting sub-tree. Constraints (2) and (3) ensure that exactly k nodes must belong to the resulting sub-tree and that the number of arcs must be equal to $k - 1$, respectively. To this end, we define the binary variable x_j used in constraint (2) for each $j \in V$, where $x_j = 1$ if and only if node j is in the solution, and $x_j = 0$ otherwise. Next, constraints (4)−(7) ensure that the resulting sub-graph must not contain sub-tours [2]. In particular, constraints (6) impose the condition that each node cannot have more than one incoming arc if it belongs to the solution. Similarly, the constraints (8)−(9) ensure that each node cannot have more than $d \in \{2, \ldots, n-2\}$ incoming and outgoing arcs from it only if it is part of the solution. These are the degree constraints related with the classical DCMST problem. Finally, constraints (10) are domain constraints for the decision variables.

Similarly, a single flow based formulation for the k-DCMST problem can be written as follows

$$P_2: \quad \min_{\{x,z,f,y\}} \sum_{(i,j)\in A} P_{ij} z_{ij}$$

$$\text{s.t.} \quad \sum_{j\in V} x_j = k$$

$$\sum_{(i,j)\in A} z_{ij} = k - 1$$

$$\sum_{l|(l,j)\in A} f_{lj} - \sum_{l|(j,l)\in A} f_{jl} = x_j - ky_j, \quad \forall j \in V \tag{11}$$

$$x_j \geq y_j, \quad \forall j \in V \tag{12}$$

$$f_{ij} \leq (k-1)z_{ij}, \quad \forall (i,j) \in A \tag{13}$$

$$\sum_{j\in V} y_j = 1 \tag{14}$$

$$\sum_{l|(l,j)\in A} z_{lj} + \sum_{l|(j,l)\in A} z_{jl} \leq dx_j, \quad \forall j \in V$$

$$\sum_{l|(l,j)\in A} z_{lj} + \sum_{l|(j,l)\in A} z_{jl} \geq x_j, \quad \forall j \in V$$

$$x, y \in \{0,1\}^n, z \in \{0,1\}^{n^2}, f \in [0,\infty]^{n^2} \tag{15}$$

We prove the correctness of formulation P_2 in the following proposition.

Proposition 1. *P_2 allows to obtain a feasible solution for the k-DCMST problem.*

Proof. First, notice that constraints (11) and (13) act as flow constraints [4]. For this purpose, we define the additional binary variable y_j being equal to one if and only if node $j \in V$ represents the root node. In particular, the right hand side in constraint (11) equals one if and only if variables $x_j = 1$ and $y_j = 0$, which means node $j \in V$ is not the root node. On the opposite, if $x_j = 1$ and $y_j = 1$, then node $j \in V$ is the root node. Next, if $x_j = 0$, then $y_j = 0$ which is implied by the constraint (12). Finally, notice that the constraint (14) implies that a unique root node must exist. This concludes the proof.

2.2 Strengthened MILP Formulations

In this subsection, we obtain strengthened MILP formulations for P_1 and P_2 while incorporating valid inequalities and reformulations that we adapt from the DCMST and dominating tree problems [2,3,8]. For this purpose, we define the sets $N_{(j)}^- = \{i|(i,j) \in A\}$, $N_{(j)}^+ = \{i|(j,i) \in A\}$, $N_{(j)} = N_{(j)}^- \cup N_{(j)}^+$, and $N_{[j]} = N_{(j)} \cup \{j\}$. Subsequently, by using the well known Handshaking lemma which states that the sum of the degrees of all vertices in a finite undirected graph equals twice the number of edges and a strengthened version of the Miller-Tucker-Zemlin constrained modelling approach [2,12], we arrive at the following reformulation of P_1 [2,8,12,13,15].

$$P_1^s: \quad \min_{\{x,u,z,\delta\}} \sum_{(i,j)\in A} P_{ij} z_{ij}$$

$$\text{s.t.} \sum_{j\in V} x_j = k$$

$$u_i \leq k x_i, \quad \forall i \in V \tag{16}$$

$$u_i \geq x_i, \quad \forall i \in V \tag{17}$$

$$\sum_{l|(l,j)\in A} z_{lj} \leq x_j, \quad \forall j \in V$$

$$u_i - u_j + (k-1)z_{ij} + (k-3)z_{ji} \leq k-2, \quad \forall(i,j)\in A \tag{18}$$

$$\sum_{l|(l,j)\in A} z_{lj} + \sum_{l|(j,l)\in A} z_{jl} = \delta_j, \quad \forall j \in V \tag{19}$$

$$\sum_{j\in V} \delta_j = 2(k-1) \tag{20}$$

$$\delta_j \leq d x_j, \quad \forall j \in V \tag{21}$$

$$\delta_j \geq x_j, \quad \forall j \in V \tag{22}$$

$$z_{ij} \leq x_i, \quad \forall(i,j)\in A \tag{23}$$

$$z_{ij} \leq x_j, \quad \forall(i,j)\in A \tag{24}$$

$$\sum_{(i,j)\in A(N_{[l]})} z_{ij} \leq \sum_{j\in N_{[l]}} x_j - 1, \quad \forall l \in V \tag{25}$$

$$x \in \{0,1\}^n, z \in \{0,1\}^{n^2}, u,\delta \in [0,\infty]^n \tag{26}$$

where the constraints (16)–(17) are constrained by the x_j variables for each $j \in V$. Notice that the constraint (18) is a stronger version of the constraint (7) [12]. Notice that the Handshaking lemma is also valid for directed graphs [13]. Subsequently, constraints (19)–(22) replace the constraints (3) and (8)–(9) in P_1. This is possible by applying the Handshaking lemma. Notice that we introduce a nonnegative variable δ to handle the degree of each node which is upper bounded by d in constraint (21). Constraints (23)–(24) are logical constraints and can be similarly applied as in the dominating tree problem [2,3]. Finally, the constraints (25) are selected valid inequalities referred to as generalized sub-tour eliminations constraints and were initially proposed for the classical minimum connected dominating tree problem [15]. Notice that these constraints are also valid for the k-DCMST problem since sub-tours are also present.

Now, we straightforwardly apply the same arguments to P_2 in order to derive an equivalent strengthened version of it. The model in this case can be stated as

$$P_2^s : \quad \min_{\{x,z,f,y,\delta\}} \quad \sum_{(i,j)\in A} P_{ij} z_{ij}$$

$$\text{s.t.} \quad \sum_{j\in V} x_j = k$$

$$\sum_{l|(l,j)\in A} f_{lj} - \sum_{l|(j,l)\in A} f_{jl} = x_j - k y_j, \quad \forall j \in V$$

$$x_j \geq y_j, \quad \forall j \in V$$

$$f_{ij} \leq (k-1)z_{ij}, \quad \forall (i,j) \in A$$

$$\sum_{j\in V} y_j = 1$$

$$\sum_{l|(l,j)\in A} z_{lj} + \sum_{l|(j,l)\in A} z_{jl} = \delta_j, \quad \forall j \in V$$

$$\sum_{j\in V} \delta_j = 2(k-1)$$

$$\delta_j \leq d x_j, \quad \forall j \in V$$

$$\delta_j \geq x_j, \quad \forall j \in V$$

$$z_{ij} \leq x_i, \quad \forall (i,j) \in A$$

$$z_{ij} \leq x_j, \quad \forall (i,j) \in A$$

$$\sum_{(i,j)\in A(N_{[l]})} z_{ij} \leq \sum_{j\in N_{[l]}} x_j - 1, \quad \forall l \in V$$

$$x,y \in \{0,1\}^n, z \in \{0,1\}^{n^2}, f \in [0,\infty]^{n^2}, \delta \in [0,\infty]^n$$

Hereafter, we denote the corresponding linear programming (LP) relaxations of P_1, P_1^s, P_2, and P_2^s by LP_1, LP_1^s, LP_2, and LP_2^s, respectively.

3 Preliminary Numerical Results

In this section, we present preliminary numerical results for all the proposed models P_1, P_1^s, P_2, P_2^s, LP_1, LP_1^s, LP_2, and LP_2^s. A Matlab program is developed using CPLEX 12.7 [17] to solve all the MILP and LP relaxations. The numerical experiments have been carried out on an Intel(R) 64 bits core (TM) with 2.6 Ghz and 8 G of RAM. CPLEX solver is used with default options. Each entry in matrix $P = (P_{ij})$ for all $(i,j) \in A$ is randomly and uniformly distributed in the interval $(0; 10]$. In Tables 1 and 2, we arbitrarily set $d = 3$. Complete and connected disk graphs instances are generated randomly in an area of $500*500\,\mathrm{m}^2$. In particular, disk graph instances are generated with a radial transmission distance of 250 ms.

Tables 1 and 2 present exactly the same column information for P_1, P_1^s, LP_1, LP_1^s, and P_2, P_2^s, LP_2, LP_2^s, respectively. More precisely, column 1 shows the instance number whilst columns 2 and 3 present the number of nodes of each graph instance and the cardinality number k. Subsequently, columns 4–8 and 9–13 present the optimal solution of the problem or best solution found by CPLEX in 2 h of CPU time, the number of branch and bound nodes required by CPLEX, CPU time in seconds, optimal solution of the LP relaxation and its CPU time in seconds as well, for the initial and strengthened formulations, respectively. Finally, columns 14 and 15 present gaps that we compute by $\left[\frac{Opt-LP}{Opt}\right] * 100$ where Opt and LP refers to the optimal solution or best solution found for the MILP and LP models, respectively. We mention that each row in Tables 1 and 2 corresponds to a same instance. We limit CPLEX to 2 hours of CPU time in order to solve each linear model. Consequently, optimal solutions are reported whenever the CPU time limit is less than 2 h. On the opposite, if the CPU time reported equals 2 hours, then the solution found by CPLEX corresponds to a best solution found.

From Table 1, we observe similar trends for the complete and disk graph instances. We obtain the optimal solution of the problem for most of the instances in less than 2 hours with the exception of instances #8–9, #15, and #17–18. In particular, we observe that the strengthened formulation allows one to find the optimal solution for the instances #9 and #18 in less CPU time. We also see that the number of branch and bound nodes is significantly reduced using the

Table 1. Numerical results obtained with CPLEX for P_1 and P_1^s.

#	n	k	P_1					P_1^s					Gaps	
			Opt	B&Bn	Time	LP	Time	Opt	B&Bn	Time	LP	Time	Gap_1 %	Gap_1^s %
Complete graphs														
1	100	25	11.54	869	3.72	6.07	0.35	11.54	1115	16.45	8.26	1.39	47.35	28.40
2	100	50	26.52	15	3.45	17.57	0.36	26.52	26	4.82	22.36	1.54	33.75	15.66
3	100	75	42.13	15575	10.23	32.94	0.35	42.13	8870	18.42	41.25	1.52	21.81	2.10
4	200	50	16.32	674	33.36	10.57	1.25	16.32	458	37.76	13.30	12.15	35.27	18.53
5	200	100	37.05	5930	36.74	26.35	1.28	37.05	3968	75.59	33.53	12.42	28.87	9.49
6	200	150	61.65	57211	118.44	50.28	1.28	61.65	12559	275.43	60.96	64.81	18.44	1.12
7	300	80	19.11	1574	732.25	11.05	16.97	19.11	1359	650.60	15.24	205.76	42.15	20.22
8	300	160	48.79	457054	7200	34.79	16.95	48.79	277819	7200	44.69	205.80	28.69	8.41
9	300	200	62.99	1192652	7200	48.44	3.09	62.99	216614	755.57	60.57	43.72	23.10	3.84
Disk graphs with radial transmission ranges of 250 ms														
10	100	25	13.26	349	14.77	6.18	1.61	13.26	158	17.68	9.62	3.89	53.39	27.45
11	100	50	38.23	8214	51.92	28.00	1.64	38.23	6403	108.55	34.89	3.80	26.76	8.72
12	100	75	65.84	6396	31.04	53.00	1.86	65.84	4033	80.60	64.92	3.36	19.51	1.39
13	200	50	22.57	19091	273.46	13.21	4.88	22.57	14359	592.87	17.19	18.49	41.46	23.83
14	200	100	52.60	45819	381.11	39.31	4.94	52.60	20827	891.18	48.85	21.57	25.27	7.13
15	200	150	97.39	934211	7200	77.42	4.88	97.39	336014	7200	95.11	17.62	20.50	2.34
16	300	80	29.56	969	62.97	19.95	2.15	29.56	245	59.46	25.71	11.61	32.53	13.03
17	300	160	70.18	3933554	7200	53.03	2.19	70.18	1080528	7200	66.21	11.89	24.43	5.64
18	300	200	99.03	5046541	7200	79.48	2.09	99.03	1046266	4595.49	96.98	11.04	19.75	2.08

Table 2. Numerical results obtained with CPLEX for P_2 and P_2^s.

#	n	k	P_2					P_2^s					Gaps	
			Opt	B&Bn	Time	LP	Time	Opt	B&Bn	Time	LP	Time	Gap_2 %	Gap_2^s %
Complete graphs														
1	100	25	11.54	248	29.18	5.97	0.48	11.54	344	44.17	5.97	1.59	48.26	48.26
2	100	50	26.52	0	22.29	17.44	0.57	26.52	0	45.40	17.44	1.63	34.23	34.23
3	100	75	42.13	224	19.08	31.75	0.41	42.13	74	41.35	31.75	1.36	24.64	24.64
4	200	50	16.32	0	461.86	10.42	3.18	16.32	19	419.21	10.42	13.23	36.13	36.13
5	200	100	37.05	1176	446.49	26.17	3.82	37.05	1317	743.13	26.17	14.36	29.36	29.36
6	200	150	61.65	5200	344.44	48.69	1.38	61.65	2725	480.00	48.69	14.06	21.03	21.03
7	300	80	19.11	0	1817.27	10.87	6.43	19.11	0	2497.98	10.87	45.73	43.11	43.11
8	300	160	48.79	2247	1861.88	33.93	11.66	48.79	1412	2698.01	33.93	48.77	30.46	30.46
9	300	200	62.99	866	1610.63	47.73	16.73	62.99	321	2475.56	47.73	55.65	24.22	24.22
Disk graphs with radial transmission ranges of 250 ms														
10	100	25	13.26	0	5.25	5.98	0.34	13.26	0	8.73	5.98	0.62	54.93	54.93
11	100	50	38.23	314	11.54	27.68	0.39	38.23	433	21.34	27.68	0.64	27.60	27.60
12	100	75	65.84	137	7.44	51.40	0.29	65.84	110	11.78	51.40	0.51	21.94	21.94
13	200	50	22.57	394	132.18	12.94	1.60	22.57	239	134.66	12.94	3.77	42.66	42.66
14	200	100	52.60	373	134.40	38.49	1.69	52.60	134	221.11	38.49	3.78	26.83	26.83
15	200	150	97.39	1491	97.26	76.14	0.87	97.39	1455	213.14	76.14	3.36	21.82	21.82
16	300	80	29.56	0	577.99	19.74	3.95	29.56	0	903.36	19.74	13.67	33.24	33.24
17	300	160	70.18	960	581.33	51.86	3.85	70.18	496	2653.09	51.86	13.36	26.10	26.10
18	300	200	99.03	542	473.62	77.25	5.17	99.03	0	1374.68	77.25	14.63	22.00	22.00

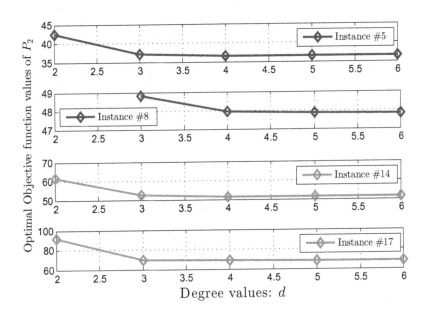

Fig. 1. Objective function values obtained with P_2 while varying the degree of all nodes in the network.

strengthened model which confirm the favorable effect of adding valid inequalities. Although, its LP relaxation is solved at higher CPU times. The gap columns also confirm the tightness achieved by the strengthened model compared to P_1. In particular, for the disk graph instances, these gaps are even better than for complete graphs which is an interesting result since disk graphs approaches with more accuracy real instances of wireless sensor networks. In general, we observe that these gaps get closer when the cardinality number k approaches the total number of nodes n. Finally, we conclude, from the numerical results presented in Table 1, that the strengthened formulation would benefit significantly if the CPU times required to solve the LP relaxations were reduced. This could be achieved by finding out which of the added valid inequalities are critical to solve the problem. From Table 2, we first verify that the optimal solutions are exactly the same as those obtained in Table 1 which confirms the equivalence of all these models. Next, we observe that the number of branch and bound nodes obtained with P_2 and P_2^s are significantly reduced than for P_1 and P_1^s, respectively. Regarding the CPU times required by CPLEX to solve P_2 and P_2^s, we observe that for the smaller instances, a higher CPU time is required compared to the values reported in Table 1 whilst for the large instances less CPU time is needed. We also see that all the instances are solved to optimality in less than 2 h which is not the case for the instances reported in Table 1. In general, we do not see large differences of CPU times for the LP relaxations in both tables. Further, we see that solving complete graph instances with P_2 and P_2^s require higher CPU times than solving disk graph instances of the problem. On the opposite, if we use P_1 and P_1^s, we require more CPU time to solve disk graph instances. Additionally, we observe that the gaps are not so tight when compared to those reported in Table 1. Finally, we conclude that P_2 and P_2^s outperform P_1 and P_1^s in terms of optimality, respectively.

In order to give more insight with respect to the performances obtained with P_2, in Fig. 1, we plot for the complete and disk graph instances #5, #8, and #14, #17 in Tables 1 and 2 respectively, optimal objective function values for different degree values of $d \in \{2, 3, 4, 5, 6\}$. This allows to observe how the optimal values behave while varying the degree imposed in the nodes of the network. Clearly, the lower the degree values, the larger the optimal solutions obtained. From Fig. 1, we mainly observe that the optimal values decrease rapidly while incrementing the value of d from 2 to 3 with the exception of instance #8. In this case, we obtain an infeasible solution. However, for degree values of $d \in \{3, 4, 5, 6\}$ we still observe a slight decreasing trend in the objective function values. Another observation is that for the disk graph instances, the objective values are higher than for complete graph instances. This can be explained by the fact that disk graph instances are more restrictive than complete graphs which are fully connected.

4   Conclusions

In this paper, we consider the degree constrained k-cardinality minimum spanning tree problem which arises as a combination of two classical combinatorial optimization problems, namely the degree constrained and k-minimum spanning tree problems (Resp. DCMST and k-MST). This problem is mainly motivated from the domain of wireless sensor networks where connected backbone sub-tree topologies are mandatorily required. Vertex degree constraints arise naturally in order to avoid overloaded nodes in the network. We proposed two compact formulations, a Miller-Tucker-Zemlin constrained version and a single flow based formulation that we further strengthen with valid inequalities that we adapt from the DCMST and dominating tree problems. Preliminary numerical results are given for complete and disk graph instances for different degree values. Our preliminary numerical results indicated that the flow based model outperforms the Miller-Tucker-Zemlin constrained version in terms of CPU time, branch and bound nodes and certification of optimality.

As future research, we plan to develop new approximation algorithms and stochastic modelling approaches for this problem. Finally, we plan to adapt our proposed models to more practical and realistic networks.

Acknowledgments. The authors acknowledge the financial support of Dicyt project 061713AS of VRIDi/USACH, Fondef IT17M10012, and Beca Doctorado Nacional 2016 CONICYT (PFCHA) 21161397.

References

1. Adasme, P.: p-Median based formulations with backbone facility locations. Appl. Soft Comput. **67**, 261–275 (2018)
2. Adasme, P., Andrade, R., Leung, J., Lisser, A.: Improved solution strategies for dominating trees. Expert Syst. Appl. **100**, 30–40 (2018)
3. Adasme, P., Andrade, R., Lisser, A.: Minimum cost dominating tree sensor networks under probabilistic constraints. Comput. Netw. **112**, 208–222 (2017)
4. Andrade, R.: The spanning tree polytope revisited, Relatorio Técnico, DEMA-RCA-2014A. Universidade Federal do Ceará, Departamento de Estatística e Matemática Aplicada (2014)
5. Andrade, R., Lucena, A., Maculan, N.: Using Lagrangian dual information to generate degree constrained spanning trees. Discrete Appl. Math. **154**, 703–717 (2006)
6. Arora, S.: Polynomial time approximation schemes for Euclidean traveling salesman and other geometric problems. J. ACM **45**, 753–782 (1998)
7. Al-Zaidi, R., Woods, J., Al-Khalidi, M., Hu, H.: Building novel VHF-based wireless sensor networks for the internet of marine things. IEEE Sens. J. **18**, 2131–2144 (2018)
8. Caccetta, L., Hill, S.P.: A branch and cut method for the degree-constrained minimum spanning tree problem. Networks **37**, 74–83 (2001)
9. Cardei, M., MacCallum, D., Cheng, X.: Wireless sensor networks with energy efficient organization. J. Interconnect. Netw. **3**, 3–4 (2002)
10. Chu, Z., Zhou, F., Zhu, Z., Hu, R.Q., Xiao, P.: Wireless powered sensor networks for internet of things: maximum throughput and optimal power allocation. IEEE Internet Things **5**, 310–321 (2018)
11. Bulut, E., Korpeoglu, I.: Sleep scheduling with expected common coverage in wireless sensor networks. Wirel. Netw. **17**, 19–40 (2011)

12. Desrochers, M., Laporte, G.: Improvements and extensions to the Miller-Tucker-Zemlin subtour elimination constraints. Oper. Res. Lett. **10**, 27–36 (1991)
13. Euler, L.: Solutio problematis ad geometriam situs pertinentis. Comment. Acad. Sci. Imp. Petrop. **8**, 128–140 (1736). Reprinted and translated in Biggs, N.L., Lloyd, E.K., Wilson, R.J.: Graph Theory, pp. 1736–1936. Oxford University Press (1976)
14. Garey, M.R., Johnson, D.S.: Computers and Intractability: A Guide to the Theory of NP-Completeness. W.H. Freeman, New York (1979)
15. Gendron, B., Lucena, A., de Cunha, A., Simonetti, L.: Benders decomposition, branch-and-cut, and hybrid algorithms for the minimum connected dominating set problem. INFORMS J. Comput. **26**(4), 645–657 (2014)
16. Gupta, H., Zhou, Z., Das, S.R., Gu, Q.: Connected sensor cover: self-organization of sensor networks for efficient query execution. IEEE/ACM Trans. Netw. **14**, 55–67 (2006)
17. IBM ILOG: CPLEX High-performance mathematical programming engine. http://www.ibm.com/software/integration/optimization/cplex/
18. Krishnamoorthy, M., Ernst, A.T., Sharaiha, Y.M.: Comparison of algorithms for the degree constrained minimum spanning tree. J. Heuristics **7**, 587–611 (2001)
19. Kruskal, J.B.: On the shortest spanning subtree and the traveling salesman problem. In: Proceedings of the American Mathematical Society, vol. 7, pp. 48–50 (1956)
20. Lozovanu, D., Zelikovsky, A.: Minimal and bounded tree problems. In: Tezele Congresului XVIII al Academiei Romano-Americane, Kishniev, p. 25 (1996). As cited by Ravi et al
21. Narula, S.C., Ho, C.A.: Degree-constrained minimum spanning tree. Comput. Oper. Res. **7**, 239–249 (1980)
22. Naveen, G.: Saving an epsilon: a 2-approximation for the k-MST problem in graphs. In: Proceedings of the 37th Annual ACM Symposium on Theory of Computing, pp. 396–402 (2005)
23. Prim, R.C.: Shortest connection networks and some generalisations. Bell Syst. Tech. J. **36**, 1389–1401 (1957)
24. Ravi, R., Sundaram, R., Marathe, M., Rosenkrantz, D., Ravi, S.: Spanning trees short or small. SIAM J. Discrete Math. **9**, 178–200 (1996)
25. Stankovic, J.: When sensor and actuator networks cover the world. ETRI J. **30**, 627–633 (2008)
26. Thenepalle, J.K., Singamsetty, P.: The degree constrained k-cardinality minimum spanning tree problem a lexisearch algorithm. Decis. Sci. Lett. **7**, 301–310 (2018)
27. Volgenant, A.: A Lagrangean approach to the degree constrained minimum spanning tree problem. Eur. J. Oper. Res. **39**, 325–331 (1989)
28. Wang, L., Xiao, Y.: A survey of energy-efficient scheduling mechanisms in sensor networks. Mob. Netw. Appl. **11**, 723–740 (2006)
29. Yardibi, T., Karasan, E.: A distributed activity scheduling algorithm for wireless sensor networks with partial coverage. Wirel. Netw. **16**, 213–225 (2010)

I-RP: Interference Aware
Routing Protocol for WBAN

Adnan Ahmed[1]([⊠]), Imtiaz Ali Halepoto[3], Umair Ali Khan[3],
Sanjay Kumar[2], and Ali Raza Bhangwar[3]

[1] Department of Telecommunication, Quaid-e-Awam University of Engineering,
Science and Technology, Nawabshah, Pakistan
adnan.ahmed03@quest.edu.pk
[2] Faculty of Information Technology, University of Jyvaskyla, Jyvaskyla, Finland
[3] Department of Computer Systems, Quaid-e-Awam University of Engineering,
Science and Technology, Nawabshah, Pakistan

Abstract. The Wireless Body Sensor Networks (WBSN) have witnessed
tremendous research interest because of their wide range of applications (medical
and non-medical) in order to improve the quality of life. The healthcare applications of WBSN demands dissemination of patient's data, reliably and in a timely
manner. For this purpose, medical teams may use real-time applications for
disseminating critical data such as blood pressure, ECG, and EEG. The critical
data packets are highly delay sensitive that must reach intended destination within
time constraints. Due to the exchange of real-time and multi-media data, some
nodes or links may experience the significant level of interference in the network.
Consequently, it results in transmission disruption, random number of packet
drops, insufficient buffer space and lack of availability of bandwidth. Moreover,
interference in the network strains the communication links, reduces the information delivery capacity of the network and leads to high collisions, packet losses,
retransmission and energy consumption. Therefore, incorporating interference-
awareness in routing decisions is desirable to enhance the performance of WBSN.
In this paper, we present an Interference-aware Routing Protocol (I-RP) that
makes use of composite routing metric incorporating link quality (in terms of link
delay and interference level) and path length. This multi-facet routing strategy
makes more informed routing decision regarding route selection in a way that, a
route with the minimum level of interference and path length is selected. Moreover, it also increases the link reliability and minimizes the packet losses and
retransmission. The simulation results demonstrate the improved performance of
proposed scheme when compared to existing routing scheme in WBSN.

Keywords: Interference · Wireless Body Area Network · Routing · Delay
MAC layer · QoS

1 Introduction

The constant monitoring of patients, suffering from chronic diseases, encourages the
researchers to develop special-purpose wireless sensor network's technology, called

© Springer International Publishing AG, part of Springer Nature 2018
M. Younas et al. (Eds.): MobiWIS 2018, LNCS 10995, pp. 63–71, 2018.
https://doi.org/10.1007/978-3-319-97163-6_6

Wireless Body Area Network (WBAN), that provide continuous health monitoring system. WBAN is comprised of several biomedical sensor nodes, either placed on the body or implanted in a body to collect physiological parameters such as temperature, Glucose, blood pressure, blood oxygen, Electrocardiogram (ECG) and Electroencephalography (EEG). The sensed data is transmitted to base station/medical server through coordinator nodes (via efficient routing protocols), where medical experts take adequate decisions in providing treatment. WBAN can be envisioned as a cost-effective and reliable solution in providing real-time healthcare services to the patients requiring emergency medical assistance [1].

The growing concerns in providing real-time health monitoring services requires adequate link quality to be maintained. However, the distinguished characteristics of WBAN raise various challenges in designing efficient routing protocol owing to limited resources, transmission range, data rate, frequency, operating environment, postural body movement and unreliability of low-power wireless links that lack in terms of QoS requirements, as low-power radios are very sensitive to noise and interference [2]. Most of the existing routing schemes for WBSN [3, 4] have traditionally focused on selecting routes by incorporating single routing metric (either hop count or temperature). The research has revealed that hop count may not always represent the optimal route selection. Moreover, the wireless links may exhibit variations in terms of link's interference level, capacity, path loss and delay [5–7]. Moreover, most of the routing schemes [8–10] incorporates composite routing metric (hop count, temperature and energy) to disseminate data packets. However, optimized route selection by keeping in view important design characteristics of WBSN such as QoS (in pursuit of link quality) have been overlooked in most of the previous studies. The timely and efficiently dissemination of critical data packets in healthcare applications require more realistic routing metric that keeps in view important aspects pertaining to link quality such as interference and delay. To best of our knowledge, incorporating interference awareness in routing decision has gained little attention in WBAN. The interference is one of the most significant performance bottleneck for wireless ad-hoc networks. Therefore, in this paper, an Interference-aware Routing Protocol (I-RP) has been proposed for WBAN that makes more informed decision regarding the actual link status. The proposed scheme estimates the channel contention by using the information available on MAC layer (channel interference) and conveys that information to the network layer. Based on the acquired information the route cost is evaluated, and the link having least cost (satisfies QoS requirements) is selected for packet forwarding. This multi-facet strategy optimizes the route selection in a way that the routes with minimum interference level and delay are selected which vital for timely delivery of critical data packets in healthcare applications. The simulation results prove the efficacy of proposed scheme when compared with existing routing schemes in WBAN. The rest of paper is organized as follows. The Sect. 2 presents the related literature review. The Sect. 3 demonstrate the proposed routing protocol. The Sect. 4 presents the simulation results and finally, the Sect. 5 concludes the paper with future directions.

2   Literature Review

This section presents the related review of the routing protocols proposed for WBAN. An Adaptive Transmit Power Mechanism (ATPM) scheme [11] is presented for e-health application of WBAN to improve QoS and energy conservation. ATPM based on Signal to Interference and Noise Ratio (SINR) and make use of few threshold values to make a decision. Moreover, to minimize the energy consumption ATMP also tune the parameter related to transmission power. A link quality aware with load balancing scheme namely, DSCA [12], is presented for WBAN with the aim to balance the load among the deployed body sensor nodes and maintain the quality of service. The proposed scheme consists of two phases: temporal link quality measurement and sub-channel allocation. The temporal link quality measure phase employs a probabilistic approach to measure the radio link quality between a sensor node and access point. The sub-channel allocation phase divides the available bandwidth in sub-channel to maintain QoS. A priority based routing protocol [3] is proposed for WBAN which is based on traditional AODV protocol. The proposed routing protocol places the data packets in the queue that is based on the defined priorities. The packets with the highest priority are placed in L1 queue whereas normal data packets are placed in L2 queue. A Link-Aware and Energy Efficient scheme for Body Area networks (LAEEBA) [13] is proposed for WBAN with the objective to minimize energy consumption and improve throughput. The proposed scheme comprised of four phases such as initialization, next-hop selection, routing and path loss selection phases. The proposed scheme incorporates a cost function that is based on distance to sink node, node's remaining energy and path loss model. The path loss model ensures the fewer packet losses. A Priority-based Cross-layer Routing Protocol (PCRP) [14] is proposed for healthcare application of WBAN that ensures reliable data dissemination for inter and intra-body communication. In order to provide channel access, the proposed PCRP scheme combines TDMA and CSMA/CA approaches to avoid idle listening, data losses and collisions. Furthermore, the PCRP scheme defines three classes of traffic to compliance heterogeneous QoS requirements such as general monitoring traffic, delay sensitive packets and emergency packets. A reliable and temperature aware routing protocol [15] is proposed for WBAN, which incorporates security primitives and temperature awareness to address the reliable dissemination of critical data packets and solve hotspot issue. Similarly, a Thermal-Aware Routing Algorithm (TARA) [4] is proposed to overcome the issue of temperature rise for implanted biomedical sensor nodes. A biosensor node estimates the temperature of its neighboring nodes by overhearing the packets sent and received. If the temperature rise is above the specified threshold, that specified node is considered as hotspot node thereby isolated from routing paths.

Based on the presented literature review it is observed that most of the proposed routing protocols for WBAN do not incorporate dynamic/changing network conditions such as channel interference in their routing decisions. Consequently, it leads to the selection of links that do not meet QoS requirements. Furthermore, most of the routing protocols require a special set of resources for their network operations such as tight synchronization, channel allocation requirements and asymmetric authentication. Moreover, most of the routing protocols either hop count and energy or hop count and temperature as a composite metric for route selection. However, these routing metrics does not adapt to varying traffic and channel conditions. The interference on links causes significant variations in the performance of throughput, delay and reliability. By keeping these issues in mind, Interference-aware Routing Protocol (I-RP) has been proposed that satisfy QoS requirements for critical healthcare application of WBAN. I-RP incorporates link's delay [16] and interference in routing decision and provide optimized route selection. The details of the proposed I-RP scheme are presented in the upcoming section.

3   Proposed Routing Protocol

The proposed I-RP routing scheme extends the routing mechanism of traditional AODV routing protocol where the control packets for route discovery, route request and route reply, are customized to keep information about the link's delay, interference and length. The proposed scheme comprises of two major phases: network initialization phase and QoS aware routing phase. The following sub-sections provide the details of each phase.

3.1   Network Initialization Phase

During this phase, sensor nodes identify the number of neighbor nodes in their transmission range and compute the hop-count, delay and link interference by exchanging hello packets. Upon receiving the hello packets, the receiving nodes add the relevant information (hop count, delay and estimated interference values) and rebroadcast and share with a neighbor in their transmission range. This process continues till all the nodes compute relevant information and exchange with their neighbor nodes. The process of computing the delay and link interference is discussed below.

Link Delay Estimation (LDE):   Each sensor node periodically exchanges hello packets with 1-hop neighbors in order to estimate the link delay. The delay is estimated, as shown in Eq. 1, by computing the difference between the times hello packet exchanged and its acknowledgment received. In this way, the inter-arrival time of the link formed between the two neighboring nodes is determined.

$$LDE = \frac{Hello\,Packet_{Ack} - Hello\,Packet_{sent}}{2} \quad (1)$$

Link Quality Indicator (LQI):   The LQI refer to the QoS metric in term of channel interference. LQI primarily focus of interference at MAC layer mainly attributed by the MAC based CSMA/CA protocol which prevents the nodes from transmitting on the shared medium as the channel is occupied by the transmission from another node, within their carrier sensing range. In other words, it indicates that access to medium has been deferred (node is in the back-off state) due to on-going traffic within the carrier sensing range. The higher the traffic rate, the larger the accumulative LQI value and vice versa. The LQI can be a good indicator for estimating the channel interference.

$$LQE = \sum_{link \in r} (HC + LDE + LQI) \qquad (2)$$

The integrated outcome of Hop Count, LDE and LQI lead to the formation of new routing metric, termed as Link Quality Estimator (LQE), as shown in Eq. 2. The LQE of the route r is aggregated sum of HC, LDE and LQI values for all the links in that selected route.

3.2 QoS Aware Routing Phase

The interference-aware routing process is incorporated in QoS aware routing phase which extends the route discovery mechanism of classical on-demand routing protocol, AODV, by replacing conventional hop count metric with new LQE metric (interference aware metric). The RREQ and RREP packets are customized to include LDE and LQI fields in their packet headers. The link that satisfies the requirements in LQE metric, in a way that $Min(LQE)$ value, is chosen for packet forwarding. The route with high LQE indicates that cost of the route is high in terms of hop count, link delay and channel interference. The QoS aware route discovery mechanism is explained as follows:

The route discovery process is initiated by source node by generating and broadcasting RREQ packet to their neighboring nodes. The intermediate/neighboring nodes receive the RREQ packets sets the reverse path to the node that sends the RREQ packet and appends HC, LDE and LQI values in the packet header. Afterward, it rebroadcast the RREQ packet to their downstream neighbor nodes. The same process continues till the RREQ reaches the destination or to the node having a valid route to the destination. Such node generates the RREP packet and unicast it to upstream nodes and maintain an entry for a forward route to the node that sends-out RREP. During network initialization phase, each sensor node has already estimated the LDE and LQI values. The same values are appended to RREP packet header and forwarded to upstream nodes. Finally, the source node may receive multiple RREPs from several routes. It computes the cost for each route and selects the one with minimum cost. This multi-facet strategy of I-RP helps in selecting the route that satisfies the QoS requirements (pertaining to link delay and channel interference) consequently leads to more route stability, minimized average delay, loss ratio and retransmissions which is very crucial for delivering critical data packets in WBAN.

4   Results and Discussions

This section presents the simulation results of proposed scheme via simulation parameters listed in Table 1. The performance of the proposed scheme is compared with ATMP and TARA routing protocols in WBAN, by varying the traffic load so that a more realistic scenario having high traffic (interference on the channel) is chosen in order to fairly analyze the performance.

Table 1. Simulation parameters

Simulation area	10 m × 10 m
Relay nodes	20
Biomedical sensor nodes	5
Transport layer protocol	UDP
Propagation model	TwoRayGround
Network interface type	WirelessPhy
Traffic type	CBR
IEEE 802.15.4 standard	Default values
Simulation time	500 s
Routing protocols	I-RP, TARA, AODV
Packet size	50 bytes

The efficacy of proposed I-RP scheme is measured in terms of throughput, average end-to-end delay and routing load. Figures 1, 2 and 3 present the performance analysis of I-RP, TARA and ATMP routing protocols in terms of throughput, average end-to-end delay and normalized routing load. As the ATMP and TARA routing protocols do not provide any mechanism to deal with channel interference, therefore, under heavy traffic loads they exhibit reduced performance. Initially, when more data packets are supplied, the throughput performance increases. However, when it reaches saturation point the performance of ATMP and TARA starts to decline due to high interference on links. Furthermore, TARA protocol makes use of hop count (other than temperature) for route selection, which is not an optimal choice under dynamic network conditions. As a result, both routing protocols (ATMP and TARA) exhibits increased packet losses due to significant congestion on the network. Moreover, it also results in a high number of retransmissions and route breakages under heavy network load. The high number of retransmissions and route breakages strain the communication links with control packets (new route discoveries and route maintenance). Thereby, limits the flow of data packets that affect the throughput of the network. Similarly, nodes have to suspend packet forwarding till the new routes are discovered, so it affects the end-to-end delay performance. Likewise, the flow of a higher number of control packets results in the increased normalized routing load. The proposed I-RP routing protocol outperforms the existing schemes as it makes more informed decision regarding the actual interference on the link by incorporating Link Quality Indicator (LQI). Moreover, Link Delay Estimation (LDE) also helps in selecting the routes with least communication delay, that is vital for the transmission of critical data packets in WBAN. The integrated outcome of LQI, LDE and HC leads to the formation of improved routing metric that performs optimized route selection which gives equal emphasis to all factors that are crucial for WBAN performance. Due to the adopted methodology of the proposed scheme, the selected routes remains more stable thereby the flow of packets remains consistent for an extended period of time. Consequently, it improves the overall throughput and end-to-end delay performances. Moreover, it also improves the routing load performance as fewer control packets flows in the network.

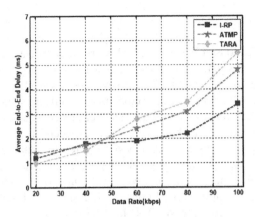

Fig. 1. Average End-to-End delay

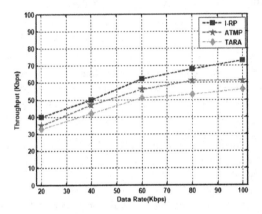

Fig. 2. Average throughput (kbps)

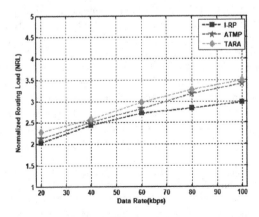

Fig. 3. Normalized routing load

5 Conclusion

The healthcare applications of WBAN are highly critical and delay sensitive, therefore, information must be disseminated reliably and within time constraints. The routing protocol responsible for delivering data packets must meet QoS requirements. The interference is one of the bottleneck factors that significantly affects the network performance. Therefore, this paper presented an interference-aware routing protocol for WBAN with the objective to make a more informed decision regarding the channel contention so that less congested links may be selected for data delivery. Moreover, link's delay and hop count parameters are also incorporated in routing decisions which ensures the selection of links with minimum delay and path length. The simulation results demonstrated the improved performance of proposed I-RP scheme as compared to existing routing protocols for WBAN. In future, we intended to propose more improved link quality metric for WBAN with its integration with security aspect so that critical patient's data should reach securely to its destination.

References

1. Zuhra, F.T., Bakar, K.A., Ahmed, A., Tunio, M.A.: Routing protocols in wireless body sensor networks: a comprehensive survey. J. Netw. Comput. Appl. **99**, 73–97 (2017)
2. Cavallari, R., Martelli, F., Rosini, R., Buratti, C., Verdone, R.: A survey on wireless body area networks: technologies and design challenges. IEEE Commun. Surv. Tutor. **16**, 1635–1657 (2014)
3. Ambigavathi, M., Sridharan, D.: Priority based AODV routing protocol for critical data in Wireless Body Area Network. In: 23rd International Conference on Signal Processing, Communication and Networking, ICSCN, pp. 1–5 (2015)
4. Tang, Q., Tummala, N., Gupta, S.K., Schwiebert, L.: TARA: thermal-aware routing algorithm for implanted sensor networks. In: International Conference on Distributed Computing in Sensor Systems, pp. 206–217 (2005)
5. Draves, R., Padhye, J., Zill, B.: Comparison of routing metrics for static multi-hop wireless networks. In: ACM SIGCOMM Computer Communication Review, pp. 133–144 (2004)
6. Campista, M.E.M.M., Esposito, P.M.P., Moraes, I.M., Costa, L.H.M., Duarte, O.C.M., Passos, D.G., Albuquerque, C.V.N.De, Saade, D.C.M., Rubinstein, M.G.: Routing metrics and protocols for wireless mesh networks. IEEE Netw. **22**, 6–12 (2008)
7. Ahmed, A., Kumar, P., Bhangwar, A.R., Channa, M.I.: A secure and QoS aware routing protocol for Wireless Sensor Network. In: 11th International Conference for Internet Technology and Secured Transactions, ICITST, pp. 313–317 (2016)
8. Rashid, T., Kumar, S., Verma, A., Gautam, P.R., Kumar, A.: Pm-EEMRP: postural movement based energy efficient multi-hop routing protocol for intra wireless body sensor network (Intra-WBSN). TELKOMNIKA (Telecommun. Comput. Electron. Control. **16**, 166–173 (2018)
9. Ahourai, F., Tabandeh, M., Jahed, M., Moradi, S.: A thermal-aware shortest hop routing algorithm for in vivo biomedical sensor networks. In: Sixth International Conference on Information Technology: New Generations, ITNG, pp. 1612–1613 (2009)
10. Hemnani, S.P., Syed, R.M., Saleem, S., Mustaqim, M., Kamlesh, N.: EBM: a cross-layer approach for wireless body area networks. J. Emerg. Trends Comput. Inf. Sci. **7**, 69–76 (2016)

11. Sarra, E., Ezzedine, T.: Performance improvement of the wireless body area network (WBAN). In: IEEE 18th International Conference on e-Health Networking, Applications and Services (Healthcom), pp. 1–6 (2016)

12. Samanta, A., Bera, S., Misra, S.: Link-quality-aware resource allocation with load balance in wireless body area networks. IEEE Syst. J. **12**, 1–8 (2015)

13. Ahmed, S., Javaid, N., Akbar, M., Iqbal, A., Khan, Z.A., Qasim, U.: LAEEBA: link aware and energy efficient scheme for body area networks. In: IEEE 28th International Conference on Advanced Information Networking and Applications, AINA, pp. 435–440 (2014)

14. Ben Elhadj, H., Elias, J., Chaari, L., Kamoun, L.: A priority based cross layer routing protocol for healthcare applications. Ad Hoc Netw. **42**, 1–18 (2016)

15. Bhangwar, A.R., Kumar, P., Ahmed, A., Channa, M.I.: Trust and thermal aware routing protocol (TTRP) for wireless body area networks. Wirel. Pers. Commun. **97**, 349–364 (2017)

16. Liang, X., Balasingham, I.: A QoS-aware routing service framework for biomedical sensor networks. In: Proceedings of 4th IEEE International Symposium on Wireless Communication Systems, ISWCS, pp. 342–345 (2007)

FDRA: Fault Detection and Recovery Algorithm for Wireless Sensor Networks

Chafiq Titouna[1]([✉]), Ado Adamou Abba Ari[2,3], and Hamouma Moumen[1]

[1] Department of Computer Science,
University of Batna 2, Batna, Algeria
`c.titouna@univ-batna2.dz`
[2] Department of Mathematics and Computer Science,
University of Maroua, Maroua, Cameroon
[3] LI-PaRAD Laboratory,
University of Versailles, Versailles, France

Abstract. Failures are inevitable in wireless sensor network, and it is important to detect and recover faulty nodes. In this paper, we present an algorithm to recover faulty nodes called Fault detection and Recovery Algorithm (FDRA). The performance evaluation is tested through simulation to evaluate some factors such as: Packet delivery ratio, control overhead, memory overhead and fault recovery delay. We compared our results with referenced algorithm: Fault Detection in Wireless Sensor Networks (FDWSN), and found that our FDRA performance outperforms that of FDWSN.

Keywords: Wireless sensor networks · Fault tolerance
Connectivity restoration

1 Introduction

A wireless sensor network (WSN) consists of a possibly large number of wireless devices able to take environmental measurements. Typical examples include temperature, light, sound, and humidity. These measurements are transmitted over a wireless channel to a base station (BS) that makes decisions based on these data. WSNs have infiltrated our daily life, such as medical monitoring [1], military surveillance [2, 3], vehicle monitoring [4], home automation monitoring [5], weather monitoring [6], building structures monitoring, and industrial plant monitoring [7–9]. Some of these WSN's applications were deployed in remote and hostile surroundings, and none can attend nodes in such environment. In addition, some nodes are failure due to energy depletion, hardware failure, communication link errors, intrusion by attackers and so on. These unattended nodes cannot be replaced or repaired. They may generate a faulty data and even cannot respond to any request. These problems may lead to network partition which decreases the cover ratio, reduces the availability of the WSN and even produces network partition. Therefore, WSN should possess a mechanism of fault tolerance. It can be defined as the ability of a system to deliver a desired level of functionality in the presence of faults [10]. Since the nodes are prone to failure, fault tolerance should

© Springer International Publishing AG, part of Springer Nature 2018
M. Younas et al. (Eds.): MobiWIS 2018, LNCS 10995, pp. 72–85, 2018.
https://doi.org/10.1007/978-3-319-97163-6_7

be seriously considered in many sensor network applications. Actually, extensive work has been done on fault tolerance and it has been one of the most important topics in WSNs [11, 12].

In this paper, we extend our preliminary work proposed in [13]. We improve the proposal algorithm which called: Fault Detection Scheme (FDS), and we present a novel one called Fault Detection and Recovery Algorithm (FDRA). The first one ensures only a detection of faulty nodes without any recovery. However, in the present scheme FDRA, we improve the previous work by ensuring this task.

The rest of the paper is organized as follows: Sect. 2 presents some related work. In Sect. 3, we describe our recovery algorithm and illustrate it through example. We provide in Sect. 4 performance results and in Sect. 5 we conclude the paper.

2 Related Works

Several works are proposed to detect and recover the faulty nodes in wireless sensor networks [14]. In [15], the authors proposed a detection technique to eliminate all erroneous sensed data generated by faulty nodes. Wang et al. [16] have proposed an approach based on cascaded movement to replace a faulty node by a nearby node, which in turn gets replaced with another and so on until reaching a redundant node. The authors in [17], proposed a few simple algorithms for achieving the baseline graph theoretic metric of tolerance to node failures, namely, biconnectivity. They formulated an optimization problem for the creation of a movement plan while minimizing the total distance moved by the robots. However in DARA [18], the main idea was to detect the failure of an actor and replace the failed actor in a cascaded manner. The previous work was enhanced in [19]. They use the connected dominating set (CDS) of the whole network in order to detect the cut-vertex node. After detecting these nodes, every node picks the appropriate neighbor to handle its failure in the case of failure in future. The objective is to choose a neighbor that may not partition the network again. In [20], the replacement of the failed node is done only by its direct neighbors. Akkaya et al. [21] presented the new distributed partition detection and recovery algorithm (PADRA, PADRA+) to handle the connectivity problem through detection of possible partitions after the failure of the cut-vertex node is observed in the network and restores the network connectivity through controlled relocation of the movable nodes. Younis et al. [22] proposed a localized distributed algorithm called recovery through inward motion (RIM) for the network partition recovery. The main idea is to move the entire neighbor node(s) towards inward direction of the failed node so that nodes can discover each other and recovery can take place. In [23], the authors presented an algorithm called Connectivity Restoration with Assured Fault Tolerance (CRAFT) to solve the problem of simultaneous sensor failures. This algorithm forms a backbone polygon around failure region. Then, CRAFT tries to fix partition problem by connection the disjoint paths to each other. A distributed fault detection algorithm for WSNs named FDWSN has been proposed in [24]. Every node discerns its own status in view of local comparisons of its sensed data with the data of neighboring nodes for q times to detect transient fault. The authors used a redundancy matrix to save all results of comparison. After, the status of the node is declared as good if the sensed data are similar. Finally, each sensor node with a defined status will broadcast its status to its neighbors to facilitate them for determining their own status. This scheme can detect and isolate faulty nodes with high detection accuracy. Transient faults are also tolerated by using time redundancy.

Contrary to the ideas proposed in the above reviewed works in which movement of sensor nodes or exchanging Hello message are required, our proposal mainly based on stationary sensor nodes that do not need any mobility.

3   Fault Detection and Recovery Algorithm

In this section, we present our proposed technique, named Fault Detection and Recovery Algorithm (FDRA). We begin first by defining some assumptions. We then provide details on the mechanism used for recovering faulty nodes. Our algorithm operates in two phases: (a) First, a tree-forming and selection of sleeping nodes are executed. (b) Second, selection of recovering nodes to recover the faulty nodes and updating connectivity table.

3.1   System Assumptions

A WSN is typically consisting of a large number of nodes scattered over a region of interest to monitor a particular physical phenomenon. Some assumptions, complying with practical aspect, have to be considered in our algorithm. The first assumption is that all sensed data are forwarded from sources to a central node called Base Station (BS), where data processing occurs. The second is that, all nodes are stationary and its batteries cannot be recharged. We recognize that local processing may occur to reduce overall communication costs. The next assumption we make is that all nodes are homogeneous in terms of energy, communication and processing capabilities, and they are assigned a unique identifier (ID). Finally, we also assume that we do not have malicious attacks on the network.

3.2   Algorithm Design

Our algorithm consists of two phases. In the following sub-sections, we describe each phase in details.

Preliminary Phase

Tree-Forming and Creation of Connectivity Table Step
Tree-forming is an efficient and effective technique for recovery process. In this paper, we are interesting to BS-based trees where it uses the BS as the core of the network. This is optimum in WSN, since the BS does not suffer from battery depletion. In Fig. 1, the initial connectivity of the network is presented, while Fig. 2, describes a BS-based tree applied on the initial topology (Fig. 1). The process of creation of BS-based tree is analytically demonstrated in [25, 26]. It is clear that this transformation leads to a creation of connectivity table which presented in Table 1. Consider the scenario shown in

Fig. 2, the table of connectivity will be presented as in Table 1. The columns describe the levels of the tree and the rows represent the ID of sensor nodes belong to each level. We consider the same example, the level 1 (L = 1) contains the following IDs: 1, 2 and 3. These nodes belong to the level 1.

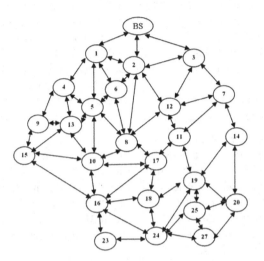

Fig. 1. Initial connectivity of the network.

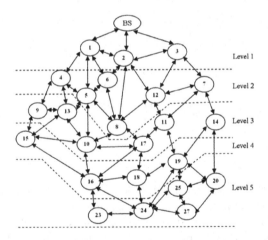

Fig. 2. Connectivity of the network after applying BS-based tree algorithm.

Selection of Sleeping Nodes Step

The BS chooses which nodes should be in sleep mode. The BS can take into account the energy remaining of nodes, the geographic position of nodes, total number of nodes presents in levels or the degree of connectivity of a node. In this paper, we are based on the degree of connectivity of nodes, i.e., the BS selects the node that has fewer neighbors. To start the selection of sleeping nodes, the BS broadcasts a *Req_nn* message to know the number of neighbors of each node. When a node receives a *Req_nn* message, it will respond with *Resp_nn* message to inform the BS the number of neighbors in its transmission range. When the *BS* receives all *Resp_nn* messages, the selection of sleeping nodes is launched by selecting only nodes with number of neighbors is less than α threshold (α can be equal to the average number of each level). The BS sends a *Select_Sleep_msg* message to all selected nodes. A response *Resp_Sleep_msg* message, it will be sent by the selected nodes to indicate to the BS that they will switch to sleep mode. E.g., consider Fig. 1. The BS selects in the 1st level the node 3. The nodes with ID 4, 6 and 7 in the second level. The nodes 9, 11 and 14 in the third level. The nodes 15, 18 in the fourth level and nodes with ID 23 and 27 in last level. The IDs of selected nodes are presented in bold in the Table 1. Figure 4 represents a message exchanging required to select sleeping nodes in level 2.

Update Connectivity Table Step
This step allows updating the connectivity table. After a phase of detection of faulty nodes (see more details in [13]) the cluster-head transmitted to the BS a black list (BL) contains all the faulty nodes detected. The *BS* updates the connectivity table, so it will proceed to an elimination of all faulty nodes'ID from the table. E.g., consider the Table 1. We suppose that nodes 5, 12 and 16 are in BL. So they should be removed from the Table 1 (we just highlighted in Table 1). The next subsections describe the steps required for the recovery phase.

Table 1. Connectivity table.

L = 1	L = 2	L = 3	L = 4	L = 5
1	**4**	**9**	**15**	**23**
2	5	13	16	24
3	**6**	10	**18**	25
	8	17	19	**27**
	12	**11**	20	
	7	**14**		

Recovery Phase

Principle
FDRA recognizes two transition states for the nodes, active and sleeping. Initially all nodes in the network are in active state. This means that all radio's nodes are on until receiving a message like "*Select_Sleep_msg*". This message comes from BS to order preselected nodes to switch their radio off and move to sleep mode. Returns back to the active state happen when the BS selects a sleeping node to recover a faulty node. To do that, BS will send a wakeup message to these nodes. Therefore, the transition between the two states is ordered by the BS and is performed by sending messages.

Selection of Recovery Nodes Step
The process of selection of recovery nodes implies the reactivation of some sleeping nodes. The BS sends a *Wake_up_msg* message to all sleeping nodes of the same level of the faulty nodes. However, the sleeping nodes which are in level that does not contain

any faulty nodes, they will not receive this message. E.g., consider the previous example, in Table 1, the sleeping nodes which receive the *Wake_up_msg* are: The nodes 4, 6 and 7 of the 2nd level and the nodes 18 and 15 of the 4th level (i.e., The message concern two levels (2 and 4), because we supposed in previous subsection that there are only three faulty nodes in BL (5, 12 and 16) which they are located in 2nd and 4th level respectively).

At receiving the *Wake_up_msg* message, the sleeping nodes turn their radio on and send back a wakeup acknowledgement message (*Wake_up_ack*) to the BS to indicate its new state (Active state). The BS sends now a request (*Req_hop_reqr*) to know the number of hops required to reach the faulty nodes from the sleeping nodes of the same level. The sleeping nodes update their routing table and respond to the BS using a simple packet (*Resp_hop_reqr*). The structure of this packet is described in Fig. 3.

When all *Resp_hop_reqr* are received, the BS creates a Hop Required Table which helps it to choose the appropriate recovery node RN. E.g., the Table 2(a) and (b) summarize the number of hops required for the nodes 4, 6 and 7 to reach the faulty nodes 5 and 12.

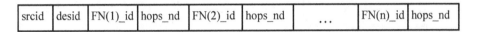

srcid	desid	FN(1)_id	hops_nd	FN(2)_id	hops_nd	...	FN(n)_id	hops_nd

Fig. 3. Packet format.

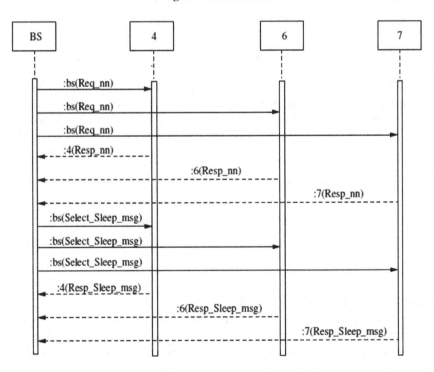

Fig. 4. Message exchanging between BS and selected sleeping node (level 2).

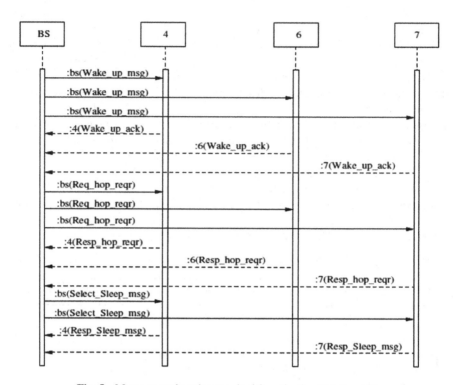

Fig. 5. Message exchanging required for selecting RN (level 2).

The BS chooses the one which requires fewer hops to reach the faulty nodes FN. E.g., consider the Table 2, the node with ID 6 need 2 hops to reach node 5 and 12. So, the BS selects it as RN. A *Select_Sleep_msg* message is sent to the not selected nodes (e.g., 4 and 7) to go back in sleep mode. A response *Resp_Sleep_msg* message, it will be sent by the selected nodes to the *BS*. Figure 5 shows the previous exchange messages.

Table 2.   (a):Hop required table (FN = 5) (b)Hop required table (FN = 12).

(a)		(b)	
Sleeping node ID	Hop required	Sleeping node ID	Hop required
4	1	4	3
6	1	6	2
7	3	7	1

Update Connectivity Table Step

The BS should update the connectivity table after each recovery phase. All sleeping nodes that are selected for covering the erroneous nodes must be mentioned in the connectivity table. E.g., consider the example in previous section, the node with ID 6 will be considered as an active node.

4 Performance Evaluation

We have conducted several series of simulations using the TOSSIM simulator [27] in order to evaluate the performance of our proposed algorithm. For comparison purposes, our proposal FDRA and FDWSN protocol are evaluated under the following metrics: (1) the packet delivery ratio (PDR); (2) the control overhead (CO); (3) the memory overhead (MO); and (3) the fault recovery delay (FRD). The key simulation parameters are summarized in Table 3.

4.1 Analysis of Packet Delivery Ratio (PDR)

Packet delivery ratio is calculated as the number of packets received by the receiver divided by the number of packets sent by the sender. This metric characterizes the percentage of successful source data packet delivery; ideally, this should be 100%. Figure 6 shows the total number of data packets received by the BS over the number of nodes (with node transmission power (TP) set to 2 mW). From this figure, we see that the amount of data collected by the *BS* from each source is much more important with our FDRA algorithm then the FDWSN protocol. This can be explained by the fact that FDWSN uses transient phase for fault detection and it does not consider the other causes of node's failures. The Fig. 7 shows the improvement in packet delivery ratio when node transmission power is equal to 4 mW. We explain this improvement by the fact that the number of neighbors of recovery node increases when we increase the transmission power. However, for FDWSN, we noticed that there is a less in packet delivery ratio because FDWSN requires a set of iterations that consume battery power which increases faulty nodes (battery depletion).

4.2 Analysis of Control Overhead (CO)

Since, the detection and recovery of faulty node is an additional task in WSN. It requires extra control packets. This metric computes the additional control packets needed to perform the recovery process. In Fig. 8, we noticed that for both FDRA and FDWSN increase with the increase of the number of nodes.

Table 3. Simulation parameters.

Parameter	Value
Area size	1000 × 1000 ms
Number of nodes	20, 40, 60, 80, 100, 200
Transmission power	2mW, 4mW
Transmission channel	Wireless channel
Propagation model log	Normal path loss model
Data packet size	32 bytes
Bandwidth	200 Kilobytes/second
Radio layer	CC2420 radio layer
Queue size	50 packets

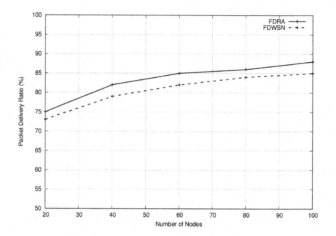

Fig. 6. PDR vs. number of nodes, TP = 2mW.

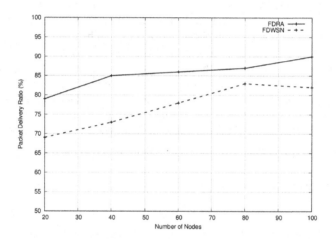

Fig. 7. PDR vs. number of nodes, TP = 4mW

More nodes require more control packets to achieve the recovery process. However, the FDWSN protocol uses more control packet comparing with our FDRA since the later does not need any iteration for the detection process. The FDWSN's detection faulty nodes process is very complicated and it is based on collecting neighbors information to detect the faulty nodes. When we increase the node transmission power to 4 mW (see Fig. 9), FDWSN needs more packet of control. However, our algorithm performs better with high transmission power because the recovery node can reach more nodes of the same level.

4.3 Analysis of Memory Overhead (MO)

This metric represents the average number of bytes needed to be stored in the memory of all nodes that are implied in recovery process. We compute for FDRA and FDWSN, the additional memory space needed to ensure the all process. We plot the result in Fig. 10. During the simulation, we notice a change in the quantity of bytes required for both algorithms. This instability in memory overhead is due to the mechanism deployed on nodes. We observe that the memory overhead in FDRA is less than in FDWSN because the later requires more memory to store transient fault matrix and other parameters. In Fig. 11 (node transmission power = 4 mW), we observe better results comparing with previous curves (transmission power = 2 mW) of two algorithms with FDRA less memory overhead.

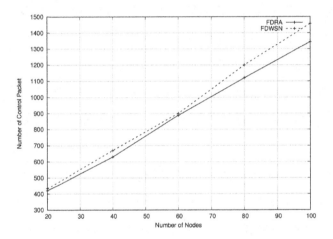

Fig. 8. CO vs. number of nodes, TP = 2mW.

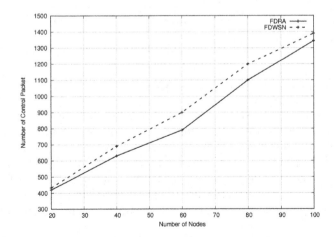

Fig. 9. CO vs. number of nodes, TP = 4mW.

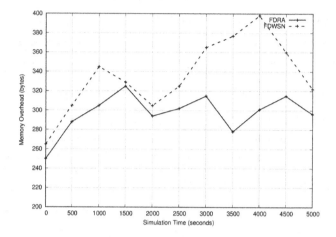

Fig. 10. MO vs. simulation time (TP = 2mW, number of nodes = 100).

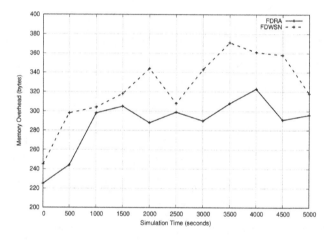

Fig. 11. MO vs. simulation time (TP = 4mW, number of nodes = 100).

4.4   Analysis of Fault Recovery Delay (FRD)

The fault recovery delay is a very important metric in the conception of a fault tolerance protocols. It is defined as the average time taken to recover from the effect of faulty node. From the Fig. 12, it is clear that our FDRA outperforms FDWSN. This is due mainly to the fact that FDWSN requires more time to create and compare transient fault matrices for each faulty node. However, the FDRA can recover a multiple faulty nodes if the position of recovery node selected is close from the faulty nodes (i.e., one sleeping node can recover multiple faulty nodes). When we increase the number of nodes in network to 200 (Fig. 13), we observe a small increase for FDRA compared with FDWSN. The later requires more time to recover from faulty nodes because it needs to compare transient fault matrices.

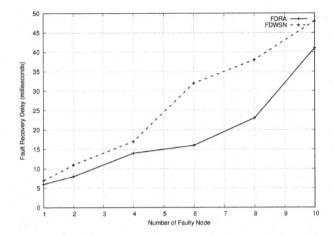

Fig. 12. FRD vs. number of faulty node (number of nodes = 100).

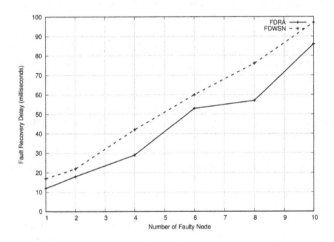

Fig. 13. FRD vs. number of faulty node (number of nodes = 200).

5   Conclusion

This paper focused on recovery faulty nodes within WSN. The main goal was to use sleeping nodes to recover faulty nodes after detection phase. In this paper we have improved our previous work to ensure a recovery process. The proposal algorithm is divided into two phases, a preliminary phase and a recovery phase. These phases are ordered by the BS and they are launched just after the detection's process of faulty nodes. The extensive simulations have demonstrated that the proposed solution permit an efficient recovery. The obtained results have confirmed also that the proposed algorithm outperforms compared to the results of the comparative algorithm FDWSN.

As a future work, we plan to formally prove the correction of the proposed algorithm. More specifically, prove that (1) it recovers all faulty nodes, and (2) it eliminates network partition.

References

1. Nourizadeh, S., Deroussent, C., Song, Y.Q., Thomesse, J.P.: Medical and home automation sensor networks for senior citizens telehomecare. In: IEEE International Conference on Communications Workshops, pp. 1–5. Dresden, Germany (2009)
2. He, T., et al.: Vigilnet an integrated sensor network system for energy-efficient surveillance. ACM Trans. Sens. Netw. **2**(1), 1–38 (2006)
3. Vicaire, P., et al.: Achieving long term surveillance in vigilnet. In: 25th International Conference on Computer Communications, pp. 1–12. Barcelona, Spain (2006)
4. Song, H., Zhu, S., Cao, G.: SVATS: a sensor-network-based vehicle anti-theft system. In: 27th Conference on Computer Communications, pp. 2128–2136. Phoenix, USA (2008)
5. Yang, L., Ji, M., Gao, Z., Zhang, W., Guo, T.: Design of home automation system based on zigbee wireless sensor network. In: 1st International Conference on Information Science and Engineering, pp. 2610–2613, Nanjing, China (2009)
6. Szewczyk, R., Mainwaring, A., Polastre, J., Anderson, J., Culler, D.: An analysis of a large scale habitat monitoring application. In: 2nd International Conference on Embedded Networked Sensor Systems, pp. 214–226. Baltimore, USA (2004)
7. Toll, G., et al.: A macroscope in the redwoods. In: 3th International Conference on Embedded Networked Sensor Systems, pp. 51–63. San Diego, USA (2005)
8. Sikka, P., Corke, P., Valencia, P., Crossman, C., Swain, D., Bishop, H.G.: Wireless adhoc sensor and actuator networks on the farm. In: 5th International Conference on Information Processing in Sensor Networks, pp. 492–499. Nashville, USA (2006)
9. Werner, A.G., Swieskowski, P., Welsh, M.: Real-time volcanic earthquake localization. In: 4th International Conference on Embedded Networked Sensor Systems, pp. 357–358. Boulder, USA (2006)
10. Demirbas, M.: Scalable design of fault-tolerance for wireless sensor networks. Ph.D thesis, The Ohio State University, USA (2004)
11. Ramanathan, N., Kohler, E., Girod, L., Estrin, D.: Sympathy: a debugging system for sensor networks. In: 29th IEEE International Conference on Local Computer Networks, pp. 554–555. Florida, USA (2004)
12. Ringwald, M., Römer, K., Vitaletti, A.: SNIF: Sensor network inspection framework. Technical report 535. ETH Zurich, Zurich, Switzerland (2006)
13. Titouna, C., Aliouat, M., Gueroui, A.M.: FDS: fault detection scheme for wireless sensor networks. Wirel. Pers. Commun. **86**(2), 549–562 (2016)
14. Mohamed, Y., Izzet, F.S., Kemal, A., Sookyoung, L., Senel, F.: Topology management techniques for tolerating node failures in wireless sensor networks: a survey. Comput. Netw. **58**, 254–283 (2014)
15. Titouna, C., Aliouat, M., Gueroui, A.M.: Outlier detection approach using bayes classifiers in wireless sensor networks. Wirel. Pers. Commun. **85**(3), 1009–1023 (2015)
16. Wang, W., Srinivasan, V., Chua, K.C.: Using mobile relays to prolong the lifetime of wireless sensor networks. In: 11th Annual International Conference on Mobile Computing and Networking, pp. 270–283. Cologne, Germany (2005)
17. Basu, P., Redi, J.: Movement control algorithms for realization of fault-tolerant ad hoc robot networks. IEEE Netw. **18**(4), 36–44 (2004)

18. Abbasi, A.A., Akkaya, K., Younis, M.: A distributed connectivity restoration algorithm in wireless sensor and actor networks. In: 32nd IEEE International Conference on Local Computer Networks, pp. 496–503. Dublin, Ireland (2007)
19. Akkaya, K., Thimmapuram, A., Senel, F., Uludag, S.: Distributed recovery of actor failures in wireless sensor and actor networks. In: IEEE Wireless Communications and Networking Conference, pp. 2480–2485. Las Vegas, USA (2008)
20. Tamboli, N., Younis, M.: Coverage-aware connectivity restoration in mobile sensor networks. J. Netw. Comput. Appl. **33**(4), 363–374 (2010)
21. Akkaya, K., Senel, F., Thimmapuram, A., Uludag, S.: Distributed recovery from network partitioning in movable sensor/actor networks via controlled mobility. IEEE Trans. Comput. **59**(2), 258–271 (2010)
22. Younis, M., Lee, S., Gupta, S., Fisher, K.: A localized self-healing algorithm for networks of moveable sensor nodes. In: IEEE Global Telecommunications Conference, pp. 1–5. New Orleans, USA (2008)
23. Sookyoung, L., Mohamed, Y., Meejeong, L.: Connectivity restoration in a partitioned wireless sensor network with assured fault tolerance. Ad Hoc Netw. **24**, 1–19 (2015). Part A
24. Lee, M.H., Choi, Y.H.: Fault detection of wireless sensor networks. Comput. Commun. **31**(14), 3469–3475 (2008)
25. Sergiou, C., Vassiliou, V.: Source-based routing trees for efficient congestion control in wireless sensor networks. In: 8th International Conference on Distributed Computing in Sensor Systems, pp. 378–383. Hangzhou, China (2012)
26. Sergiou, C., Vassiliou, V.: Tree-forming schemes for overload control in wireless sensor networks. In: 11th Annual Mediterranean Ad Hoc Networking Workshop, pp. 61–66. Ayia Napa, Cyprus (2012)
27. Levis, P., Lee, N., Welsh, M., Culler, D.: TOSSIM: accurate and scalable simulation of entire TinyOS applications. In: 1st International Conference on Embedded Networked Sensor Systems, pp. 126–137. Los Angeles, USA (2003)

Modeling the Mobile Signal Transmission Network of Earth-Moving and Construction Machines' Sensors

Tatyana Golubeva[1]([✉]) [iD], Bakhodyr Yakubov[1], Sergey Konshin[1], and Boris Tshukin[2]

[1] Almaty University of Power Engineering and Telecommunications, Almaty, Kazakhstan
ya_nepovtorimaya@mail.ru, yakubov.baxadyr@mail.ru,
ots2@yandex.com
[2] National Research Nuclear University MEPhI, Moscow, Russia
tsh-k22@mail.ru

Abstract. In this paper, the problem of performing distributed computations in signal transmission mobile network of earth-moving and construction machines' sensors is investigated. Distributed computing was performed within this mobile network. A new definition of distributed computing has been developed within this mobile network, which allows you to explore this sensor network in terms of sensors power consumption in the case of possibility to recharge the nodes from the environment.

The model of this mobile network was obtained. This model allows to estimate the power consumption by nodes of sensor network, depending on changing characteristics of the network.

Keywords: Mobile network · Sensors · Signal transmission
Earth-moving and construction machines

1 Introduction

As the result of research carried out by the authors [1–7], the structure of an automated control system of work of earth-moving and construction machines was developed. At the same time, authors have considered various aspects of the implementation of such system to automate digging, transportation and unloading processes. However, the issues of transmitting signals from sensors installed on earth-moving and construction machines have not been studied before. The use of wire connections between sensors and the controller of machine is unacceptable due to the constant movement of machine moving parts (bucket, boom, etc.). Work [8] is an example of moving parts in the theory of machines and mechanisms. Therefore, the use of a mobile network as the transmitting medium is the only correct solution.

Over the past few years, continuous progress in mobile communications has opened up new research areas in the field of mobile networks aimed at increasing access to data networks in environments where wired solutions are virtually impossible. For example, work [9] deals with Vehicular Ad-hoc Networks (VANET) modeling. The authors

M. Younas et al. (Eds.): MobiWIS 2018, LNCS 10995, pp. 86–98, 2018.
https://doi.org/10.1007/978-3-319-97163-6_8

presented «VanetMobiSim», a freely available generator of realistic traffic paths for network simulators. The article [10] provides information of the computer simulation results for determining technical characteristics of fractal antennas used to transmit information in mobile networks.

The research and development of new sensor types for various devices with wireless data transmission are being actively conducted. For example, wireless sensor Vibration Energy Harvester (VEH) [11]. VEH is designed to be installed on rotating parts, for example, on train wheels, and performs several functions: measuring the temperature, transferring the measured data to the operator, generating the necessary electric energy from mechanical vibrations. According to the information from developers, VEH does not require additional maintenance, and is ideal to be installed in train wheels, as in addition to borrowing energy, the sensor instantly captures the critical temperature rise in the bearings. This helps to prevent major repairs.

And in work [12] the wireless switch "Cherry Energy Harvesting Wireless Switch" which produces the electric power, sufficient for transfer a turn on signal or short retransmission is offered. The distance to which the signal can be transmitted due to the generated energy depends on the operating frequency. For transmission at 10 m, the frequency is 2.4 GHz, for transmission at 300 m, the frequency is 868 MHz. The power generated by pressing the button can reach 0.5 mW. As an additional feature of the "Energy Harvesting Wireless Switch", one can be a work in wireless sensor networks (for this purpose, a unique identifier that eliminates erroneous operations is implemented in the switch), as well as a "pairing" function that allows several switches to be used for one receiver or vice versa.

At the same time, Energy Harvesting technology need to be given special attention, since this technology allows sensors to operate autonomously. Autonomy is achieved due to low power consumption and independent electricity generation on account of mini solar panels, vibration process or like ones. The main methods of the "Energy Harvesting" are based on converting light energy, kinetic energy and energy of the temperature difference between the environment and the heat source into electrical energy. For example, a wireless sensor network node with extremely low power consumption, which borrows and converts solar energy, thereby demonstrating that such a solution is convenient for wireless sensor network applications [13]. Borrowing the energy of the environment in a wireless network is especially important if a node battery is difficult to replace or it have a high cost. A node that borrows solar energy performs monitoring and supports wireless interface functions at levels requiring low power consumption. The presence of an additional input source makes it possible to take energy from other alternative energy sources (radio frequency radiation, vibrations, etc.) at step of energy management, in case if solar batteries are discharged or can't be accessed at the moment. The interaction of data networks is discussed in detail using the example of modeling using the NetCracker 4.1 program [14].

However, the development of mobile networks to automate the work of earth-moving and construction machines with data transfer from sensors to controllers, was not considered in the literature.

The analysis and review of the literature made it possible to simulate the mobile network for sensors signal transmission of earth-moving and construction machines.

2 Materials and Methods

Agent-based modeling is well suited to simulate the concept of such mobile network [15]. Agent-based modeling can be defined as a special case of simulation modeling, which focuses on the study of the global system state, depending on a behavior of agents which are system components. In the case of a mobile network for sensors signal transmission, a similar approach is observed, as network nodes are distributed throughout the territory, actively interact with the environment and neighboring nodes, and a behavior and technical characteristics of an individual network node affect the network performance. In the case of traditional simulation, the simulated system is considered as a linear aggregate of passive elements in the general process, and the elements' behavior is pre-established. In the case of discrete-event approach, attention is given to a particular process that is already considered nonlinearly, the stages of a particular process are analyzed.

In the case of agent-based modeling, each network component has its own behavior scenario, which affects the task quality. Thus, agent modeling is a convenient approach for describing systems consisting of components whose behavior is ambiguous and depends on many factors.

To perform the simulation, Matlab was used - a high-level programming language and the same name environment for modeling, scientific and engineering calculations, which is based on the interpreter of the native language Matlab. The algorithms implemented in Matlab, for the most part, use vectors and matrices to handle large amounts of data.

The availability of specialized tools (processing of big data, the ability to operate with neural networks) is the main reason for choosing Matlab as a tool for modeling distributed computing in mobile network for sensors signal transmission of earth-moving and construction machines.

Nodes in sensory zones are unevenly distributed. There are nodes with large number of sensors. And there are nodes with 1–2 sensors.

In this case, the simulated system is the set of nodes of mobile network, the environment in which they are located, the scenario of their behavior, the goal to be achieved by the simulated system in the course of its work.

Simulation is carried out in order to determine the advisability of organizing distributed computing in our mobile network. For this, it is necessary to simulate the system with the absence and support of distributed computing and to perform the comparative analysis of the results obtained.

The control method of the mobile network for sensors signal transmission of earth-moving and construction machines was developed on the basis of neural networks, taking into account the Energy Harvesting technology, which, through specially built-in modules for the sensor network, allows to transform various types of renewable energy into electrical one to recharge network nodes from the environment. "Energy Harvesting technology" is to collect variety of energy from the environment and converting it into electrical energy to power the autonomous miniature devices. Any natural and physical processes and phenomena - from sunlight to any mechanical vibrations can be used as energy source [16]. The developed work algorithm of our mobile network is based on the mathematical apparatus of theory of automatic control "Neural Networks" section and supplemented with the possibility of "Energy Harvesting".

In mobile network model, being developed, a node is considered as an in-dependent intellectual object that changes its state depending on changes in the parameters of the unit itself or environmental parameters. At first sight, it would be ideal to imagine a network consisting of this type of nodes, in the form of a finite automaton. But to solve the problem of controlling transitions between possible states of a node, the method of neural networks is chosen, that is, another abstraction of the description of the technical object behavior.

Subjectively, the method of neural networks is more convenient, since errors are possible during development, since the automatic design of the FSM (Finite state machine) provides the developer with more free description of the technical object behavior. While the solution of the task using neural networks is reduced to the problem of classifying an arbitrary combination of input data in accordance with a set of states similar to FSM.

Let's describe the model, compiled using the object-oriented language Java [17].

Input data:

- size of earth-moving and construction machine;
- node count in earth-moving and construction machine;
- node distribution law;
- initial energy reserve of nodes;
- Constants for calculating formulas in accordance with the protocol;
- transmitter and receiver parameters.

Output data (being measured in the network, in addition to the values of sensors them-selves):

- value of energy remaining on network nodes;
- transmitted packets count;
- number of nodes whose energy was exhausted before the claimed number of work rounds was expired.

Functions:

- input data initialization;
- creation, training of a neural network;
- initialization of the mobile network;
- node parameters analysis;
- choice of state for each network node.

The network nodes independently choose one of four states: computer, receiver, transmitter, scavenger, depending on current parameter values of nodes of the mobile network. The node parameters, depending on the current state, are stored on the node as attributes of selected class. Depending on the selected state, one of the attribute blocks is activated, and the remaining blocks are blocked. The choice of the node state at the current time is made by the method of neural networks, depending on the node param-eters at the current moment and the parameters of the task that requires calculations.

After completing the training, the sensor network will independently select the parameters in accordance with the possible energy from the environment and the requirements of the task at any given time.

3   Results

The class diagram of wireless network model with support for distributed computing was developed (Fig. 1).

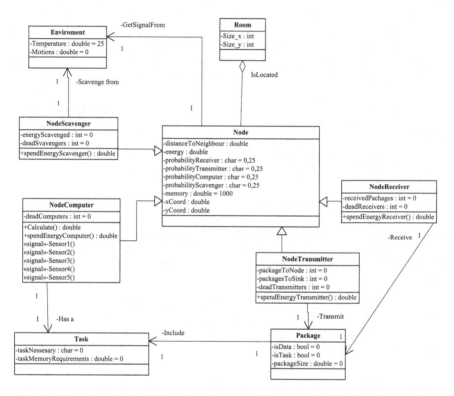

Fig. 1. Class diagram of wireless network model with support for distributed computing

According to Fig. 1, the base class is the Node class. Extended classes NodeScavenger, NodeComputer, NodeReceiver, NodeTransmitter enter into the generalization relationship with the base class Node.

The environment in which the node is located is indicated by the Room and Enviroment classes and is related with the Node class. We can say that the Room class includes several nodes and, thus, enters into the aggregation relationship with the Node class. The Enviroment class interacts with both NodeScavenger class (in the charging process) and with Node class (in the process of data collection by the node sensors).

The Task class enter into the association relationship with NodeComputer class and the Package class. The Task class is typical only for the NodeComputer state, since the calculation of the task is unacceptable when the node is in other states (it is impossible to charge the node when it is not in the NoseScavenger state). The association relationship with the Package class is explained by the fact that the task itself is transmitted over the network in the broadcast packet structure.

The Package class enters into the association relationship only with the Node-Receiver class and NodeTransmitter class, because, in one of these states, the node can receive or transmit data packets.

Mathematical modeling of the task was carried out. The parameters for calculating the power consumption are given in Table 1 and are constant. These parameters are used to calculate the energy consumption in the LEACH (Low Energy Adaptive Clustering Hierarchy) protocol [18], with which the comparison is made. The calculation of the energy consumption takes place using formula (1), according to which the current value of energy is reduced by an amount depending on the distance parameter. The distance parameter, in turn, varies depending on the nodes location according to formula (2).

$$Node(i).Energy = Node(i).Energy - ((ETX + EDA)(4000)Emp * 4000 * \tag{1}$$
$$(distance * distance * distance * distance))$$

$$distance = \sqrt{(Node(i).xd - Node(n+1).xd)^2 + (Node(i).yd) - (Node(n+1).yd)^2} \tag{2}$$

Table 1. Data for calculation of energy consumption, being inputted at the simulation

Parameter	Data
ETX	50*0.000000001;
ERX	50*0.000000001
Efs	10*0.000000000001
Emp	0.0013*0.000000000001
EDA	5*0.000000001

In the process of studying the developed model, it is planned to change the following input parameters in order to reveal the trend in energy consumption by the network:

- node density;
- node count;
- number of work rounds.

For example, the location and density of nodes can vary. In Fig. 2, there are 9 nodes, in Fig. 3 there are 40 nodes. These Figures show the distance in meters and the location of the nodes on abscissa and ordinate axes for two different types of earth-moving machines.

It is proposed to study and compare the proposed method on the basis of neural networks and the existing LEACH protocol by evaluating the following output characteristics:

- total values of energy, remaining at network nodes, depending on changing input parameters;

- number of nodes whose energy was exhausted before the claimed number of work rounds was expired.

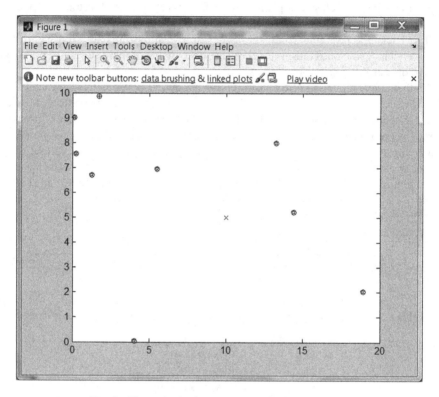

Fig. 2. The nodes location of sensor network for n = 9

After the simulation of our mobile network, the following results were obtained:

1. dependence of residual energy on the number and density of nodes;
2. dependence of residual energy on the number of work rounds.

In the first item, the variable parameter is the node count of simulated network, with the unchanged size of machine, where they are. That is, the increase in the density of the sensor network nodes is investigated. Also, depending on the number of nodes, the quantitative ratio between nodes of different types (NodeScavenger, NodeReceiver, NodeTransmitter, NodeComputer) varies, therefore the data of energy consumption is changing.

The results obtained are given in Table 2, to which the graph in Fig. 4 corresponds.

Method 1 - the method to be developed with the support of distributed computing. Method 2 - the method based on the LEACH protocol without the support of distributed computing.

Based on the results obtained in Table 2 and Fig. 4, it can be concluded that with an increase in the number of nodes of the sensor network that can be recharged from the environment, the amount of energy on the nodes of the sensor network, that remains after the expiration of the claimed number of work rounds, is increasing. That is, in terms of energy efficiency, it is advantageous to increase the density of the nodes of the sensor network.

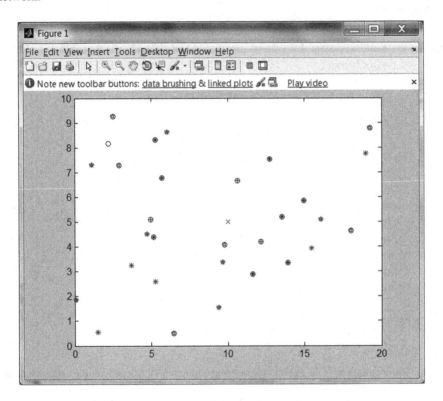

Fig. 3. The nodes location of sensor network for n = 40

In the second item, the variable parameter is the number of rounds of the simulated network with an unchanged number of nodes. That is, the energy consumption depending on its operation time is studied. It would be logical to assume that with increasing rounds, the network will expend more energy. But it is necessary to investigate how much the availability of the possibility of borrowing energy from the environment effects energy consumption, and also to compare the values of the residual energy in compared approaches.

For this, let us consider two methods. Method 1 - the method to be developed with the support of distributed computing. Method 2 - the method based on the LEACH protocol without the support of distributed computing.

The results suggest that with an increasing the number of work rounds of the sensor network and the availability of energy borrowing, energy consumption is decreases, and when this number reaches 400–500 rounds, energy consumption increases. This is evidenced by dependence graph of residual energy at the network nodes from the number of work rounds. That is, the result obtained differs from expected one.

Table 2. Results of the study on dependence of network power consumption on the density of the nodes location

	Node count	9	15	20	25	30	40	45
Method 1	Residual energy, J	29,46	46,08	62,08	79,42	98,9	130,5	148,8
	«Dead» nodes	0	0	0	0	0	0	0
Method 2	Residual energy, J	9,204	15,94	20,65	26	30,62	41,08	46,61
	«Dead» nodes	0	0	0	0	0	0	0

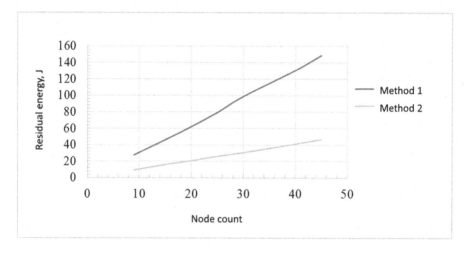

Fig. 4. The dependence of the network power consumption on the density of the nodes location.

It is interesting to note that after reaching the number of rounds of 100, the increase in the gain in energy consumption slows down (Fig. 5).

Thus, from the point of view of energy efficiency, it is advantageous to increase the number of rounds to just about 350.

The results obtained are shown in Table 3 and in Figs. 5 and 6.

Table 3. The results of the study on the dependence of the network energy consumption on the number of rounds

	Number of rounds	15	25	50	100	200	300	400
Method 1	Residual energy, J	64,94	75,25	95,96	116,27	121,07	122,58	121,92
	«Dead» nodes	0	0	0	0	0	0	0
Method 2	Residual energy, J	20,06	22,75	30,84	56,72	190,65	649,48	2196
	«Dead» nodes	0	0	0	0	0	0	0

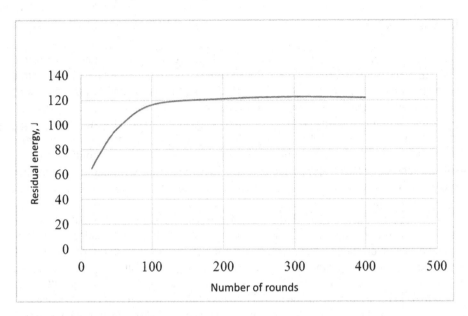

Fig. 5. The graph of the dependence of the network power consumption on the number of rounds for Method 1

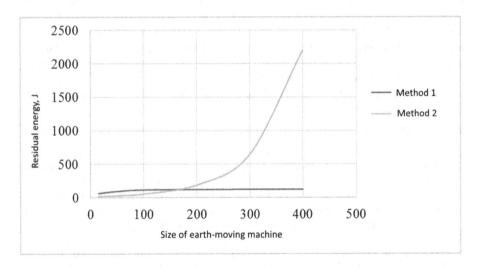

Fig. 6. The graph of the dependence of the network power consumption on the size of earth-moving machine.

The results of research, presented in Fig. 6, shows that method 2 (without the distributed computing support, based on the LEACH protocol) is not suitable for simulation the big size earth-moving machines, such as, for example, a multibucket excavator. Method 1 (with the distributed computing support) gives an adequate result for any size of earth-moving machine, allowing the data transfer without additional power consumption.

4 Conclusion

Thus, it can be concluded that the network model being developed contains data transfer nodes that interact primarily with each other, rather than with the server of the central dispatch room for control the work of earth-moving and construction machines, and send data without the participation of coordinator.

Research in this and related areas is mainly carried out to develop the most energy efficient routing protocols, which seek to solve the problem of uneven power consumption by network nodes. All energy efficient protocols use dynamic reconfiguration of network topology. The proposed method also uses dynamic reconfiguration, since the state in which each node of the sensor network is located varies over time, and this change affects the network state.

In the paper, the problem of urgency of executing distributed computations in a mobile network for sensors signal transmission of earth-moving and construction machines is investigated. The implemented model with the support of distributed computing, within the framework of the experiment simulation, has limitations that relate to the physical part of data transmission. In further studies, additional attention needs to be given to improving the model of the mobile network for signal transmission.

As a result of the research, the following conclusions can be drawn. Current energy-efficient protocols for sensor networks do not take into account the charging of the sensor network nodes from the environment. A new definition of distributed computing within the mobile network for sensors signal transmission of earth-moving and construction machines has been developed, which allows to explore this sensor network in terms of energy consumption in case if nodes can be recharged from the environment. The model of the mobile network for sensors signal transmission of earth-moving and construction machines which allows to estimate the energy consumption by the nodes of the sensor network, depending on the changing characteristics of the network was obtained.

References

1. Golubeva, T., Pokussov, V., Konshin, S., Tshukin, B., Zaytcev, E.: Research of the mobile CDMA network for the operation of an intelligent information system of earth-moving and construction machines. In: Younas, M., Awan, I., Holubova, I. (eds.) Mobile Web and Intelligent Information Systems. MobiWIS 2017. LNCS, vol. 10486, pp. 193–205. Springer, Cham (2017). https://doi.org/10.1007/978-3-319-65515-4_17
2. Golubeva, T., Konshin, S.: Improving of positioning for measurements to control the operation and management of earth-moving and construction machinery. In: 13th International Conference on Remote Engineering and Virtual Instrumentation (REV), 24–26 February 2016, pp. 112–115. IEEE, UNED, Madrid, Spain (2016). https://doi.org/10.1109/REV.2016.7444450. 978-1-4673-8245-8/16/$31.00
3. Golubeva, T., Zaitsev, Y., Konshin, S.: Research of 3G-324 M mobile communication protocol in the management and control system of work of earth-moving machines and data transfer. In: 2016 10th International Symposium on Communication Systems, Networks and Digital Signal Processing (CSNDSP), 20–22 July 2016, pp. 1–3. IEEE, Prague (2016). https://doi.org/10.1109/CSNDSP.2016.7573995. WOS:000386781300099

4. Golubeva, T., Zaitsev, Y., Konshin, S.: Research of electromagnetic environment for organizing the radio channel of communication of operation control system of earthmoving and construction machines. In: 19-th International Symposium on Electrical Apparatus and Technologies (SIELA 2016), 29 May–1 June 2016, pp. 1–4. IEEE, Bourgas (2016). https://doi.org/10.1109/SIELA.2016.7543006. WOS:000382936800035

5. Golubeva, T., Konshin, S.: The research of possibility of sharing use of wireless and mobile technologies for organizing the radio channels of operation control system of earthmoving and construction machines. In: 2016 International Conference on Intelligent Networking and Collaborative Systems (INCoS), 7–9 September 2016, pp. 9–14. IEEE, Ostrava (2016). https://doi.org/10.1109/INCoS.2016.24. WOS:000386596100002

6. Golubeva, T., Zaitsev, Y., Konshin, S.: Research of WiMax standard to organize the data transmission channels in the integrated control system of earth-moving machines. In: 2016 17th International Conference of Young Specialists on Micro/Nano Technologies and Electron Devices (EDM), June 30–July 4 2016, pp. 91–95. IEEE, Erlagol (2016). https://doi.org/10.1109/EDM.2016.7538701. WOS:000390301500024. Electronic ISSN: 2325-419X

7. Golubeva, T., Zaitsev, Y., Konshin, S.: Improving the smart environment for control systems of earth-moving and construction machines. In: 2016 IEEE 4th International Conference on Future Internet of Things and Cloud (FiCloud), 22–24 August 2016, pp. 240–243. IEEE, Vienna (2016). https://doi.org/10.1109/FiCloud.2016.42. WOS:000391237900034. ISBN: 978-1-5090-4053-7

8. Ivanov, K., Tultayev, B., Balbayev, G.: A single speed (CVT) transmission. In: Joint International Conference of the 12th International Conference on Mechanisms and Mechanical Transmissions, MTM 2016 and the 23rd International Conference on Robotics, Robotics 2016, Aachen, Germany, 26–27 October 2016, vol. 46, pp. 125–131. Mechanisms and Machine Science (2017). https://doi.org/10.1007/978-3-319-45450-4_13. ISSN: 2211098, ISBN: 978-331945449-8

9. Harri, J., Fiore, M., Filali, F.: Vehicular mobility simulation with VanetMobiSim. Simul. Trans. Soc. Model. Simul. Int. **87**(4), 275–300 (2011). https://doi.org/10.1177/0037549709345997. WOS:000289161600001. ISSN: 0037-5497

10. Solochshenko, A.V., Kulikov, A.A., Satimova, Y.G., Rutgayzer, O.Z.: The study of influence of changes of fractal antennas forms during using affine "compression" transformation on its characteristics. Int. J. Appl. Eng. Res. **12**(1), 7–10 (2017). ISSN: 09734562

11. Lee, O.B., Ket, T.C., Keat, Y.C., Aziz, R.A.: Applications of vibration-based energy harvesting (VEH) devices. In: Biologically-Inspired Energy Harvesting through Wireless Sensor Technologies, pp. 1–26 (2016). https://doi.org/10.4018/978-1-4666-9792-8.ch001. ISBN: 978146669792?

12. Cherry – Energy -harvesting wireless switches for industrial applications, 10 July 2015. https://www.electropages.com/2015/07/cherry-energy-harvesting-wireless-switches-industrial-applications/

13. Silicon Labs Energy Harvesting Applications // Silicon Labs Home page. www.silabs.com/energy-harvesting/

14. Yakubova, M., Serikov, T.: Development and imitating modeling in the developed network consisting of several knots removed among themselves on NetCracker 4.1. In: 2016 17th International Conference of Young Specialists on Micro/Nanotechnologies and Electron Devices (EDM), June 30–July 4 2016, pp. 210–213 (2016). https://doi.org/10.1109/EDM.2016.7538726. Electronic ISSN: 2325-419X

15. Macal, C.M., North, M.J.: Agent-based modeling and simulation. In: Proceedings of the 2009 Winter Simulation Conference, pp. 86–98. IEEE (2009). 978-1-4244-5771-7/09/$26.00 ©2009

16. Hagerty, J., Helmbrecht, F., McCalpin, W., Zane, R., Popovic, Z.: Recycling ambient microwave energy with broad-band rectenna arrays. IEEE Trans. Microw. Theory Tech. **52**(3), 1014–1024 (2004). https://doi.org/10.1109/TMTT.2004.823585
17. Hilton, A.D., Duvall, R., Rodger, S.H., Astrachan, O.: Programming Foundations with JavaScript, HTML and CSS. https://www.coursera.org/specializations/java-programming
18. Sarr, Y.M., Sarr, C., Gueye, B.: Reduction of single clusters in LEACH protocol for wireless sensor. Open Access Libr. J. **2**(e2251), 1–8 (2015). https://doi.org/10.4236/oalib.1102251

Web and Cloud Services

Analysis of the Use of System Resources for Cloud Data Security

Josef Horalek and Vladimir Sobeslav[✉]

Faculty of Informatics and Management, University of Hradec Kralove,
Hradec Kralove, Czech Republic
{josef.horalek,vladimir.sobeslav}@uhk.cz

Abstract. The article presents results of the analysis of the use of system resources for data security via client-side encryption. The research was focused on efficiency of the usage of system resources by open-source tools that are used for client-side data encryption before saving them to cloud environment. Based on the acquired results the proper client-side encryption tool can be selected depending on type and size of encrypted data.

Keywords: CPU · System resources · Boxcryptor · Cryptomator · Viivo

1 Introduction

Security risks associated with cloud storage data [1] is a topic being currently discussed, because information saved in public cloud storages is accessible to a public cloud operator. Not only that, the information is secured by means provided by an operator of that particular cloud storage. It is important to mention that commonly used cloud storages such as Google Drive, Dropbox, Amazon Drive, Microsoft One Drive, iCloud Drive, Mega or Wedos Disk do not offer an option of a client-based encoding, even for paid users. The security of stored data and the Directive 95/46/ES (General Data Protection Regulation (GDPR)) taken into an account, one of the options to secure the data effectively is to use client-side encryption and sending only encrypted data to the cloud storage. Using such a method also provides an option to save the data. This solution is more and more common and to some extent it solves a problem of data retention in the public-cloud. There are various applications available nowadays which directly communicate with the aforementioned cloud storages, offering appropriate client-side security data encryption. Their use is affected by the degree of impact for the end-user's everyday work. That is a reason why a research has been made, focused on the use of selected system environments with a standard use of an endpoint device. A set of measurements, with selected software tools, was made providing a client for the endpoint device, which provides more than the only standard encryption AES 256 [2], but also sends data to a chosen cloud storage while running automatically in the background. The tools selected were chosen on the basis of a simple survey among users from the university affiliated with the authors. However, the research is not a subject of the present article. The choice of testing and measuring of selected system sources Memory and CPU was chosen

© Springer International Publishing AG, part of Springer Nature 2018
M. Younas et al. (Eds.): MobiWIS 2018, LNCS 10995, pp. 101–111, 2018.
https://doi.org/10.1007/978-3-319-97163-6_9

considering the efficiency of these critical system resources in the user-work routine. It was assumed that encryption and data backup to the chosen cloud-storage is fully automatic as a process running in the background, and that a user should not notice any significant decrease in available system sources for other running processes. From this point of view, it is more efficient for users and for the operating system to use linear system sources with a minimum number of significant performance fluctuations, even at the cost of a longer processing time. From this perspective, it is more efficient for users and the operating system to use system resources linearly with a minimum number of significant performance deviations even at the costs of longer processing time. Such an approach is preferred in case of standard non-preemptive or voluntarily preemetary operation systems; furthermore, with a well-chosen system of planning processes utilizing the possibility of using external priorities, it is also frequently used.

Data security for the cloud environment is a highly topical issue. Yan et al. [3], who has been dealing with the issue of security of cloud computing via identity management based on a hierarchical identity, points to the issue of data security in the cloud. Kamara and Lauter [4] in the article called Cryptographic Cloud Storage, deal equally with this issue. To secure data in the cloud using cryptographic devices and their effective deployment is being dealt by [5, 6]. The use of selected cryptographic methods in the third-party cloud environment is dealt by [7, 8]. Generally speaking, the issue of data security in cloud-storages is directly solved on the given cloud solution and architecture. The solution for a non-negligible group of users, both in a private and a corporate sphere, is to use public-cloud storages even in a paid form. However, they demand a high level of security for their data as well as privacy. These requirements are not reflected by operators; therefore, a relevant solution is to use the cloud for storing encrypted data which are automatically encrypted on the client-side.

2   Presentation of Tested Tools

The present research utilizes three selected freely available tools sharing the use of basic AES algorithms in their 256 version. A common feature for all selected representatives is that they provide a client for the end-user on all the most commonly used architectural platforms of operating systems. Another common denominator for selected tools is the ability of a direct cooperation with a wide array of cloud-storages.

2.1   Boxcryptor

Boxcryptor [9] is software which is used for data encryption on a cloud-storage. It was developed by the German company Secomba GmbH and is among the most popular products in its category. It has always been used in a combination with a specific cloud-storage solution. Currently it supports a large number of common and less popular cloud solutions. The list is available on the product's pages [10]. Boxcryptor is designed according to the zero knowledge paradigm. It means only the owner has access to the data and no one else may access it. There is a wide range of mobile and desktop platforms supported. Boxcryptor combines the possibilities of asymmetric and symmetric ciphers.

Each file has its own randomly generated key which occurs during a file creation and is used for encryption and decryption of the data files. The basic algorithms used are: 256-bit AES variant in a combination with CBC and PKCS7, 4096-bit RSA variant in a combination with OAEP. A detailed description of the technical data is available on the product's pages [10]. Boxcryptor supports a large number of mobile and desktop platforms.

- Windows (version 7, 8, 10)
- macOS (version 10.9 and higher)
- Android (version 4.0.3 and higher)
- iOS (version 8.2 and higher)
- Windows Phone (version 8 and higher)
- Blackberry OS (version 10. 2 and higher)

There is also a portable variant for 64-bit Linux and macOS, followed by 32-bit Windows and finally a Google Chrome add-on.

2.2 Cryptomator

Cryptomator [11] is the second tested external tool, which can be used for encrypting of personal data in a cloud storage. It is a highly solid German product offering many kinds of security. The first functionality is a virtual file system. This system makes sure that there are no unencrypted copies of user data anywhere on the disc. SHA1PRNG service takes care of randomly generated encrypted keys. The next layer of protection is the main key protected by the user password itself. The individual encrypted files have their own encryption key, which is additionally protected by the main key. An interesting fact is that the file name is encrypted separately as well as a file header and the content itself. The algorithms used are AES-CTR in a combination with AES-SIV. The keys are concentrated in a so called "vault", where all the data is secured. Access is possible with the user password. Cryptomator is not dependent on the cloud storages itself. What suffices is the insertion of a specific encrypted data-unit (the vault) to the file storage and the rest of the process runs as normally as it runs when synchronizing common files. Every vault is encrypted by the aforementioned 256-bit algorithm. The supported operational systems are:

- Windows (Windows Vista SP2 and higher)
- Mac (OS X 10.8.3)
- Linux (may vary for each distribution)
- Other platforms supporting Java

2.3 Viivo

Viivo [12] is a product used for user-data security in a cloud. The solution from a PKWARE company is to secure the data before it is sent. After that it might be synchronized, which increases the protection of data abuse and unauthorized reading. Server providers cannot access the unencrypted copies of stored data as well as the keys. The user itself manages the keys used for the secured data. Viivo uses several layers of encryption. At the first level key pairs are being exchanged. They are encrypted by a 2048-bit variant of RSA algorithm. The user-private RSA key je protected by password the user chooses. The password is protected by a strong PBKDF2, HMAC and SHA256 combination. Finally, the files themselves are encrypted by the 256-bit algorithm AES. In the case of security files sharing, each file is encrypted by a randomly generated unique relational encrypted key. Such key is used only for one file. It is never used for more or other files. The software cooperates with a number of popular storages, for example: Dropbox, Box, Google Drive, Microsoft OneDrive. An interesting fact is that you it may be deployed in a private cloud solution. The application also takes care of data compression to save space in the storage. Viivo, unlike other products, does not have such a large number of supported platforms. Supported platforms include:

- Mac OS
- Windows
- iOS
- Android

3 Testing Methods

The subject of testing was the analysis of the use of system resources in the implementation of the security and data synchronization process which will be encrypted using the tools presented above. Because the data sync rate is a real incomparable variable whose speed and efficiency depend on a number of factors, one of Google's most commonly used cloud storages - Google Drive, was used for testing. The standard with standard parameters was selected for testing, so the obtained results were as objective as possible, taken from the perspective of a standard user:

- operating system: Windows 7 SP1 build 7601 (64-bit version)
- processor: Intel Core i5 2430M (2,40 GHz)
- operating memory: 8 GB
- HDD and SDD drives

Internal tools implemented in the operating system were used for performance-monitoring analysis. This procedure was chosen for the maximum objectiveness of the obtained data to eliminate an influence of third-party software on the operation system. The operation system provides an internal analytic tool – Windows Performance Monitor. This tool may be used by Windows to monitor how running programs affect computer performance either in real time or by using gathered protocol data for further analysis. Windows Performance Monitor uses performance counters, event data tracing and configuration information. Such information from these counters was used for the present analysis.

It was also necessary to generate general test data. For this purpose, File Generator (version 3.6.0) – available freely, was used. It is a part of a system toolkit – Disk Tools software [13]. 10 000 files were generated with each of them having a size of 4096 B (bytes) and one file of 1024 MB. In the framework of the following analysis, system sources and their use by individual tools for encrypting and synchronization of encrypted data to the cloud storage were monitored. The Windows Performance Monitor counter was set to a scanning interval of one second.

The internal tool available in the operation systems from Windows NT family – Windows Task Manager was used to analyze and measure the use of system resources. The performance tracking progress was initiated at the same time as the entire encryption process started and it ended right after the encryption process had finished. It is obvious that the completion process of synchronization is substantially influenced by the actual use of local network connectivity. From this very reason it was not the goal of the realized measurements because of possible non-objectivity. With all three tools, all activities in the Google Drive folder were running simultaneously and so it was necessary to take into account possible latency caused by sending data to the server.

It was essential for the measurement methodology that the measurement itself was running as a simulation of normal computer operation. Therefore, the system sources were occupied by other processes as well. The task of this controlled simulation was to get as close as possible to the standard user working mode in which they use the tested encryption tools. The mode of power consumption which could affect CPU usage has not been regulated in any way.

4   Results Evaluation

The results relevance is important so each measurement was repeated 20-times to re-evaluate the data using Student's t-distribution procedures. Due to repeated measurements, any extremes can be excluded from individual measurements and the statistical functions – Median and Arithmetic mean – were used applied to the results. The final results were obtained as average values of each individual function from each of the 20 executed measurements.

4.1   Evaluation of CPU and Memory Usage for File Size of 1024 MB

The measured data characterize the use of Memory in the encryption process and it is possible to find clear differences in Memory utilization from the percentage point of view. These differences have a maximum value of 3.5%, which is something that cannot be considered as a significant difference. The data table below show that Memory usage oscillated around the average value, which can be seen from the small difference between the Median and the Arithmetic mean as well. The graph captures the process of Memory use at the time data was encrypted by individual tools. The exception is the ending encryption process using the Boxcryptor too, where a significant decrease in Memory and CPU usage is typical. There is not a complete release of system resources, but the software continues to operate. This characteristic decrease in Memory and CPU usage was recorded in each measurement when processing a 1024 MB file.

From the data in Table 1 it is clear that the most linear CPU usage for encrypting a single 1024 MB file is performed by the Boxcryptor tool. On the other hand, Cryptomator software is a clear opposite. It starts the CPU with a relatively high load after the initial preparation phase, which, however, lasts shortly compared to other tested tools. Viivo shows similar features, however, CPU usage over Cryptomator is one-third and the time of this increased CPU load is three times longer than Cryptomator. Boxcryptor processed the data for the longest period of time and as it has been already mentioned above, it shows a typical behavior when processing one 1024 MB file. CPU takes approximately half of the usage time oscillating around the arithmetic mean and half of the time when the process associated with the Boxcryptor instance, assigned to CPU, oscillates in values about 1% (Fig. 1).

Table 1. Memory usage and processor for file size 1024 MB

Memory usage in time [%]			
	Boxcryptor	Cryptomator	Viivo
Median	18,475	22,160	20,256
Arithmetic mean	18,744	22,209	20,290
CPU usage in time [%]			
Median	2,940	0,310	9,844
Arithmetic mean	2,773	7,038	7,353

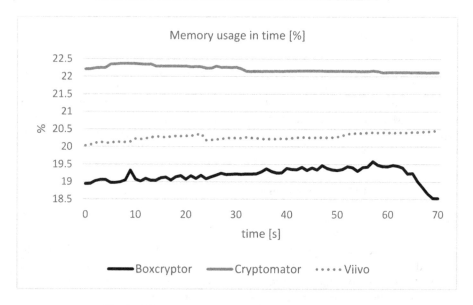

Fig. 1. Memory usage in time [%] for file size 1024 MB

When evaluating CPU usage over time, the behavioral characteristics of each application used were significantly more dynamic (Fig. 2).

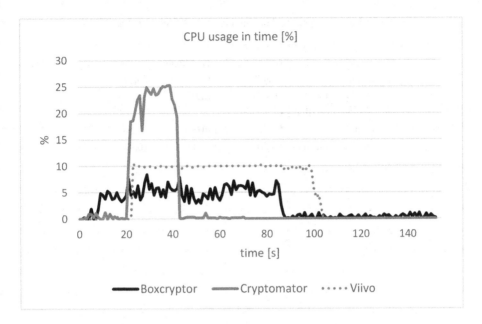

Fig. 2. CPU usage in time [%] for file size 1024 MB

4.2   CPU and Memory Usage Evaluation for 10 000 Files of Size of 4096 B

When processing 10 000 small 4096 B files, looking from the overall perspective the Memory and CPU usage is highly similar to the previous example. As expected, encryption time was longer and there was a slight increase in the use of allocated system sources. Significant differences were apparent in the time distribution of the use of system sources throughout the data processing time.

The Memory usage in time for Viivo is significantly different. Not only compared to Boxcryptor and Cryptomator, but also compared to its own behavior when processing a single file of size 1024 MB. The Viivo tool used about 30% of the available memory in the first third of its processing. Right then, there was a significant decrease of 10%. This way of using Memory was reflected in all the measurements that have been made. Both remaining testing tools – Boxcryptor and Cryptomator – showed stable Memory usage throughout the whole encryption process, as the evidence shows minimal differences in Median and Arithmetic mean values (Table 2).

The tested tools showed similar behavior during Memory usage as well as CPU usage. Compared to the behavior of the tested tools when encrypting a single 1024 MB file, there is a significant change in Cryptomator's behavior, which significantly approached Boxcryptor thanks to the linear CPU usage. Sporadic peaks occurrences were measured during repeated measurements although their duration lasts in units of seconds and so can be attributed to other standard operations on the tested device. However, as these peaks occurred at all measurements, they were not identified as random measurement errors (Figs. 3 and 4).

Table 2. Memory usage and processor for 10 000 files of size 4096 B

Memory usage in time [%]			
	Boxcryptor	Cryptomator	Viivo
Median	20,470	21,122	25,974
Arithmetic mean	20,671	21,207	28,081
CPU usage in time [%]			
Median	5,476	1,408	8,438
Arithmetic mean	5,426	1,554	16,742

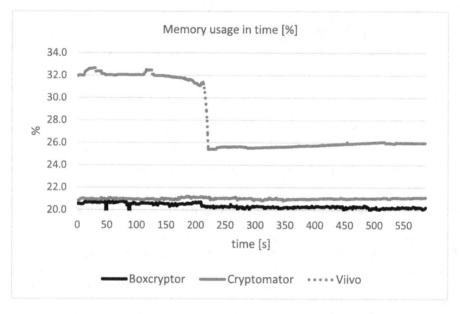

Fig. 3. Memory usage in time [%] for 10 000 files of size 4096 B

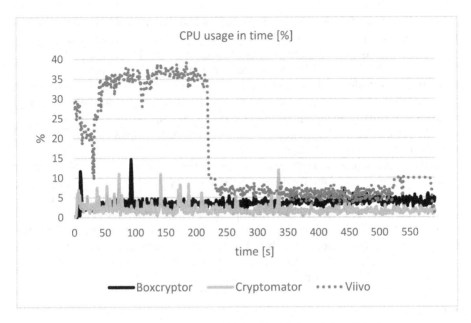

Fig. 4. CPU usage in time [%] for 10 000 files of size 4096 B

5   Conclusion

The issue of data storing to public storages and the security is a topical issue and it is being dealt by a wide range of available commercial tools or by freely accessible tools. A frequently used option is a choice of storing data in the cloud storage in an encrypted form. Encryption is being done on the endpoint device and so the already encrypted data is sent to the cloud storage. There are many tools available for this means of security in the cloud. The tools we have chosen were selected on the basis of a simple survey among users affiliated with the authors' university; this research, however, is not the subject of the present article.

The testing and measurement of selected system resources of Memory and CPU has been chosen considering an efficient use of these vital system resources for the routine user-work. We assumed that encryption and data backup on the selected cloud storage is processed automatically as a process running as a background service so the user should not notice any significant decrease of the system resources for other running processes.

From this point of view, it is more efficient for users as well as the operating system to use system resources linearly with a minimum number of significant performance fluctuations, even at the cost of longer processing times. This approach is preferred in standard non-preemptive or voluntarily preemetary operating systems and is also often used. Important is to choose the right planning system considering the possibility of using external priorities.

From this perspective, Boxcryptor is the most advantageous tool based on measurements and the relative use of system resources. The Boxcryptor's system requirements show their linear usage with moderate system requirements. The next tested tool was Viivo which showed significantly higher system requirements especially when processing 10 000 files of the size of 4096 B. There were also significant processing spikes which could affect the availability of system resources for other running processes. Overall, it can be argued that Viivo tool uses significant amount of system resources for data encryption together with major changes of their capacity which is based on their size and processing.

The last tested tool was Cryptomator with system requirements highly influenced by the amount of processed data. Based on a file size variety that users usually work with, it is not possible to simply predict the behavior of this tool and thus major peaks in system resources usage can be expected, depending on the actual size of data.

This work and the contribution were supported by project of specific science "Computer networks for cloud, distributed systems, and Internet of Things", Faculty of Informatics and Management, University of Hradec Kralove, Czech Republic. We would like also thank to students Lubos Mercl and Pavel Blazek.

References

1. Rauber, K.: Cloud cryptography. Int. J. Pure Appl. Math. **85**(1), 1–11 (2013). https://doi.org/10.12732/ijpam.v85i1.1. ISSN 1311-8080. http://www.ijpam.eu/contents/2013-85-1/1/. Accessed 18 Oct 2017
2. Schneier, B.: Applied Cryptography: Protocols, Algorithms, and Source Code in C, 20th Anniversary edn. Wiley, Indianapolis (2015). ISBN 9781119096726
3. Yan, L., Rong, C., Zhao, G.: Strengthen cloud computing security with federal identity management using hierarchical identity-based cryptography. In: Jaatun, M.G., Zhao, G., Rong, C. (eds.) CloudCom 2009. LNCS, vol. 5931, pp. 167–177. Springer, Heidelberg (2009). https://doi.org/10.1007/978-3-642-10665-1_15
4. Kamara, S., Lauter, K.: Cryptographic cloud storage. In: Sion, R., Curtmola, R., Dietrich, S., Kiayias, A., Miret, J.M., Sako, K., Sebé, F. (eds.) FC 2010. LNCS, vol. 6054, pp. 136–149. Springer, Heidelberg (2010). https://doi.org/10.1007/978-3-642-14992-4_13
5. Singh, M.D., Radha Krishna, P., Saxena, A.: A cryptography based privacy preserving solution to mine cloud data. In: Proceedings of the Third Annual ACM Bangalore Conference on COMPUTE 2010, pp. 1–4. ACM Press, New York (2010). https://doi.org/10.1145/1754288.1754302. ISBN 9781450300018. http://portal.acm.org/citation.cfm?doid=1754288.1754302. Accessed 18 Oct 2017
6. Grobauer, B., Walloschek, T., Stocker, E.: Understanding cloud computing vulnerabilities. IEEE Secur. Privacy Mag. **9**(2), 50–57 (2011). https://doi.org/10.1109/msp.2010.115. ISSN 1540-7993. http://ieeexplore.ieee.org/document/5487489/. Accessed 18 Oct 2017
7. Jaber, A.N., Zolkipli, M.F.B.: Use of cryptography in cloud computing. In: 2013 IEEE International Conference on Control System, Computing and Engineering, pp. 179–184. IEEE (2013). https://doi.org/10.1109/iccsce.2013.6719955. ISBN 978-1-4799-1508-8. http://ieeexplore.ieee.org/document/6719955/. Accessed 18 Oct 2017

8. Cao, N., Wang, C., Li, M., Ren, K., Lou, W.: Privacy-preserving multi-keyword ranked search over encrypted cloud data. IEEE Trans. Parallel Distrib. Syst. **25**(1), 222–233 (2014). https://doi.org/10.1109/tpds.2013.45. ISSN 1045-9219. http://ieeexplore.ieee.org/document/6674958/. Accessed 18 Oct 2017

9. Technical Overview. Boxcryptor. Secomba, Augsburg. https://www.boxcryptor.com/en/technical-overview/. Accessed 5 May 2017

10. AES encryption for all cloud storage providers. Boxcryptor. Secomba, Augsburg. https://www.boxcryptor.com/en/providers/. Accessed 5 May 2017

11. Security Architecture. Cryptomator. Skymatic UG, Sankt Augustin. Dostupné z. https://cryptomator.org/architecture/. Accessed 5 May 2017

12. Viivo. Milwaukee: PKWARE (2016). https://viivo.com/. Accessed 5 May 2017

13. Free Disk Tools software. Download software tools (2014). http://www.soft.tahionic.com/download-file-generator/index.html#file_generator. Accessed May 5 2017

Towards the Cloud Solutions in Aspects of Distributed Business Services

Aneta Poniszewska-Maranda[1(✉)], Bartosz Ignaczewski[1], and Erich Markl[2]

[1] Institute of Information Technology, Lodz University of Technology, Łódź, Poland
aneta.poniszewska-maranda@p.lodz.pl
[2] University of Applied Sciences Technikum Wien, Vienna, Austria
erich.markl@technikum-wien.at

Abstract. Cloud solutions in the business are nowadays becoming more and more popular. Many companies decide to deploy their applications in the cloud or migrate them from their non-cloud based solutions. It allows them to focus on functionalities and turn over the work connected with setting up and managing an infrastructure (with its issues such as scalability or availability) to the cloud providers.

This paper provides an in-depth analysis of cloud solutions in aspects of distributed business services. It is supported by a web application that is responsible for testing the provided services to supports the analysis.

1 Introduction

Once upon a time, when software engineering and computer industry in general were still in a very early stage of development, creations of applications were fairy simple in terms of the amount of technologies and tools used as well as the infrastructure setup. Basically, when the first two phases of software development process (requirements gathering and the design) were finished, the next steps were almost always the same. Firstly, a developer picked up a programming language and technology he was about to use. After that, he installed operating system and other libraries required to run, test and deploy the application (usually the same software as in a production environment). Finally, he was ready to start the implementation phase. The created program was a monolith – it did not have many components nor required to be highly scalable.

Nowadays, the applications are very complicated in terms of requirements, architecture and amount of technologies that are being used, not mentioning the collaboration with many developers (and others) included in the projects' contributions. The software stack is huge, every element (loosely coupled with the others) has its own core solution that is being used and usually different teams of developers are responsible for developing and maintaining it [34].

The distribution of services brings a lot of challenges: beginning with data consistency, availability and partition tolerance problems to applications performance and scalability issues. In addition, it is extremely hard to foresee the number of users that are going to use the systems that were built and with all

© Springer International Publishing AG, part of Springer Nature 2018
M. Younas et al. (Eds.): MobiWIS 2018, LNCS 10995, pp. 112–125, 2018.
https://doi.org/10.1007/978-3-319-97163-6_10

the infrastructure set up the costs of maintaining it on site are enormous. These are the main reasons why cloud solutions began to be so popular: they allow expenses reductions by handling all the traffic adjustments in the real time and (relatively) easy infrastructure set up. Amazon [1], Google [2] and Microsoft [3] are the biggest players on the market as they provide huge amount of different cloud services which can be used within minutes after an account creation. The questions are: what exactly do they provide and how do they differ?

This paper provides an in-depth analysis of cloud solutions in aspects of distributed business services and answers the given questions. It is supported by a web application (written in the Ruby on Rails framework) that is responsible for testing the provided services. The objective of this work is to analyse the cloud solutions in aspects of distributed business services and to design and implement a web application that supports the analysis.

The paper is structured as follows: Sect. 2 includes a general overview of the cloud computing topic in the aspects of distributed business services. Section 3 presents an analysis of cloud solutions given by specific cloud providers – it covers their infrastructure capabilities, popularity, locations, support for different needs and systems. Section 4 describes the project that is used to support the analysis of the cloud solutions, while Sect. 5 provides information about realization of functional tests, which were gathered during a web application deployment to the clouds. Section 6 presents the data that was gather through the tests (both functional and non-functional) that were made by the built application.

2   Why Do We Need Cloud Computing?

Cloud computing is an extremely broad topic that covers or connects with many more such as software engineering, web engineering, systems architecture, security [32]. There are many definitions of what exactly cloud computing is, e.g. by National Institute of Standards and Technology definition [4] or by Amazon definition [5].

Looking at these definitions it can be said that *cloud computing is the on-demand service that allows the management of various IT resources via the Internet which has certain characteristics and models.*

Cloud computing, as a solution, is a response to some problems that occur during the development process in the (especially) last years. Its advantages are the best seen in large project, which require for instance high availability, performance and scalability that can be achieved without building an own data centre [33].

As the software grows, more functionalities are added and more technologies are used. The developers decide to split the monolith they created with only one language and one framework for easier testing, deployment and project management itself. They start to create components and they move towards using a micro-services architecture [6] to support more platforms and be ready to scale it in every possible way.

In general, not only there are many services that support different operations, but the whole system is now distributed among many servers. The projects are now really big and it is very common that the components and services are divided for example into:

- web front-end (for instance in React.js),
- background workers (supported by a language such as Python),
- databases (PostgreSQL and NoSQL solutions),
- back-end (for example in Ruby on Rails or Node.js),
- a proper server like Puma or Unicorn),
- queues (like Redis),
- API endpoints.

3 Analysis of Cloud Providers' Solutions

There are many cloud providers that allow to use their infrastructure to support their clients' needs, especially when it comes down to distributed business services due to their complexity and broad requirements. However, the three most popular cloud providers are going to be described in this paper: Amazon, Google and Microsoft.

3.1 Compute Services

Compute Services are one of the most important aspects that exist in the cloud. They allow to run business services (also distributed ones) in the cloud and without them it would not be possible. They are virtual machines that allow to be set up very quickly and clients choose how many resources (like RAM or CPU capabilities) they need in order to run their software.

Every cloud provider calls them differently: Virtual Machines (VMs) by Microsoft [8], Amazon Elastic Compute Cloud (Amazon EC2) by Amazon [9] and Compute Engine by Google [10].

Not many companies are going to use them as they will simply not need that much of computing power. That being said, the main difference is the pricing. However, as this changes a lot, it is outside of scope of this work and it is extremely hard to compare due to many pricing models and discounts that can be applied in various scenarios. Because of that, it was relied on a very broad cloud costs analysis that is shared online by *RightScale*. In summary, Amazon tends to be the most expensive provider for more powerful instances whereas Google is the cheapest one.

3.2 Locations

Locations of the infrastructure that are being used is a very important aspect that should not be neglected, especially when it comes down to distributed business services (as they may be deployed in many different locations). There are two reasons for that:

1. As stated it may be necessary to deploy the application or store data in a country where it is used – it may be required by law.
2. It allows to have better performance with lower latency (the lower the distance between the client and the server the better).

In other words, the more locations are available, the better. That being said, for the time of writing this paper Amazon allows to use 43 availability zones within 16 geographical regions [11]. Microsoft has 36 regions [12] and Google has 12 regions and 36 zones [13]. Each of the providers is planning to add more locations in the following months.

3.3   Available Features and Technologies

When it comes to the terms how many *features and technologies* the cloud providers have available and how mature their products are, Amazon and Microsoft are both clear winners [14]. Google lacks many services that its competitors have and many of them are in a BETA phase, so they can contain bugs and behave in an unexpected way. In other words, they might be good for experimenting, but not for serious production applications, especially distributed business services, which rely on multiple different technologies.

What is more, even when it comes to available technologies Google lacks many that are present on the competitors' side. For instance, Google allows to use only two relational database engines (MySQL and PostgreSQL, whereas the latter is only in BETA phase [15]) and Amazon has six of them.

3.4   Storage

Storage, apart from computing capabilities, is the second most important aspect of cloud providers solutions. The mentioned databases are based on it and it allows to store in reality any file that a client would like to, from blobs and queues to caches. This is extremely important for distributed business services, as they rely on many types of technologies and solutions that require different kinds of files.

Obviously, it can come down to sending files to Google Drive [16], iCloud Drive [17] or similar websites from other vendors, but other cloud models (Infrastructure as a Service and Platform as a Service) are communicated through Application Programming Interfaces or other technical ways.

There are many services being offered by each vendor (for different types of files, Fig. 1). The most general ones will be discussed below – the ones built to support *Object Storage*.

3.5   Documentation and Different Tools Support

Documentation is a very important aspect that basically describes the existing services: what they offer, how they work, how they can be used etc. It cannot

Object Storage	Azure Storage (Blobs, Tables, Queues, Files)	Amazon Simple Storage (S3)	Cloud Storage
Block Storage	Azure Blob Storage (how to)	Amazon Elastic Block Storage (EBS)	Persistent Disk
Hybrid Cloud Storage	StorSimple	AWS Storage Gateway	None
Backup Options	Azure Backup	Amazon Glacier	Google Cloud Storage

Fig. 1. Comparizon of storage services offered to clients from Microsoft, Amazon and Google [14]

be neglected as it is the most in-depth resource that a company can provide for its clients.

Amazon offers the most extensive one. Its long presence on the market allowed it to create, test and document very well its services. Microsoft and Google try to catch up with their main competitor, they lack a lot in comparison to Amazon [18]. Amazon and Microsoft have definitely the best tools (from command-line and APIs to SDKs) to use their services [19,20]. They offer support for a lot of languages and systems, whereas Google seems to have around half of them [21].

3.6 Free Tiers

It is mentioned in the Subsect. 3.1 that services prices are outside of scope of this paper. However, every cloud provider allows to try and test their product for free with some limits. The services and allocated resources that can be used are not enough to launch a real world project on a production level, but they are sufficient to see how a simple application or a prototype can be deployed and run.

Amazon offers a variety of services (like *Amazon CodeCommit, Amazon ElastiCache, Amazon Elasticsearch Service*) that can be used without costs in the first year and sometimes beyond, for unlimited amount of time [22]. Among others, the free tier covers 5 GB of Amazon S3 storage, 750 h per month for both relational database usage and Amazon EC2 computing with the tiniest instance (*t2.micro* – 1 vCPU, 6 CPU credits per hour, 1 GiB of memory). It is structured in a way that cannot be used in a production environment but is sufficient to launch a simple prototype and to see how AWS in general works.

On the other hand, Google not only allows to use free tier for unlimited amount of time (it is always there), it also gives 300$ that can be used on any product for the first 12 months [23]. As Amazon, for the always free tier they share many services, among which there can be listed Google Compute Engine (with montly 30 GB HDD storage and 1 *f1-micro instance* – 0.2 vCPU, 0.6 GiB of memory available only in the US regions except Northern Virginia) or Google Cloud Storage with 5 GB per month regional storage (only in the US regions except Northern Virginia).

Microsoft, just like Amazon and Google, also offers a free tier that can be used in order to get familiar with its products [24]. Customers can always use for free for instance the App Service, which allows to "Quickly build and host up to 10 web and mobile apps on any platform or device" [24], Azure Search or Azure Machine Learning.

Presented cloud solutions, given by the three main cloud providers (Amazon, Google and Microsoft), are very sophisticated systems which allow switching from on-premise servers to the infrastructure held by the mentioned deliverers. They offer a lot of computing power and storage (literally unlimited and extremely reliable), they can be accessed anywhere and anytime and they allow to use multiple number of services with many kinds of APIs.

Due to this, they seem to be a perfect fit for distributed systems with microservices architecture. In addition, a client can place its infrastructure in many locations all over the world in the matter of seconds if it is required to do so. What is interesting, the research has shown that clients usually tend to use multiple cloud providers for their systems (a "hybrid" cloud). For instance, they use Amazon for computing, Google for one of their specific APIs and Microsoft for databases.

Moreover, it is possible to test the given solutions with the provided free tiers, where the analysis will continue. To do that, a project (named *CloudM*) was built to assess different aspects of them, giving more in-depth knowledge and practical information. It is extensively described in the following sections.

4   Project *CloudM*

Project *CloudM* was built with an idea that an application administrator, even with almost no knowledge of cloud computing or computer science in general, could use it after a short introduction of the action flow in the settings panel. It is a prototype that integrates with Amazon Web Services and allows extremely simplified deployment and migration of business services and data.

The base project consists of two main panels: end users and administrator panels. The first one is designed to be used only by that "real" application users that put, update and delete data (posts with titles and bodies, Fig. 2), whereas an administrator can change application settings, connect with the cloud and create an infrastructure to support it.

It is crucial to list what exactly can be assessed and how a cloud can be evaluated in general. Before going straight to the tests, it is important to mention on what solutions and technologies the *CloudM* project is exactly based on and what can be done within the free tiers.

In general, it consists of two main components: a web application (written in *Ruby on Rails*) and a database (*PostgreSQL*). The application (as a whole) is deployed on public clouds (Amazon's, Google's and Microsoft's) within a *Platform as a Service* model (as it is the suggested one for developers who would like to quickly run it without unnecessary infrastructure configurations).

As mentioned in above, after deploying the project (and looking into a functional side of the specific vendors' solutions along with a support for the mentioned software stack) the performance tests are to be run. Nonetheless, it is very important to first describe the main framework that the whole application is based on (and dependent).

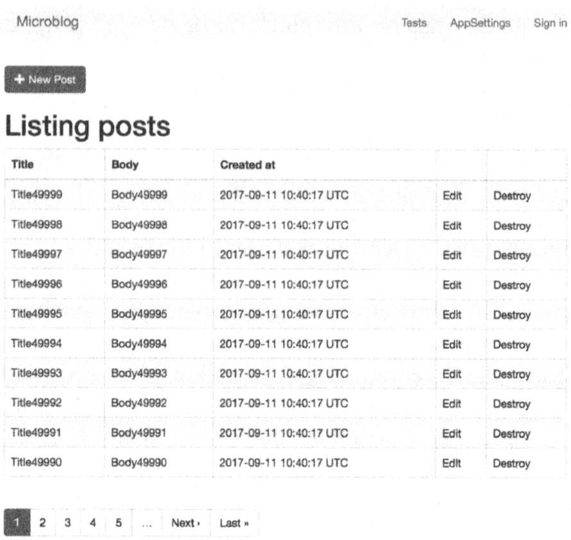

Fig. 2. Application users panel in *CloudM* project that allows to put, update and delete data (posts with titles and bodies)

4.1   Testing Cloud Services

Testing cloud services is a very complicated topic that consists of many parts and kinds of tests [25,26]. It is important to notice that different service and deployment models can be tested. For instance, tests concerning Infrastructure as a Service have other requirements than Software as a Service ones and public cloud should be more security-wise focused than it would be with private cloud.

However, they all share some high-level sections and usually it is a matter of increased focus on some types of tests than big differences in between. That being said, we can categorize two main kinds of them: functional and non-functional tests. The functional tests (which are unfortunately very often neglected as almost everyone focuses on technicalities) come generally with:

- making sure that clients get exactly what they signed up for and that it meets their expectations,
- that all elements and services work together seamlessly, so there are absolutely no issues between them, for instance a web application has a constant and proper connection with a database,
- the infrastructure and the overall setup has to work on many platforms (like mobile or desktop) and can be moved from one cloud to the other.

The non-functional tests are more complicated as they require a lot of resources to be used. They can be generally divided into the following:

- *Performance testing* – this is in one of the broadest type of tests as almost everything else can actually be taken as a performance in some ways. However, it comes down to taking into account times of queries, computing, etc. It is extremely dependent on a built infrastructure and its possibilities.
- *Latency testing* – it is a very important type of test as the cloud has to support global access and it is directly dependent on locations of the infrastructure. It is a difference of time between client's request and provider's (service) response.
- *Stress and load testing* – these ones can also take into account response times (as the tests mentioned above), but they are more focused on scalability (resizing, adding or removing resources when they are needed). It can be done manually, but it is a standard that it is done automatically (depends on the stress and load levels).
- *Availability testing* – this one describes for how long an infrastructure is "on the run" and can be accessed without any issues. These tests are ones of the most crucial types as they directly try to measure the given Service Level Agreements (SLAs) terms.
- *Fail-over testing* or *disaster recovery testing* – these tests can be characterized by answering a question: *when there is any kind of failure or breakdown, how much time will it take to (fully) recover and what are the possible losses (for instance of data)?*.
- *Security testing* – this is an enormous topic in itself, probably the biggest one of all of types of non-functional tests. It differs drastically depending on deployment and service models. As it was said, public clouds are the most "dangerous" ones as they are open to everyone in the world whereas private clouds depend solely on people having a direct access and being on-premises. In addition, multi-tenancy testing is very important (as it could be considered as a subsection of security testing) and it is partially also referencing performance testing. The reason is that many users share hardware so that the load of one of them affects the other ones and there may be a breach causing not privileged access to others' people data.

These businesses are also capable of using many tools that exist only to test specific aspects of both software and hardware, like Selenium [27], JMeter [28] or Wireshark [29]. Basically, the only kind of non-functional tests that can be performed (still in limited ways) with a good degree of accuracy are performance tests, which were done. From the functional tests side simple deployment, along with documentation reading and using provided by vendors tools gives already a lot of insight how everything works.

Microsot Azure is the equivalent for AWS Elastic Beanstalk solution. Unfortunately, it has a very poor support for Ruby on Rails framework. It covers Java, Node.js, ASP.NET, PHP and Python for web applications.

To start with the web application deployment the first thing that is needed to be done is a resource group creation (in the same manner as it was made with

PostgreSQL database). Then there is an *App Service* which setup allows to host the project itself. However, running it causes a problem: the *−sku FREE* attribute is invalid, as the FREE pricing model cannot be used with Linux virtual machines. There is a necessity to choose a paid plan. It means that a virtual machine running Linux has to charge money whereas a Windows one not.

Afterwards there is the moment to create the web application stack itself. There are two things worth mentioning. First of all, the runtime is set to "ruby—2.3". The second worth writing thing is that deployment is going to be done from a local Git repository. To finish and put the project online all that it is left to be done (theoretically) is pushing all files from Git to the Microsoft created service and restart it.

This is basically the moment where all the support for Ruby and Linux goes down. In this case, we wanted to look into the application logs. However, it was impossible to do: even after turning on every possible logs, the live-streaming log service did not show any output and when it was tried to download a .zip file with all the logs, it had 1 KB of size and an error when trying to unpack it. When we could not see the logs and a possible solution was based on a feeling, we realized that deploying an application in these technologies (that are available only in the Preview mode) is practically undoable, especially when it comes down to relying on it. The project has two main components and even with them there are issues. We do not see any possibility to deploy more complex, distributed systems when there are problems with smaller projects that depend on only two technologies.

Deploying web applications or distributed business services to the cloud is a complicated process that needs to be done very thoroughly, without neglecting anything. Depending on a vendor and its solutions it may be relatively easy with everything ready and fully functional or many errors can occur on the way.

Amazon seems to be (so far) the best provider. Not only their support for different technologies is amazing and almost uncountable, they also provide brilliant documentation (with minor ambiguities) with quite straightforward articles. Everything just works fine and we are certain that if we were to deploy a distributed system that consists of many components there would be no problems with it. Unfortunately, Google Cloud could not be tested as it does not offer its free tiers to either private or corporate entities (as the project has no revenue that can be gained) in the European Union. Microsoft apparently tries to catch up with Amazon. However, they have a very poor support for selected technologies: there are many errors with their solutions and extreme inconsistencies and ambiguities in their documentation. It is a huge problem to deploy a web application that consists of two components. We cannot imagine trying to deploy a distributed system which stacks have multiple different technologies.

5   Results of Performance Tests

The project-level description of the performance tests was given in Subsect. 4.2. It is important to mention that all tests were done on Amazon Web Services as this is the only vendor that cloud allowed to deploy the whole application. With Google Cloud it was impossible to do due to regulations and being localized in the European Union. Microsoft beta-versions (Preview modes) of its services along with a very poor support for the chosen technological stack (Ruby on Rails, PostgreSQL) disallowed to have a fully functional system available.

5.1   Amazon Web Services' Free Tier Instances

Amazon's free tier allows to use *t2.micro* and *t1.micro* EC2 instances ("the free tier for Amazon EC2 provides you with 750 h usage of Linux [any combination of *t2.micro* and *t1.micro* instances])" [30]. In this case, the application is tested on *t2.micro* instance as it is just a next generation (and a replacement) of the latter one. Note that AWS Elastic Beanstalk is based on EC2 instances. From the specification point of view, the micro EC2 instance has 1 GB of memory and 1 vCPU with a 2 h 24 min burst mode. From the business costs point of view, for the time being of writing this paper it is valued at $0.013 per hour (Linux on demand, Ireland region). PostgreSQL service differ mostly in prices (at $0.020 hourly on demand in Ireland region) and that it is allowed to use micro RDS instances as well (with 1 GB of memory) [31]. For the purpose of these tests, the option with 5 GB storage is used (with a SSD disk type by default).

5.2   Results of Performance Tests on AWS Instances

The results consist of four different tests: two computing ones (named *Squre root* and *Square*) and two database queries ones (named *Posts create* and *Posts query all*). They were chosen because the *CloudM* project consists of two components: the web application and the database. We wanted to measure the performance of both components. Each of these tests was run three times with three different parameters values so that the load was increasing. Then, the average result for computing power (processing time) was calculated for every parameter and run. After that, the average times were compared to see if the load influenced the performance. Ideally, it should not at all.

Square Root Test. This test calculates square roots from 1 to the given number in a loop and the processing time required to do it. Programmatically it can be presented as:

$$x.times\{|i|Math.sqrt(i)\} \tag{1}$$

The tests considered the following x parameters: 10000000, 100000000 (10 times more than the first one) and 500000000 (50 times more than the first one).

After all the tests were run (with an increased load each time) the average times were compared (Fig. 3). To do it properly, the average times were divided by a number of times the parameter value was higher than the first parameter. In other words, if the second parameter was 10 times higher than the first one, the average result for it in the comparison was divided by 10.

Having all the times properly compared we can draw a conclusion that the computing power of the micro EC2 is very reliable, as the final results are almost identical for all the tests. In other words, the load does not seem to affect the overall performance, which is a highly desirable situation.

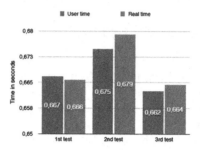

Fig. 3. Square root tests average times results comparison

Square Test. This test is almost identical to the previous one, but it differs with the calculation algorithm:

$$x.times\{|i|i * *2\} \qquad (2)$$

This test is only to support the results and conclusions from the previous one, as the formula checks the performance of the EC2 instance in a very similar way. The comparison of average values is given in Fig. 4. The final results confirm the conclusion from the previous test: the EC2 instance is very reliable as the average computing times are very close to each other. The difference between the average values from the first parameter tests and the second ones is $\sim$1,5%, whereas the difference between the average values from the first parameter tests and the third ones is even lower ($\sim$0,1%). The load does not seem to affect the performance almost at all.

Performance tests allow to see what is the real computing power and database capabilities with the given instances. They are extremely important as without them the administrators would not know if they need to scale and change their infrastructure on which applications and distributed business services are based.

The *CloudM* project allowed to test the configured AWS infrastructure. As the application consist of two parts, there was a need to create performance tests specific for both of them: the application server, which were responsible for measuring the computing power and the database server, responsible for calculating queries processing or execution times.

In the conclusion, despite having only the free tier available to be used, Amazon Web Services behaved very well during the performance tests. Both EC2 and RDS instances worked as expected. They did not slow down when they had higher amounts of data to process nor they responded with errors. There were absolutely no issues with them and they were highly reliable.

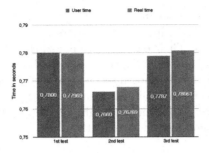

Fig. 4. Square tests average (User and Real) times results comparison

The free tier should not be ever used in a production environment, so the real-world application should not be deployed using the instances that it offers. However, when the instances that are reachable within the free tier meet the requirements of reliability and are not prone to performance fluctuations, it gives a very good prognosis for the instances with more computing power. Particularly, that they may be very capable of handling multiple, heavy requests that the distributed business services are constantly hit by.

6 Conclusions

Cloud computing is a very broad and advanced topic that connects with a lot of fields in computer science. Due to Internet accessibility and speed it is very convenient (and affordable) to use it. Many people do not even know that they do it on daily basis: by storing images in their iCloud accounts, sending emails through Inbox by Google and so on.

It is even more complex when it comes down to distributed business services, as they are very peculiar with their requirements. They are usually huge systems, consisting of multiple components, having sometimes millions of users. Because of these, they have to be highly available, scalable, reliable. Obviously they are extremely dependent on the infrastructure that they are based on and if they are hosted in the cloud they also have to have full support for the technological stack that they use. In other words, not only theoretical work had to be done in order to see what are the cloud possibilities. The real-world assessments also had to be held to see the real support for distributed systems, which came down to functional and non-functional tests realizations.

Three main cloud vendors were taken into account for testing purposes: Google, Microsoft and Amazon. To assess them properly and in a practical manner this paper presented the *CloudM* project that was capable of deploying and migrating business services and data to the cloud. After modifying it the added test page allowed (after deployment) to see what are the infrastructure capabilities (via live tests) in production environments.

The whole process of deploying and testing the given cloud solutions drew many conclusions. From all three tested vendors only Amazon was practically perfect in their solutions. Their offerings are amazing, extremely reliable, with many features, brilliant support and a very, very good documentation. Microsoft had a very poor support for the chosen technological stack, having many services only in Preview modes which practically made testing production environment impossible via the built application. Google on the other hand did not even allow deploying the mentioned system to their cloud whereas due to the law regulations set by them.

The analysis of cloud solutions in aspects of distributed business services given in this paper is complex and it provides a lot of information with a strong focus on mentioned three vendors. However, it should not only be seen through them: the extension built on top of the *CloudM* project allows testing infrastructure in any environment, even on-premises. When used properly, it answers many questions regarding capabilities, possibilities and when taking into account also the theoretical knowledge, if selected solutions should be used for current needs.

To answer even more questions, the extension and the base of the *CloudM* project itself can be developed further in many ways: form adding more integrations with different cloud providers to performing other measurements and tests, not only performance ones. In addition, more components and business services could be connected with it so that more complex tests can be run (both functional and non-functional). For instance a server that handles background processing, another one for caching or queueing. However, to do it in the cloud it requires a lot of resources – both time and money.

References

1. Amazon Web Services main website. https://aws.amazon.com
2. Google Cloud Platform main website. https://cloud.google.com
3. Microsoft Azure main website. https://azure.microsoft.com
4. The National Institute of Standards and Technology Definition of Cloud Computing website. http://nvlpubs.nist.gov/nistpubs/Legacy/SP/nistspecialpubli cation800-145.pdf
5. AWS Cloud Computing intruduction website. https://aws.amazon.com/what-iscloud-computing/
6. Microservices architecture pattern explained website. http://microservices.io/patterns/microservices.html
7. Information about cloud computing statistics document website. http://assets.rightscale.com/uploads/pdfs/RightScale-2017-State-of-the-Cloud-Report.pdf
8. Virtual Machines (VMs) by Microsoft website. https://azure.microsoft.com/en-us/services/virtual-machines/
9. Amazon Elastic Compute Cloud (Amazon EC2) by Amazon website. https://aws.amazon.com/ec2/
10. Compute Engine by Google website. https://cloud.google.com/compute/
11. AWS Global Infrastructure website. https://aws.amazon.com/about-aws/globalin frastructure/

12. Microsoft Azure regions website. https://azure.microsoft.com/en-us/regions/
13. Google Cloud Locations website. https://cloud.google.com/about/locations/
14. Compare Services & Features Between Microsoft Azure vs. Amazon Web Services vs. Google Compute website. https://stackify.com/microsoft-azure-vsamazon-web-services-vs-google-compute-comparison/
15. Google Cloud SQL website. https://cloud.google.com/sql/
16. Google Drive website. https://www.google.com/drive/
17. iCloud Drive website. https://www.apple.com/icloud/icloud-drive/
18. Service Level Agreement for Microsoft Azure Storage website. https://azure.microsoft.com/en-us/support/legal/sla/storage/v1_2/
19. Tools for Amazon Web Services website. https://aws.amazon.com/tools/
20. Microsoft tools and SDKs for Azure website. https://azure.microsoft.com/en-gb/downloads/
21. Google Cloud Platform tools and SDKs website. https://cloud.google.com/sdk/
22. Amazon Free Tier website. https://aws.amazon.com/free/
23. Google Free Tier website. https://cloud.google.com/free/
24. Microsoft Azure Free Tier website. https://azure.microsoft.com/en-us/free/pricingoffers/
25. Testing Cloud Services. How to test Saas, Paas and Iaas. https://www.polteq.com/wp-content/uploads/2013/11/2013_EuroSTAREbook.pdf
26. Getting Started with Cloud Testing. http://www.softwaretestinghelp.com/getting-started-with-cloud-testing/
27. Selenium main website. http://www.seleniumhq.org
28. JMeter main website. http://jmeter.apache.org
29. Wireshark main website. https://www.wireshark.org
30. Amazon Web Services Free Tier limits website. http://docs.aws.amazon.com/awsaccountbilling/latest/aboutv2/free-tier-limits.html
31. Amazon RDS Free Tier website. https://aws.amazon.com/rds/free/
32. Poniszewska-Maranda, A., Wieczorek, B.: Aspects of application security for internet of things systems. In: Younas, M., Awan, I., Holubova, I. (eds.) MobiWIS 2017. LNCS, vol. 10486, pp. 163–176. Springer, Cham (2017). https://doi.org/10.1007/978-3-319-65515-4_14
33. Poniszewska-Maranda, A., Matusiak, R., Kryvinska, N.: Use of salesforce platform for building real-time service systems in cloud. In: Proceedings of 14th IEEE International Conference on Services Computing, IEEE SCC 2017, pp. 491–494 (2017)
34. Kaczor, S., Kryvinska, N.: It is all about services - fundamentals, drivers, and business models. Soc. Serv. Sci. J. Serv. Sci. Res. 5(2), 125–154 (2013)

Web Service Composition on Smartphones: The Challenges and a Survey of Solutions

Gebremariam Mesfin[1], Gheorghita Ghinea[1],
Tor-Morten Grønli[2(✉)], and Muhammad Younas[3]

[1] Department of Computer Science, Brunel University,
London, UK
{gebremariam.assres,george.ghinea}@brunel.ac.uk
[2] Mobile Technology Laboratory, Department of Technology,
Westerdals Oslo ACT, Oslo, Norway
tmg@westerdals.no
[3] School of Engineering, Computing and Mathematics,
Oxford Brookes University, Oxford, UK
m.younas@brookes.ac.uk

Abstract. Today, smartphones are capable of hosting a large variety of applications as clients for the classical as well as service-based business applications. They can also be envisaged for composing and hosting service-based thick client applications aiming at exploiting users' creativity and resolving mobile connectivity challenges, respectively. However, the challenges in input mechanisms, storage, and screen size of smartphones all limit the operations of Web service composition. These challenges can be addressed through a criteria-based selection process of appropriate Web service and associated technologies. Accordingly, the REST services, semi-automatic service composition with Web 2.0 technologies (HTML5, and JavaScript APIs), JSON-based messaging and data serialization format, as well as the cross-platform mobile client application development approach are found more suitable for composing Web services on the constrained smartphone. All together, they constitute a stack of appropriate technologies to implement resource-oriented architecture on the smartphone.

Keywords: Web service · REST · SOAP · Mobile · Smartphone · JSON · Web 2.0
HTML5 · JavaScript APIs · Cross-platform · Composition techniques
Semi-automatic · SOA · ROA

1 Introduction

The smartphone landscape has made significant leap and transformed the phone from a handset used merely for voice calls into a state-of-the-art mobile computing device [1]. Today, smartphones are capable of hosting a large variety of client-side applications in areas such as banking, education, and health. There are also attempts to turn the smartphone into a development environment such as the Android IDE[1].

---

[1] https://www.android-ide.com/.

© Springer International Publishing AG, part of Springer Nature 2018
M. Younas et al. (Eds.): MobiWIS 2018, LNCS 10995, pp. 126–141, 2018.
https://doi.org/10.1007/978-3-319-97163-6_11

On the other hand, developing applications using service-oriented architecture (SOA) and resource-oriented architecture (ROA) has paramount importance [2]. In this regard, client-side applications which are composed of SOA/ROA based Web service components can also be hosted on the smartphones. However, to the best of our knowledge, the smartphone is not yet in use as a Web service composition device.

The end-user development research community, on the other hand, confirms that end-users can innovatively develop their own applications with little or no programming knowledge [3, 4]. Thus, a possibility of composing Web services on smartphones would enable the exploitation of smartphone users' creativity so that they can develop their own applications and also contribute their work to app stores for use by others. For example, a supplier may need a custom made application for his smartphone to find customers with the best price offer for products to sale, negotiate a contract, arrange billing details, and logistics for shipment as shown in Fig. 1.

Figure 1 depicts a system design (a scenario) of Web service composition on a smartphone. The figure demonstrates Web services being provided from customers' devices (left), the smartphone being used in the wiring of workflows for composing Web services (middle), and Web services being provided from third-party organizations' devices (right). Accordingly, the supplier performs Web service composition by wiring interfaces of the exposed services.

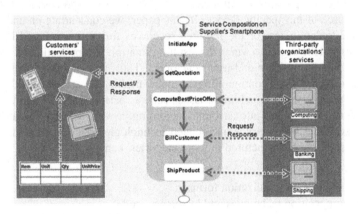

Fig. 1. Service composition on smartphones

The above described scenario requires identifying the most appropriate Web service and associated technologies for simplicity of composing on smartphones. In this regard, although many of the available mash-up tools are claimed to be for end-users too, they are generally targeted towards data integrators for use on classic computing devices. Moreover, practice shows that they also require significant programming skill [5].

Additionally, a client application is required to be thick enough for interactive business applications [6]. It is also worth mentioning the situations of low bandwidth and intermittent Internet connectivity like the case of many developing economies [7]. Thus, hosting composite applications on the smartphone as a thick-client would compensate the negative impact of intermittent and low bandwidth mobile connectivity. However, to the best of our knowledge, there is no established trend in the hosting of service-based (composite) client-side applications on the smartphone.

Thus, composing Web services directly on the smartphone and hosting the resulting client-side application on it has paramount importance. However, smartphones are still constrained in terms of input mechanisms, storage, and screen size and these are essentially the challenges which could limit the operations of Web service composition and hosting.

In fact, service composition is an existing challenge already [8]. For example, Beaton et al. [9] reveal that service consumers encounter challenges such as fragmentation of the discovery user experience across multiple interfaces, confusing hierarchies of service navigation, lack of business modeling support, hidden relationships between services, and inconsistent Web service interface design. Some of the manifestations of these challenges are through the difficulties developers encounter while assembling data structure in Web service parameters, cycles of errors due to unclear control parameters in data structures, and difficulties to understand long identifier names.

Thus, the fast proliferation of Web services and dynamically changing user requirements are demanding increasing design consistency and simplicity of Web services. In addition, addressing design issues for the use of Web services in smartphone applications development challenges even more [8].

In smartphone application development, the software design process is driven by the limited resource of the specific device. In this paper, we concentrate on and examine Web service technologies for the required resources for composing and hosting on smartphones and the degree to which the resulting smartphone application is lightweight and usable enough to please end-user developers. Thus, the small and diverse screen sizes, storage capacity, and configurations of the smartphone need to be considered when developing Web services. In addition, issues such as performance, footprint size, and usability must all be taken into account. Accordingly, we conduct a literature-based survey of available Web service and related technologies relevant to compose Web services on smartphones structured in four categories, namely:

- Types of Web services;
- Messaging and data serialization formats;
- Service composition techniques and languages; and
- Mobile client application development approaches.

In addition, we evaluate candidate technologies for their desirable features and limitations and proposed stack of appropriate technologies aimed towards tailoring Web service composition environment for a smartphone. Thus, the paper is organized as follows. In Sect. 2, we present a survey of Web service and associated technologies in each of the above mentioned categories. Sections 3, 4 and 5 respectively detail evaluation of these technologies, discussion of results, and the conclusions drawn.

2   Survey of Web Services and Associated Technologies

Web services are implementation technologies of SOA and ROA. They are inspired by the need to integrate and reuse software for the dynamically changing and highly collaborative stakeholder needs of today's businesses. Additionally, we provide the associated technologies which are used for developing applications using Web services as presented below. Accordingly, we approached the survey by classifying the Web services and associated technologies in four categories as depicted in Fig. 2.

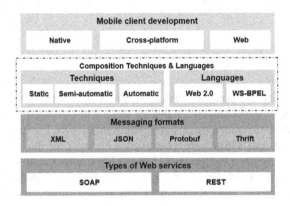

Fig. 2. Web service technologies in categories

Figure 2 shows a client-server interaction between mobile clients and Web services through messaging formats. In addition, the composition techniques and languages component in the figure signifies the technology with which the code logic of a mobile client can be developed. Accordingly, these Web services and associated technologies are described next.

2.1   Type of Web Service

Web services can be broadly categorized into SOAP (Simple Object Access Protocol) and REST (Representational State Transfer). SOAP services work in the context of SOA based-on foundational Web technologies like the DOM, URL based discovery, and HTTP messaging with XML [10]. REST services, on the other hand, correspond to the ROA which works based-on the concept of Web resources' URL addressability and the mechanism of passing-in parameters via the URL [10, 11]. A review on the challenges of composing Web services on smartphones is presented next.

In SOA, self-contained software services are used to build applications or other software services and the process is called Web service composition. Thus, software components are made interoperable leveraging the flexibility to meet customers' use cases, to have access to data in a unique context, and to meet customers' preferences to interact from a smartphone device [12].

Srirama et al. [8] pointed out that the smartphone can be used as a Web service requestor, and as a host. However, it faces a number of hardware challenges such as the small screen size which would limit the use of the smartphone as Web service composition device [19].

The composition of Web services on smartphones could also be challenged due to usability limitations of the Web services themselves. For example, usability of Web services could be impeded due to the complex data structures in SOAP; and the manual operation in REST [9, 11]. Thus, from the perspective of type of Web service, composition requires programming skill which prohibits non-programmers for building applications [5].

2.2 Messaging Format

The type of messaging and data serialization format is among such associated technologies for Web service composition. Nurseitov et al. [15] pointed out that the choice of data format can have significant consequences on data transmission rates and performance. Today, many data formats are available like XML, JSON, Protobuf, efficient XML interchange (EXI[2]), and Thrift [17]. However, with the ever increasing access to a diversity of Internet-connected devices, choosing the appropriate data serialization format for use on the constrained smartphone has become a challenge [16]. Thus, comparing data format as text versus binary with respect to the smartphone has paramount importance.

2.3 Web Service Composition

Orchestration and choreography are among the service composition techniques applicable on both SOAP and REST Web services and selecting among them is dependent on the purpose of the application in question [18]. In this paper, we concentrate on the use of a smartphone as a coordinator in the orchestration of Web services for building applications. However, the difference in the conventional practices of the SOAP and REST services has induced differences in the composition techniques and languages.

Thus, service composition approaches can be categorized either as control flow, data flow, and assisted by service consumer [19]; or as static, automatic, and semi-automatic [20]. The composition languages, on the other hand, are BPMN, WS-BPEL and HTML5 together with JavaScript APIs; these can all be categorized as graphical modeling, XML-based, and Web 2.0 technologies, respectively. Both the BPMN and WS-BPEL have standard business process execution engines. Here our intention is not to provide generic comparison of such a varying collection of technologies and their variants like the BPEL for REST services[3] in the WS-BPEL. Accordingly, we concentrate on the WS-BPEL industry standard for its role in the composition of SOAP services [18], and HTML5 which is in use as a mash-up language together with JavaScript APIs (in the Web 2.0 context) for REST services as representative alternative technologies for our

---

[2] http://www.w3.org/XML/EXI/.
[3] http://ode.apache.org/.

perspective. These technologies are evaluated with respect to the requirements of composing on smartphones.

2.4 Mobile Client Application

The composition tool in use also influences the task of composing Web services on smartphones. Essentially, this represents the mobile client application and it denotes the Web service consumer in the composition. Due to the proliferation of smartphones, it is a common practice today that Internet users employ mobile Web client applications such as Opera, Chrome, and Safari browsers for their Web experiences [1]. In addition, native and cross-platform smartphone application development approaches are also employed to communicate with Web services [21]. Thus, studying the characteristics of mobile client applications with respect to the goal of composing Web services on smartphones and the need to host the composite applications is of paramount importance.

In general, the existing literature provides significant insight into the Web services and the associated technologies; and Web service composition. However, to the best of our knowledge, composition with respect to the resource limited smartphone environment is not sufficiently explored. Thus, further review of literature focusing on the influence of the technologies for enabling composition on smartphone platforms is presented next.

3 Evaluation of Technologies

3.1 Methodology

This study was conducted using literature survey on Web services and associated technologies according to the four categories depicted in Fig. 2. Performance, amount of communication and storage footprint; and the level of simplicity to work on the constrained input components and the small but variable screen real-estate of the smartphone landscape were given due consideration for evaluating each category presented in the previous section. Thus, description of each evaluation criteria is presented next.

Type of Web Service. Here, we concentrated on the distinct features and shortcomings of the SOAP and REST services with respect to the smartphone platforms [14]. That is, the SOAP service uses a standard XML-based message envelope and a set of rules for exchanging structured information which means it has a significant message payload, a parser, and an explicit interface description with WSDL. The REST service, on the other hand, is a lightweight implementation which uses HTTP and URIs to characterize its addressability, uniformity, connectivity and statelessness [14]. Thus, the literature indicates that these inherent characteristics leverage for using complexity, performance, flexibility, footprint, reusability, usability, and scalability as evaluation criteria (see Table 1).

Table 1. Literature summary on the evaluation of Web service technologies

Category	Technology	Criteria						
		Complexity	Performance	Flexibility	Footprint	Reusability	Usability	Scalability
Types of Web services	SOAP services	Generating client code from WSDL requires tools and resulting in **high complexity** [13]	The tools used to consume SOAP degrade performance to **low** [14]	Client code is **stiff** to change because of the structured nature of WSDL [9]	SOAP envelope for operations attributed to **more** footprint [9]	Its highly structured nature **restricts** reusability [23]	The lengthy process required to locate, contact, and invoke makes it **less user friendly**	Tightly coupled and **less** scalable [28]
	REST services	Light weight design makes **less** complex even on thin clients [25]	Significantly **faster**	REST is designed for loose coupling [25], hence **flexible**	Directly invoked with HTTP, **no overhead** [26]	Virtually **unlimited**	Simple but the lack of tools attributed to more **user concern**	Loosely coupled and the **Web** is evident for its scalability
Messaging formats	XML	Text based formats are more easier for human readers but parsing is **complex** for machines	Quantitative results in [16] showed XML's serialization speed is the **slowest**	Human-readability of text-based formats makes them **better** choice for flexibility [16]	Results in [16] showed it produces the **largest** footprint	Text based data can be reformatted for cross-platform **reuse**. XML and JSON can also be parsed by many APIs	XML and JSON are **better** for readable, large user base, and documentation [16]	Scalability can **be achieved** based on the schemas defined by each format and the context of use
	JSON		Much **faster than XML**		Smaller **than XML**			
	Thrift	Binary based formats, can only be parsed by tools makes its usage on smartphones **complex** [16]	**Faster than JSON**	Binary formats are platform specific and **less** flexible	**Smaller** than both text-based formats	Platform dependency makes binary less reusable	Usability is **limited** to the specific platform where the parser is deployed	
	Protobuf		The **fastest** of all		The **smallest** of all formats included in the study			
Composition techniques	Static	**Complex**		**Stiff**		User involvement	Static and semi-automatic showed usability **limitation** [4]	**Custom made**
	Semi-automatic	Challenging for non-programmers [20]	The task of composing services is generally is user-assisted which lead to **better** performance	study in [4] showed that it is the most **flexible**	No article discussed about this, but size of the footprint can be influenced by the language it uses	**enhanced** the reuse [20]		**High** end user developer [24]
	Automatic	**Simple**	Transforming natural language **slows** it	**Stiff**		Reuse is **limited**	**Better** user experience	**Limited** [4]
Composition languages	Web 2.0 technologies	**Simpler** than WS-PBEL [28]	**Faster**	Literature showed that it is more **flexible** in use than WS-BPEL	It is described for its **small** footprint size [22]	**High** because of the Web 2.0 technologies [19]	**Less** due to lack of tool support for automatic compo.	Composing REST with Web 2.0 is **more** flexible
	WS-BPEL	**Complex** to track states and transitions	Associated tools **slowed** its performance	It is generally **stiff** [30]		**Low** due to WSDL's structure	**Better** supports automatic approach	**Lower**
Mobile client development approaches	Cross-platform client	**Small effort** needed [32]	Thick clients have **better** communication speed [14]	**Flexible** for multiple platforms	**High** due to verboseness of XML	Generally, this can be achieved depending on the design goal of the applications	**Less** than native [21]	**Better** due to the absence of centralized host
	Native client	**Complex** to deploy		Platform **dependent**	Thick clients owe **high** storage footprint		**Excellent**	
	Web client	Generally **simple**	**Offloads** client-side processing	**Flexible** for updates [21]	**High** communication footprint		**Less** than native	**Lower**

Messaging Format. Messaging is a fundamental function in distributed environment that requires data serialization and de-serialization. Thus, the literature shows performance, footprint, and usability as major evaluation criteria for XML, JSON, Protobuf, and Thrift with respect to their appropriateness for smartphone platforms [16]. In addition, we extend these criteria by adding complexity, flexibility, reusability and scalability for their influence during service composition and invocation (see Table 1).

Composition Techniques and Languages. Here, our literature survey was focused on identifying the criteria for static, semi-automatic, and automatic composition techniques as in [19, 20]; and the WS-BPEL and Web 2.0 languages (see Sect. 2). Thus, we found out that performance, footprint and usability are significant criteria for the resource-constrained smartphone [8, 19]. In addition, the use of WS-BPEL standard with SOAP services versus Web 2.0 with REST have strong influence on performance, footprint, and usability [18, 22]. Hence, we adopted these as our criteria along with complexity, flexibility, reusability and scalability evaluate the technologies with respect to the smartphone platform (see Table 1).

Mobile Client Application. In a similar context, we identified criteria to evaluate the mobile client application development approaches. In this regard, Dalmasso et al. [21] used criteria like software quality, usability, development cost, time to market, adaptability, and extensibility when comparing the native, Web, and cross-platform mobile client development approaches. These in many ways represent our complexity, performance, flexibility, footprint, reusability, usability, and scalability criteria described above with respect to evaluating the client development approaches (see Table 1).

In general, the mapping of the Web service and associated technologies into the smartphone environment is influenced by complexity, performance, flexibility, footprint, reusability, usability, and scalability. Thus, evaluation of the four categories technologies conducted by mapping against the criteria as presented next.

3.2   Evaluating Types of Web Service

SOAP service consumers use the SOAP protocol to locate, contact, and invoke the service while the standard HTTP verbs and URIs are sufficient for the REST [23]. In order for a client to use SOAP Web services, it must generate a client code from the WSDL interface which is quite a complex effort [13]. This complexity is also magnified by the fact that developers must produce the same mobile application for several platforms. REST, however, is designed to operate with thin clients without a strict prerequisite for explicit interface description [25]. Thus, REST is less complex than its SOAP counterpart.

In the SOAP service, the process of generating client code from WSDL must make use of heavyweight parsers which are too heavy for the resource-constrained smartphone [9]. This leads to greater performance degradation of the application that employs SOAP services [14] as compared to the WSDL-less REST counterpart [26].

The SOAP service is highly structured which implies that changing a service requires a significant change in the corresponding WSDL and hence change of client code [26].

Moreover, disseminating such change for multiple smartphone platforms is cumbersome. Although similar descriptive languages like WADL and WSDL 2.0 are proposed for the REST services, they do not represent its resource-centric, self-descriptive, and loosely coupled nature [13, 18]. Thus, making a change in a REST service does not significantly affect client code, which makes it a more flexible approach than SOAP.

In the SOAP services, a SOAP protocol specifies an XML-based message envelope and a set of rules for converting platform specific data types into XML representations [14]. With large message payloads, the footprint for enveloping and setting the rules require more memory to be composed on the smartphone. However, the REST service is directly invoked with HTTP and the response is a representation of the resource itself [25]. Thus, no XML overhead is needed for encapsulating communication interfaces, and specifying input/output data types. As a result, the amount of storage and communication footprint of REST is significantly lower for the smartphone than its SOAP counterpart [26].

SOAP service uses a complex data structure which generally restricts its reusability [9, 23]. Reusability of the REST, on the other hand, takes the advantage of the Web 2.0 paradigm which prefers direct access to Web resources [19]. Similarly, the complex data structure attributed to SOAP makes the composition difficult and error prone [9]. In addition, the lengthy process used to locate, contact, and invoke the service limits developer productivity [23]. These characteristics of the SOAP service limits its usability. Unlike SOAP, however, the URI accessibility of REST services attributes to its ease of reuse. Thus, REST services are widely used to build composite applications [27]. However, they also have usability challenges due to the difficulty of encoding a large amount of input data in the resource URIs and the lack of automated tools [26].

For many of the above mentioned reasons, SOAP services also have scalability limitations. The REST services, however, are designed to support caching and parallelization on URIs. For example, GET responses can be cached in proxies and gateways. Moreover, compared to the ad-hoc partitioning of operations behind SOAP interfaces, REST provides a very simple way to support load balancing based on URI partitioning. Hence, together with the possibility of making stateless interactions, the REST service can enable the building of more scalable systems; and the fact that the whole Web is built on REST principles proves its scalability [28].

3.3   Evaluating Messaging Format

XML and JSON are text-based formats which need to be parsed character by character, hence demand heavyweight parsing [16]. However, Protobuf and Thrift are binary formats and use a technique called positional-binding to store a message's name part of the name-value pair in a separate file [16]. In addition, binary formats incur an extra step because they are language dependent and therefore need to be compiled before use. Thus, both text-based and binary formats exhibit a certain level of complexity.

Sumaray and Makki [16] pointed out that XML produces the largest amount of data, followed by JSON, and then Thrift, with Protobuf being the smallest, hence serialization performance is inverted. A related study by Pentland et al. [7] also confirmed that the data transfer speed of JSON is better than XML. Any change on the data serialization format of the service being invoked may introduce system faults. As long as the substitute data serialization format and the services are compatible with the client's technology, the choice of data format is not a real concern. However, the human-readable characteristic of the text-based protocols is generally a better choice for subsequent use of the data [16].

Because XML and JSON are easily read by human, the resulting data can be reformatted as required and also opens an opportunity for cross-platform compatibility. In addition, XML and JSON are supported by a multitude of programming language APIs. Thus, a Web service that implements XML or JSON as its data format is generally more reusable [16].

The human-readability characteristic of XML and JSON is especially important for reading the context of the data while debugging and making them more usable than the binary formats. Yet, the usability of XML and JSON prevails over the binary formats because they have better documentation and user base [16].

The scalability criteria of data formats can be seen from the perspectives of the data and the application that uses it. Thus, XML is scalable and the scalability of JSON can also be achieved using JSON-schema⁴. However, the ability to support multiple platforms and the need to minimize footprint size as more services are invoked makes the choice of data serialization format a design trade-off. Thus, the literature shows that text-based messaging and data serialization formats appear to be highly important for smartphone.

3.4   Evaluating Composition Technique and Language

Among the composition techniques described in Sect. 2, the semi-automatic is regarded as difficult for nonprogrammers while the automatic technique is the simplest [4, 20]. Similarly, the complexity of a composition language depends on how the states and transitions are managed. Thus, WS-BPEL is more complex than Web 2.0 as it needs to track the states and transitions between the client and each Web service [28].

Automatic service composition, on the other hand, strives to automate user goals extracted from the request and builds the causal link matrix among the inputs and outputs of the services participating in the composition [20]. Thus, transforming natural language into formal requests, the discovery of services and execution sequencing are all made using an automated tool, which significantly degrades the performance of smartphone applications. However, Web 2.0 applications are lightweight and run faster than WS-BPEL based tools which need to execute a graphical workflow designer, process flow logic template, and the BPEL engine on the client [29].

Arguably, questions of flexibility are not appropriate for static techniques. However, the semi-automatic technique has a higher flexibility compared to the automatic [4]. For the languages, the use of HTML5 together with JavaScript APIs to compose a set of loosely-coupled REST services is more flexible when compared with the WS-BPEL standard which is generally used to aggregate the structured WSDL interfaces of SOAP services [30].

---

⁴ http://json-schema.org/.

Regarding communication and storage footprint, the language of choice is more important than the composition technique. Thus, the Ajax feature of Web 2.0 intrinsically provides an asynchronous function in which a partial page refresh would reduce the amount of content drawn into the smartphone resulting in a smaller footprint, while the verbose nature of XML leads to a greater footprint in WS-BPEL [22].

One of the goals of Web services and compositions is to promote service reuse [4]. When considering the service composition techniques and languages, however, it is imperative to explain the reusability of the end result instead of the techniques. The lack of user involvement in the automatic composition limits reusability of the end result, however. Hence, static and semi-automatic techniques provide an opportunity for users to manipulate the result for future reuse [20]. Similarly, reusability of a Web service resulting from WS-BPEL is restricted by the highly structured nature of the WSDL [23]. HTML5/JavaScript APIs, on the other hand, takes advantage of the reusability of Web 2.0 [19].

The automatic composition provides a system for managing services' compatibility [4] which makes the process more user friendly than static and semi-automatic; and the set of automated composition tools associated with WS-BPEL makes it preferable in terms of usability. However, the promise of uniform service interface standards has proven elusive, and absolute automation is unattainable which makes the usability arguable [28].

Web 2.0 is rich in user experience, however, the REST lacks a formal framework to describe, find and orchestrate the services [20, 28]. Thus, the capability of the Web 2.0 technologies is restricted to the use of static or semi-automatic, and the choice of a composition language is a technology selection tradeoff with respect to usability criterion.

Wajid et al. [4] also revealed that the automatic composition technique has limitations in scalability, as it is criticized for its not accommodating user preferred services on templates. The impact of a composition language on scalability is, however, more dependent on the service itself, implying that REST based applications developed with Web 2.0 technologies are more scalable than SOAP service composed with WS-BPEL [28]. In general, our survey indicated that the choice of a composition technique and language generally influences the composition of both the SOAP and REST services.

3.5   Evaluating Mobile Client Development Approach

In the mobile Web client, entering a URL into a general purpose mobile Web browser is the only necessary condition that a user is required to fulfill, which makes it a simple process. The cross-platform and the native mobile clients, however, need to be searched, downloaded, and installed on the mobile client before their actual use. The native approach is even more complex for service consumers because it requires recompiling the resulting code for many different smartphone platforms [21].

The performance of a mobile client application can also be influenced by its processing capacity and communication latency [14]. In fact, the processing capability of smartphone appliances is growing fast and surpasses the bandwidth and latency of a wireless infrastructure where a thick client plays significant role. For example, in the context of developing countries, the quality of installation and maintenance of wireless data communication infrastructure is much less than the market penetration of state-of-the-art smartphones which are usually limited to offline use. In addition, a mobile client should be thick enough to meet the fast response rate of interactive business applications [6]. Thus, while native and cross-platform approaches can implement a thick client and enhance communication performance by placing a considerable processing and caching load on the client side, the Web client does the converse and offloads client side processing.

Flexibility is another important aspect of a mobile client application that describes the ease and cost of propagating changes to each mobile user. In this case, a Web client (mobile Web browser) just sends requests to the server and presents the response content back onto the screen, which makes it the most flexible approach of all. This is followed by the cross-platform approach for its deployment on many platforms, with the native client being the least flexible [21]. A mobile Web client avoids the need for client side processing and storage, but, also incurs a considerably large amount of communication footprint.

In view of reusability, it is important to mention the fact that mobile clients can employ composition tools to aggregate multiple Web services together and result in specific applications or other reusable services [20]. That is, a mobile Web client owner executes the logic of a composite application which is exclusively located on a remote server and also stores the resulting data back. In the cross-platform and native mobile client approaches, however, the logic of a composite application and its data are stored on the smartphone. Thus, depending on the design goal, all mobile client approaches can be used to generate reusable results.

Usability is another criterion that is employed in the selection of an appropriate mobile client development approach. Thus, studies reported in [21] revealed that the native approach has the highest usability, and that the cross-platform approach provides a user experience similar to the mobile Web.

Scalability is also an important aspect in the design of a mobile client because a growing number of connected mobile clients can lead to the risk of a single point of failure, with consequent limitations in extensibility. Thus, the Web client is highly centralized while the thick client approach (cross-platform and native) would enhance scalability [6, 31]. In general, the choice of a mobile client application development approach generally influences the characteristics of a service composition environment on the smartphone.

4   Results

Our analysis has identified SOAP and REST services as the main candidate technologies for service composition on smartphones. Regarding SOAP, studies in [8, 26] suggested kSOAP2 and kXML2 should be used for resource-limited smartphones. However, Mohamed and Wijesekera [26] pointed out that REST services are generally less resource consuming and more efficient to implement on smartphones. That is, the fact that REST services focus on the description of resources rather than describing how operations are performed presents a fundamental difference for consumers compared to the use of SOAP [27]. Thus, although SOAP services have been in use for long and appear as the only choice, REST services have come into the frame backed by quantitative data as a better choice for building flexible, scalable and loosely-coupled applications on smartphones (see Table 1).

In the messaging and data serialization formats category, the text- binary feature has made clear distinctions. That is, the text-based formats are generally characterized as human-readable and platform independent, and the quantitative data in [16] reveals their low serialization speed and large footprint compared to binary formats. In addition, Sumaray and Makki [16] recommended that unless there is a compelling reason, XML must be avoided from mobile applications. However, although JSON's serialization speed is a bit lower than that of the binary formats, its human-readability and platform independence outweigh this slight performance limitation.

Our analysis has also revealed important characteristics of the composition techniques and languages in view of implementing on smartphones. Thus, as described in Table 1, the semi-automatic composition technique prevails in respect of many of the specified criteria, with the exception of usability. Similarly, although Web 2.0 technologies lacks standard tool support for composing services, it is best suited for the smartphone when compared to WS-BPEL in respect of many of the criteria, including performance. In addition, the capability of Web 2.0 technologies to write and parse JSON data on any platform leverages its use on smartphones.

The mobile client application development approaches category also showed significant prospect. That is, the literature-based summary in Table 1 demonstrates that among other criteria, communication performance of the native and the cross-platform mobile client approaches outweigh those of the mobile Web client, while being characterized by a lower processing performance and a high storage footprint.

Thus, the cross-platform approach can be tweaked just like the native approach for better usability and reaching a large number of users of different platforms; and it is more appropriate to design a thick cross-platform client to compensate for the communication bandwidth and latency limitations of the smartphone.

Overall, our analysis of the state of the art of technological readiness for Web service composition on smartphones has portrayed important insights into the selection of appropriate technologies. Accordingly, we present our findings based on the features and shortcomings identified during the mapping of technologies to the smartphone platform as follows.

- The REST service works based on limited standards and tools, however, its lightweight, easily accessible, scalable, and self-descriptive design makes it more appropriate for service composition on smartphone.
- Semi-automatic composition of REST services using Web 2.0 technologies enables the achievement of flexibility, performance, and simplicity. In effect, the matching of Web 2.0 technologies with the REST service [22] can reward certain limitations of the recommended technologies such as easing usability during semi-automatic composition.
- Regarding the messaging and data serialization formats, we highlighted earlier that JSON has an acceptable data serialization speed and that it can be written and parsed

on any platform. In addition, the fact that JavaScript contains APIs which can easily parse JSON data makes it well-matched to Web 2.0 technologies provisions.

- Similarly, the cross-platform mobile client application development approach is found more appropriate for reasons explained in the above sections. In addition, our previous research [24, 32] pointed out that a cross-platform approach can be used to implement a REST service composition tool with Web 2.0 technologies.

Overall, the REST services, semi-automatic service composition with Web 2.0 technologies, messaging and data serialization with JSON, and the use of cross-platform mobile client approaches all together constitute a stack of appropriate technologies.

5 Conclusion

The purpose of this paper is to conduct a literature-based survey of available Web service and associated technologies relevant to compose Web services on the smartphone environment. Accordingly, because REST services are light-weight, easily accessible, scalable, and self-descriptive, they are found more appropriate for composing Web services on smartphones. In the same setting, semi-automatic composition with Web 2.0 technologies demonstrated appropriate combination of composition approach and language mainly because of better flexibility, performance, and simplicity.

In the case of messaging and data serialization formats, JSON is found more appropriate given its human-readability, platform independence, acceptable data serialization speed and ease of data parsing with JavaScript APIs. Similarly, approaches for mobile client development are evaluated and the cross-platform approach was found to best suit our study's criteria, mainly for compensating potential bandwidth and latency limitations, a better user experience and reaching a large audience while fully exploiting a smartphone device's capability.

In general, the REST service, semi-automatic composition with Web 2.0 technologies, messaging and data serialization using JSON and the cross-platform mobile client approach constitute a stack of appropriate technologies for the composition of Web services on the constrained smartphone platform. However, these set of technologies revealed usability limitations due to lack of standards and automated composition tools. In addition, issues such as security are not included in the scope of this study. Our future work will address both limitations.

References

1. Grønli, T-.M., Hansen, J., Ghinea, G., Younas, M.: Mobile application platform heterogeneity: Android vs Windows Phone vs iOS vs Firefox OS. In: IEEE 28th International Conference on Advanced Information Networking and Applications (AINA), pp. 635–641. IEEE, May 2014
2. Mesfin, G., Grønli, T.-M., Ghinea, G., Younas, M.: Adopting SOA in public service provision. In: Younas, M., Awan, I., Holubova, I. (eds.) MobiWIS 2017. LNCS, vol. 10486, pp. 279–289. Springer, Cham (2017). https://doi.org/10.1007/978-3-319-65515-4_23

3. Lieberman, H., Paternò, F., Klann, M., Wulf, V.: End-user development: an emerging paradigm. In: Lieberman, H., Paternò, F., Wulf, V. (eds.) End User Development. Human-Computer Interaction Series, pp. 1–8. Springer, Dordrecht (2006)

4. Wajid, U., Namoune, A., Mehandjiev, N.: A comparison of three service composition approaches for end users. In: AVI, p. 407, May 2010

5. Lin, J., Wong, J., Nichols, J., Cypher, A., Lau, T.A.: End-user programming of mashups with vegemite. In: Proceedings of the 14th International Conference on Intelligent User Interfaces, pp. 97–106. ACM, February 2009

6. Satyanarayanan, M.: Pervasive computing: vision and challenges. Pers. Commun. IEEE **8**(4), 10–17 (2001)

7. Pentland, A.S., Fletcher, R., Hasson, A.: Daknet: rethinking connectivity in developing nations. Computer **37**(1), 78–83 (2004)

8. Srirama, S.N., Jarke, M., Prinz, W.: Mobile Web service provisioning. In: International Conference on Internet and Web Applications and Services/Advanced International Conference on Telecommunications, AICT-ICIW 2006, p. 120. IEEE, February 2006

9. Beaton, J., Jeong, S.Y., Xie, Y., Stylos, J., Myers, B.: Usability challenges for enterprise service-oriented architecture APIs. In: IEEE Symposium on Visual Languages and Human-Centric Computing, VL/HCC 2008, pp. 193–196. IEEE, September 2008

10. Raman, T.V.: Toward 2 W, beyond Web 2.0. Commun. ACM **52**(2), 52–59 (2009)

11. Mesfin, G., Ghinea, G., Grønli, T-.M., Alouneh, S.: REST4Mobile: a framework for enhanced usability of REST services on smartphones. In: Concurrency and Computation: Practice and Experience (2017)

12. Treiber, M., Scherling, C., Dustdar, S.: Applying SOA Principles on Mobile Platforms (2010)

13. Wagh, K., Thool, R.: A comparative study of soap vs rest Web services provisioning techniques for mobile host. J. Inf. Eng. Appl. **2**(5), 12–16 (2012)

14. AlShahwan, F., Moessner, K., Carrez, F.: Evaluation of distributed SOAP and RESTful mobile Web services. Int. J. Adv. Netw. Serv. **3**(3 & 4), 447–461 (2010)

15. Nurseitov, N., Paulson, M., Reynolds, R., Izurieta, C.: Comparison of JSON and XML data interchange formats: a case study. Caine **9**, 157–162 (2009)

16. Sumaray, A., Makki, S.K.: A comparison of data serialization formats for optimal efficiency on a mobile platform. In: Proceedings of the 6th International Conference on Ubiquitous Information Management and Communication, p. 48. ACM, February 2012

17. Tamayo, A., Granell, C., Huerta, J.: Using SWE standards for ubiquitous environmental sensing: a performance analysis. Sensors **12**(9), 12026–12051 (2012)

18. Pautasso, C.: RESTful Web service composition with BPEL for REST. Data Knowl. Eng. **68**(9), 851–866 (2009)

19. Beletski, O.: End user mashup programming environments. In: T-111.552 Seminar on Multimedia, April 2008

20. Laga, N., Bertin, E., Crespi, N.: User-centric services and service composition, a survey. In: 32nd Annual IEEE Software Engineering Workshop, SEW 2008, pp. 3–9. IEEE, October 2008

21. Dalmasso, I., Datta, S.K., Bonnet, C., Nikaein, N.: Survey, comparison and evaluation of cross platform mobile application development tools. In: 9th International Wireless Communications and Mobile Computing Conference (IWCMC), pp. 323–328. IEEE, July 2013

22. Marino, E., Spini, F., Paoluzzi, A., Minuti, F., Rosina, M., Bottaro, A.: HTML5 visual composition of REST-like Web services. In: 4th IEEE International Conference on Software Engineering and Service Science (ICSESS), pp. 49–55. IEEE, May 2013

23. Erl, T.: SOA: Principles of Service Design, vol. 1. Prentice Hall, Upper Saddle River (2008)

24. Mesfin, G., Grønli, T.-M., Midekso, D., Ghinea, G.: Towards end-user development of REST client applications on smartphones. Comput. Stand. Interfaces **44**, 205–219 (2016)
25. Fielding, R.T.: Architectural styles and the design of network-based software architectures. Doctoral dissertation, University of California, Irvine (2000)
26. Mohamed, K., Wijesekera, D.: Performance analysis of Web services on mobile devices. Procedia Comput. Sci. **10**, 744–751 (2012)
27. Pautasso, C., Zimmermann, O., Leymann, F.: Restful Web services vs. big'Web services: making the right architectural decision. In: Proceedings of the 17th International Conference on World Wide Web, pp. 805–814. ACM, April 2008
28. Lanthaler, M., Gütl, C.: Towards a RESTful service ecosystem. In: 4th IEEE International Conference on Digital Ecosystems and Technologies (DEST), pp. 209–214. IEEE, April 2010
29. Schroth, C., Janner, T.: Web 2.0 and SOA: converging concepts enabling the internet of services. IT Prof. **9**(3), 36–41 (2007)
30. Peltz, C.: Web services orchestration and choreography. Computer **10**, 46–52 (2003)
31. Tanenbaum, A.S., Van Steen, M.: Distributed Systems. Prentice-Hall, Upper Saddle River (2007)
32. Mesfin, G., Ghinea, G., Midekso, D., Grønli, T.-M.: Evaluating usability of cross-platform smartphone applications. In: Awan, I., Younas, M., Franch, X., Quer, C. (eds.) MobiWIS 2014. LNCS, vol. 8640, pp. 248–260. Springer, Cham (2014). https://doi.org/10.1007/978-3-319-10359-4_20

Server-Based Indoor Location Detection System

Osman Kerem Perente$^{(\boxtimes)}$ and Tacha Serif

Yeditepe University, Atasehir, 34755 Istanbul, Turkey
{kperente,tserif}@cse.yeditepe.edu.tr

Abstract. With the advancement of technology and telecommunication services, data consumption rates are increasing ever since. People for long have started using applications with the help of contextual information to improve their user experience. Thus, providing a cross-platform location service to further enrich such applications has become a necessity. For this purpose, numerous client-based indoor location systems on mobile devices are developed to perform this task. Nevertheless, most of the time these systems suffer from elimination of features from operating systems for security purposes. Indeed, with the current security trends, to ensure the privacy of mobile users, mobile operating system designers are progressively eliminating certain low-level features such as reading RSSI and introducing randomized MAC addresses. Thus, in this study, the authors propose, design and implement a server-based indoor positioning system to eliminate platform dependency and to provide the location detection in wide range of devices. The designed server-based system is scalable and platform independent; hence can run on virtually any family of smart device. Furthermore, the evaluation findings indicate that the proposed system performs in acceptable accuracy to client-based systems compared to more complex and costly implementations.

Keywords: Server-Based · Location detection · RSSI · Indoor positioning

1 Introduction

Mobile devices are used in every field in our lives. With the advancing technologies and telecommunication services, data consumption rates have been increasing with an exponential pace. People use applications with the help of contextual information to improve the user experience. Thus, providing an accurate location service to further enrich such applications has become a must.

Although Global Positioning System (GPS) is widely adopted as the standard positioning system for outdoor environments, it lacks the required accuracy in indoor environments where a clear view of sky is not available. Therefore, it is necessary to use different techniques for indoor location detection, such as Wi-Fi IEEE 802.11, Bluetooth 4.0 radio signals. Many of these systems use client-based positioning approach where location estimation is done on the user's device. However, in recent releases of mobile operating systems (OS), many low-level functionalities are gradually being disabled or becoming harder to access due to security and privacy concerns. As an example, such feature restrictions include the elimination of RSSI reading of wireless access points and randomized MAC addresses to disguise the device in iOS 7 and later [1]. Therefore,

© Springer International Publishing AG, part of Springer Nature 2018
M. Younas et al. (Eds.): MobiWIS 2018, LNCS 10995, pp. 142–153, 2018.
https://doi.org/10.1007/978-3-319-97163-6_12

the implementation of some low-level functionalities in some OSs can be more cumbersome and harder to achieve compared to other OSs.

In this paper, a server-based location estimation system is proposed and evaluated for accuracy and performance. The proposed system uses sniffer devices to gather signal information from mobile devices. The position calculation is done on the server which enables platform independency. Accordingly, this paper is structured as follows; Sect. 2 reviews and details similar location-aware systems. Section 3 elaborates on the location estimation techniques and methodologies and Sect. 4 details the requirements and the proposed designed of the system. Section 5 depicts the prototype implementation and Sect. 6 details the approach used to conduct the evaluations and discusses the findings. Finally, Sect. 7 draws conclusions and highlights the possible future development venues.

2 Background

The lack of consistent and reliable location detection mechanism for indoor environments attracted a lot of interest from both academia and industry. As a result, over the last decades many localization techniques were developed and tested with various properties. Among the proposed techniques, the most popular ones utilized radio signals as their key component.

In 2001, the Bat location sensor system [2] is developed by AT&T Laboratories in Cambridge using ultrasonic personalized badges known as Bats. Trilateration technique works by emitting an ultrasonic signal from the badge and using the receivers on the ceiling to calculate time-of-flight values of the signal. Trilateration technique is then utilized to perform location detection. The test results indicated that the Bat location sensor system estimated the location of badge wearing personnel with 3 cm error rate 95% of the time. Bergamo and Mazzini [3], which used triangulation on Wireless Sensor Networks by the received signal powers from two wireless beacons that were placed to two known locations. Their work focused on improving accuracy by modeling wireless fading when movement is present. Following this trend, Bahl and Padmanabhan [4] designed an RF based localization system based on empirical and signal propagation models in location estimation and compared several methods in each model. Empirical method based on fingerprinting achieved distance error of just less than three meters.

Generally, the positioning systems are designed and tested in relatively small or controlled environments where systems behave optimally. Hence, the test results do not always reflect the real-life performance of these proposed systems. Accordingly, Wirola et al. [5] has comparatively highlighted the requirement and methodology differences between implementing indoor positioning system in a large and small scale indoor environments. Li et al. [6], developed a positioning system at Queen Mary University in London which aims to identify room the user is currently in. The system is deployed on the second and third floors of Electronic Engineering building. In this study, they incorporated Wi-Fi RSSI positioning system with GSM-based approach and their results indicate that the proposed system achieved room level positioning with 72% accuracy. Similarly, Mathisen et al. [7] evaluated several positioning techniques utilizing the existing Wi-Fi infrastructure in a university hospital floor of 160,000 m^2. Their proposed system, for various algorithms, achieved a mean error-rates from 8 to 15 m relative to ground positions.

3   Methodology

Accordingly, this section details the methodologies and algorithms that are used to implement location detection and estimation systems.

3.1   Distance Determination

Determining the distance between two points is the first step of location detection. One of these points has a fixed location with known coordinates and, generally the other one is a mobile device whose location will be determined. There are several methods that can be used to determine the distance. Such as time of arrival (ToA), time difference of arrival (TDoA), angle of arrival (AoA) and received signal strength indicator (RSSI). These methods utilize radio signals and their propagation characteristics in free space.

3.2   Received Signal Strength Indicator

Most of the techniques discussed above require line-of-sight (LOS) operation. However, indoor environments seldom have direct LOS, which degrades the value of the time and the angle information extracted from the received signal due to multipath effect [8]. On the other hand, RSSI method performs well both in LOS and non-LOS environments, changing with respect to the distance from the transmitter. RSSI distance determination mainly uses IEEE 802.11 wireless local networking standard, with wide availability in many consumer handsets and extensive deployment in many urban areas.

RSSI is a good option for determining the distance between devices because of the attenuation property of radio signals when the distance between the receiver and the transmitter increase. Also, it is an easier method to implement and it does not have the complexities of the other methods. Using the RSSI method, the distances between two points of measurements in terms of signal propagation can be calculated using the Euclidean distance theorem (Eq. 1).

$$d = \sqrt{\sum_{i=0}^{n} \left(q_i - p_i\right)^2} \tag{1}$$

3.3   Fingerprinting

Fingerprinting is a technique that is evolved to increase the positioning accuracy in non-LOS indoor environments by constructing a radio map at pre-determined target locations. It is performed by sampling more than one RSS measurement over time in each target reference point to better map the environment. Once the signal map of the environment is constructed, the location detection can be achieved by comparing the real-time signal information with the signal map and calculating the position using a subset of signal information contained in the map.

To utilize this technique, location detection procedure is broken down into two distinct phases – offline and online phase.

Offline Phase. This phase can also be called learning phase, implying that the necessary signal characteristics of the environment is constructed for the real localization.

Firstly, the indoor environment is evaluated and the locations for signal sampling are determined. These locations are called reference points (RP), with each point having a distinct x and y coordinate and an array of average signal values. As the RSSI value collection and signal map generation can be a time-consuming process, an offline phase tool is needed to help the collection of acquirable signal strengths of access points (AP) at RPs.

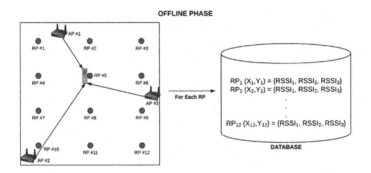

Fig. 1. Offline phase of fingerprinting technique

As depicted in Fig. 1, the idea is to move the mobile device through the RPs one by one, collecting RSSI samples at each RP. For a single RP, the mobile device collects a pre-determined number of RSSI values for each AP received from each accessible AP and stores the average of these AP-specific RSSI values in signal map database. The average of RSSI samples measured at every RP is inserted into the database, as RP Data (RPD) vector in the form $\{ID, S_1, S_2, S_3\}$ where ID identifies the reference point, whereas S_i denotes the signal strength received from the AP_i at a specific RP.

Online Phase. In this phase, the real-time localization operation is performed. Accordingly, the mobile device initiates the collection of RSSI values from each available AP at the point where the location is to be determined. Euclidean distances are calculated by using the collected RSSI of the available APs and signal map retrieved from the database. Since the signal map contains signal measurements done at each RP in the environment, the Euclidean distance calculation is performed for each RP present in the signal map. Thus, for every RP in the signal map, the distances between MU and each RP is obtained (Fig. 2). After this step, K-Nearest Neighbor (KNN) algorithm is used to calculate location of the MU by selecting the closest RPs. The steps of this operation are given in detail below.

- For a given test point (TP), make at most 10 observations per each available AP using mobile device and store them in the observation set (OS). Here OS_i denotes observation stack of ith AP. $OS_i = \{O_1, O_2, \dots O_{10}\}$
- For each AP, calculate the average of all observations in OS, and generate the average signal strength (SS) vector of MU. $SS = \{s_1, s_2, \dots s_n\}$ (Here n represents the number of available APs at the location of mobile device)
- For each RP calculate the Euclidean distance between the RP and TP using the RPD and SS vector.
- Perform KNN algorithm for the closest k neighbors (RPs). The weighted average of the x and y coordinates of the candidate RPs are the estimated MU location.

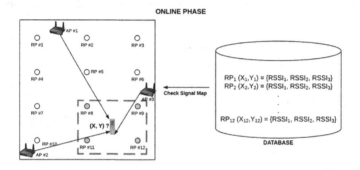

Fig. 2. Online phase of fingerprinting technique

3.4   K-Nearest Neighbor (KNN) Algorithm

K-nearest neighbor algorithm is a very simple classification and regression machine learning algorithm. It involves k-nearest training data to classify or determine value of an object by measuring its distance to that of the training data. K is a pre-determined number, which can be selected to optimally represent the class or value of an object.

To determine the closest training data, distance must be measured. One way to measure the distance between the object and training data is to use Euclidean distances. This distance value can also be used to improve regression based KNN, in which case the algorithm evolves in to weighted k-nearest neighbor (WKNN) algorithm. The weight can be taken as the inverse of the distance 1/d, to improve the weight of the closer training data during calculation. The localization accuracy can be further improved by using WKNN, in such case that the weights are taken using the complementary neighbors.

$$x = \frac{\sum_{i=1}^{4}\left(x_i * d_{4-i}\right)}{\sum_{i=1}^{4} d_i} \quad y = \frac{\sum_{i=1}^{4}\left(y_i * d_{4-i}\right)}{\sum_{i=1}^{4} d_i} \tag{2}$$

In Eq. 2, x_i denotes the x-coordinate of RP_i, y_i denotes the y-coordinate of RP_i and d_i denotes the measured distance between the user position and RP_i. By multiplying x_i and y_i with d_{4-i}, the weight can be incorporated in to the algorithm (Fig. 3).

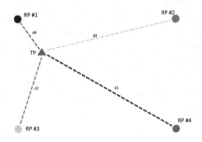

Fig. 3. WKNN in fingerprinting

4 Analysis and Design

The system architecture of the proposed system can be seen in Fig. 4. This location detection solution is composed of a server and at least three wireless sniffer devices, where each device is connected to the server via Ethernet connection. The server hosts database where the signal map of the environment and sniffer device information is stored. By making use of this architecture adding additional sniffer devices for increased coverage becomes very easy and affordable.

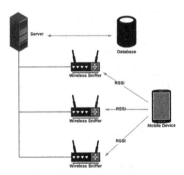

Fig. 4. System architecture

In this scenario, sniffer devices are required to capture 802.11 frames over the air and filter them according to the MAC addresses of the mobile device that needs its position estimated. For this scenario to work, the mobile device is required to be connected to a wireless infrastructure to initiate server registration for its MAC address, and also to generate wireless traffic for the sniffers to capture. This wireless traffic between the MU and the wireless network is essential because the system exploits the packets captured from this traffic to determine the position of the user. Therefore, to make this system work, an additional access point is needed for the mobile device to connect and communicate.

Accordingly, the infrastructure requirements of the proposed system is as follows; the server platform should be capable of performing the necessary calculations in a short amount of time and handle large number of consecutive requests of position estimations. Also, since the mobile devices runs on battery and have limited resources, the mobile application must be relatively simple and straightforward to minimize battery consumption. Therefore, the system should follow the thin client and thick server model. Considering, the size of the location detection area cloud systems can be used. However, in our proof of concept, the server should be able to handle requests sent from a single device within medium-sized room.

As depicted in Fig. 5, the sequence diagram of the system, once the client is connected to the AP serving internet access, the client can send the system startup command to start the positioning process. Then the server contacts to wireless sniffers to start Airodump processes for capturing 802.11 frames. Once the general system startup is accomplished, the client can send positioning request periodically, the server requests new station data from the sniffers and performs positioning algorithm to calculate user position. The server then sends the calculated user position back to the client.

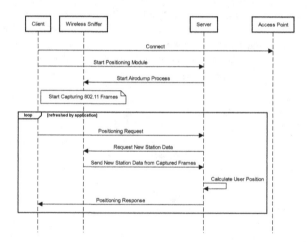

Fig. 5. Sequence diagram of the system

5   Implementation

5.1   Wireless Sniffer Modules

As wireless sniffer devices, three Linux PCs with Ubuntu operating system are employed. These PCs are regular desktop stations with Mid ATX chassis, but in a real-life scenario these PCs can be substituted with mini-PCs.

The sniffing process is performed using a special wireless application suite called Aircrack-ng [9]. From the suit member application, our study makes use of Airodump-ng application, which enables the wireless network interface adapter to sniff wireless packets in the environment. The sniffer function requires special wireless adapters which can be put into the monitoring mode. Therefore, TP-Link 802.11n wireless adapter with model number WL722 N is selected. This device utilizes an Atheros chipset, which can easily put into monitoring mode and coupled with Airodump-ng. After the monitoring interface is created, Airodump-ng process is executed. Then, Airodump-ng simply uses this newly created monitoring interface and listens to all available wireless packets across all Wi-Fi channels. Collected wireless data is then used to create device lists on the terminal. The data then can easily be dumped to a CSV that contains the following information: MAC address of the station, first time seen, last time seen, signal strength of the station, and information whether a station is connected to an AP, and if connected, the MAC address of this AP.

Bearing in mind the MAC address of the device that requested position estimation, the data from CSV file can be parsed to get its signal strength. Consequently, its MAC address along with its signal strength values are send to the server every time a sniffer captures 802.11 frames containing this MAC address.

5.2 Server-Side Implementation

Server-side application is implemented in Java programming language along with a JDBC database. The server has separate components for configuring and running the positioning system. These components (Fig. 6) are; offline phase calibration, online phase localization, sniffer registration, and database management. Sniffer registration module accepts the addition of new sniffer modules for later expandability, in our case three sniffer modules are generated. Offline phase calibration is responsible for creating the signal map by the help of sniffer modules. Online phase module is responsible for real-time localization and mobile device connection management. Database module is responsible for database connection and management.

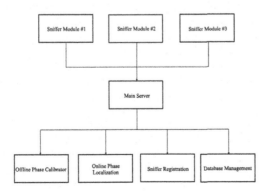

Fig. 6. Server modules

In the case of a positioning request from the mobile device, the server contacts the sniffer module and requests the most recent signal data for the device in question. Since sniffing and the signal strength collection is a continuous process, the online phase module extracts the required data from the database via the help of the database management module and performs necessary positioning calculation. The result of this calculation is written to the database continuously and updated in every few seconds when necessary data is gathered for another location update. For the online phase localization WKNN algorithm is chosen and deployed in the server. The k value in the WKNN algorithm is chosen to be four, which gives the best results in the test environment the system is implemented.

6   Tests and Results

6.1   Test Environment

The proposed system is implemented and evaluated in the Pervasive System Laboratory in the Engineering Faculty. The test environment was the whole of the laboratory, which is approximately 47 m^2. In order to cover the entire test environment, the sniffer PCs are sporadically spread around the laboratory, so they were as far away from each other as possible. On the other hand, 15 reference points (RP) are selected and each one of them is distributed with 1.4-m intervals. Furthermore, 10 test points (TP) are selected at random locations to estimate the location and calculate the error-rate. The coordinates of each sniffer PC, RP and TP is calculated in reference to the test bed and implemented on the database to be used in location determination.

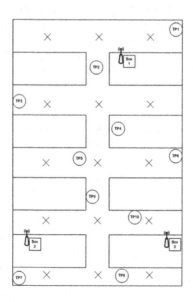

Fig. 7. Test environment

A detailed depiction of the test environment is provided in Fig. 7, where the RPs are marked with "X"s, sniffer PCs with an antenna, and the TPs with their TP numbers. In order to measure the error-rate of the proposed solution, a number of measurements are conducted on 10 test points by utilizing the fingerprinting and finding how they compared with the actual coordinates within the test environment.

6.2   Evaluation Results

In order to evaluate the proposed system for its performance, 10 pre-determined test points were set. At each of these test locations, the system tried to capture 20 airborne packets that were transmitted from the mobile device and by making use of the collected packet information to perform the location estimation. According to the CDF for location estimation error-rate in Fig. 8, the systems performs within 3 m positioning error-rate 70% of the time.

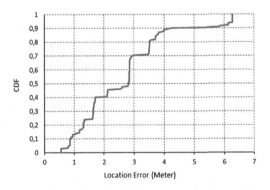

Fig. 8.   CDF location estimation

As it can be seen from Table 1, where the results are given in centimeters, the mean system location estimation error-rate ranged between 105.85 cm and 615.15 cm. Overall mean of location estimation error-rate of this solution was 266.15 cm and standard deviation was 38.77 cm. To elaborate more on the single test results, it can be seen that 5th test point has the lowest error with 55.44 cm. Whereas 1st test point has the greatest error with 626.99 cm.

It can be noted that test points (2, 4, 5, 9, 10) that are covered within reference points has lower location estimation error, whereas test points (1, 3, 6, 7, 8) which are not covered within the reference points and reside on the outer radius and extremities of the room has greater error-rate (Fig. 9). This phenomenon can be the result of the WKNN algorithm itself, where the candidate location estimate is calculated using the nearest four RPs. In the case of test points that reside in the locations that are not directly covered within RPs, the WKNN algorithm cannot perform optimally, thus it increases the error-rate.

Table 1. Detailed test results

TP	N	Mean	Std. deviation	Std. error	Minimum	Maximum
1	20	615.51	22.47	5.03	538.52	626.99
2	20	184.66	67.57	15.11	117.00	372.65
3	20	321.96	57.61	12.88	255.16	425.03
4	20	105.85	21.94	4.91	85.56	131.31
5	20	126.97	51.38	11.49	55.44	170.66
6	20	293.09	23.55	5.27	285.35	371.32
7	20	350.99	0.99	0.22	348.62	353.62
8	20	257.62	102.94	23.02	133.27	399.53
9	20	121.46	36.75	8.22	79.88	167.17
10	20	283.41	2.47	0.55	278.98	291.27
Total	200	266.15	38.77	8.67	55.44	626.99

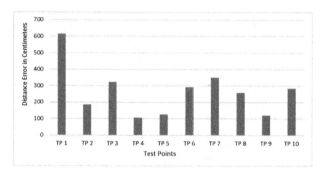

Fig. 9. Test results per TP

7   Conclusion

In this paper, a study is undertaken to evaluate a server-based indoor positioning system that is platform independent. The server-based system proposed to be scalable mainly for large area deployment and mobile OS independent. Therefore, it does not suffer from client-based systems where they need OS API compatibility. The server-based positioning system aimed to perform in similar performance accuracy to client-based systems albeit a more complex design process. The findings show that it performs within these expectations. The average positioning error for server-based system is 266 cm which is comparable to the tested systems when they are evaluated.

For the future work, the server-based system can be improved by adding hybrid functionality with sensor-based methods. Such system with iBeacon and PDR support, can choose the most accurate method on-the-go and cut down the positioning error even in large real-world environments. Furthermore, the algorithm can be improved such as adding probabilistic approaches to plain Wi-Fi and Bluetooth techniques. Consequently, the accuracy and performance of the server-based system can be tested in a large indoor environment such as the supermarket branch used in Wi-Fi positioning system.

References

1. iOS 7 Eliminates MAC Address as Tracking Option, Signaling Final Push Towards Apple's Own Ad Identifier Technology. https://techcrunch.com/2013/06/14/ios-7-eliminates-mac-address-as-tracking-option-signaling-final-push-towards-apples-own-ad-identifier-technology/. Accessed 1 Apr 2018

2. Addlesee, M., Curwen, R., Hodges, S., Newman, J., Steggles, P., Ward, A., et al.: Implementing a sentient computing system. IEEE Comput. **34**(8), 50–56 (2001)

3. Bergamo, P., Mazzini, G.: Localization in sensor networks with fading and mobility. In: 13th IEEE International Symposium on Personal, Indoor and Mobile Radio Communications (2002)

4. Bahl, P.N., Padmanabhan, V.: RADAR: An in-building RF-based user location and tracking system. In: 19th Annual Joint Conference of the IEEE Computer and Communications Societies (2000)

5. Wirola, L., Laine, T.A., Syrjarinne, J.I.: Mass-market requirements for indoor positioning and indoor navigation. In: International Conference on Indoor Positioning and Indoor Navigation (2010)

6. Li, K.J., Bigham, J., Bodanese, E.L., Tokarchuk, L.: Location estimation in large indoor multi-floor buildings using hybrid networks. In: IEEE Wireless Communications and Networking Conference (2013)

7. Mathisen, A., Sorensen, S.K., Stisen, A., Blunck, H., Gronbaek, K.: A comparative analysis of indoor WiFi positioning at a large building complex. In: 2016 International Conference on Indoor Positioning and Indoor Navigation (2016)

8. Hightower, J., Borriello, G.: Location Sensing Techniques, University of Washington, Paper# UW-CSE-01-07-0 (2001). ftp://ftp.cs.washington.edu/tr/2001/07/UW-CSE-01-07-01.pdf. Accessed 2 Apr 2018

9. Aircrack-ng. https://www.aircrack-ng.org. Accessed 2 Apr 2018

Web and Mobile Applications

Analysis of Technical Devices Relevance for Remote Readings of Electric Meters

Josef Horalek and Vladimir Sobeslav[✉]

Faculty of Informatics and Management,
University of Hradec Kralove, Hradec Kralove, Czech Republic
{josef.horalek,vladimir.sobeslav}@uhk.cz

Abstract. The following article presents analysis results of technical devices relevance for remote readings of electric meters. Real communiqués of reading centrals with selected types of meters were charted by using different protocols for individual readings. Types of stored data, the system of their collection and results of analysis from different points of view were described. The analysis of individual data transition ratio was done initially; next, times of readings for selected types of meters, total readings of data and error rate of meters according to used transmission protocols VDEW, DLMS and SCTM were assessed for continuous period of four months. Results presented here are based in real operations and they are important for effectivity evaluation of the currently used system of electro meters remote readings and its next development.

Keywords: Smart metering · AMR · GPRS · SCTM · VDEW · DLMS

1 Introduction

At the beginning of building the remote communications with meters in Czech Republic, it was important that the offtake site was equipped with connection to public phone network. This requirement transferred part of expenses in form of providing phone lines to operators of offtake sites. At first this included mostly big customers, transfer sites in the system, and producers of high voltage and extra-high voltage electricity. The situation changed slowly after implementation of GSM and GPRS technology because all expenses for remote readings go to the energy company. Considerable increase of offtake sites with remote communication was, inter alia, contributed by new legislation connected with electric energy market liberalization. At this point the progress concerned the exchange of real data among market participants with help of direct reading technology: electro meter – data central – invoice system (i.e. SAP). In the mid 1990s only several dozens of sites were read remotely, primarily in properties of energy companies. After development of technologies at the time of data analysis realization, there were ten thousands sites in the Czech Republic. Data collection standard is an automatic electro meter reading technology as can be found in [1, 2] (AMR), which belongs to Smart metering group [3–5], which is a fundamental cornerstone for creating Smart Grids as mentioned by authors [6] or [7–9]. However, AMR system only allows sending data from electro meters to reading central [10]. It is, however, only one-way

© Springer International Publishing AG, part of Springer Nature 2018
M. Younas et al. (Eds.): MobiWIS 2018, LNCS 10995, pp. 157–166, 2018.
https://doi.org/10.1007/978-3-319-97163-6_13

communication that allows arbitrary data readings and lowers expenses of manual collection of data by a reader. GSM and GPRS technologies are still used for data transfer between metres and data central. Despite GSM technology being proven with years, it is unsuitable for remote meters readings for its financial costs. Especially when there is a need to read more sites. Therefore, GSM technology is used mostly as a backup line when GPRS is unavailable or absent. An integral part of data collecting is communication protocols defining rules of transfer between electro meters and the reading central. Serial Code Tele Metering (SCTM) is among the oldest used protocols, which is used exclusively on the meters of older production date; details about this protocol can be found i.e. in [11]. Two different protocols have the largest percentage of use: one of them is VDEW protocol based on three-layered architecture EPA described in detail in [12] and DLMS protocol which had become international communication standard working on server-client principle and its specification is stated in [13]. Some electro meters can work with both mentioned protocols or with only one of them. Therefore, the statements above show the significance of analysis of current results from the point of view of reliability and effectivity of readings in real-time operations that can point out potential imperfections of used technical equipment and individual protocols. Potential high level of unreliability and error rate has a wide range of impact not only for technical solution itself but also economic impact in a form of redundant expenses invested in human resources, and non-effective expenses in communication and technical equipment.

2 Selected Meters Testing Procedure

Group of meters including the most commonly used types for high voltage and extra-high voltage levels disturbed in the Czech Republic were chosen for the testing. Testing and analysis realization took place in 60 places, while the emphasis was put on that the metres were located in electric distribution network of ČEZ Distribuce, a.s. company, and in the location with sufficient mobile operator signal or trouble-free lines in case of PSTN technologies readings. Data readings were done with the help of mobile operator (O2) and they were realized by GSM or GSM/GPRS technology, where GSM held a backup way of reading if GPRS was non-functional. All meters had to use modems supplied and recommended by their producers. Data collection was executed with the help of data central Converge from Landis&Gyr company. Meters samples from all meter technology producers were used and from every line 5 m with corresponding modems were integrated into the analysis. The exception was a meter group from the same type line communicating in multi-master operation (cascade) with 11 pieces. Data for analysis were acquired from data/reading central Converge in version 3.9.7 from Landis&Gyr company and managed by ČEZ Distribuce, a.s. company.

2.1 Testing Data Use Overview

Two types of data are saved in electro meters to two different memories (buffers). First data area includes Load profile (sometimes labelled as Last profile), which is a data row containing measured physical unit values with time mark and with possible status of the respective value. For reading measurement in offtake sites measures with three profiles are used. One profile is used for active offtake and two for reactive energy. Electro meters with six profiles (6LP) are used when measuring producers of electric energy and transferring places between distribution systems. There two profiles measure active offtake and supply. The other four is used for reactive energy. The principle comes from a four-quadrant model of measuring electric energy where the difference among three profiles has no significant role and from the time point of view is negligible. All tested meters use fifteen-minute time period for measuring the profiles, which is the highest reached average maximum per time unit.

The second data area includes register values (BV – Billing Values) that contain information about parameters of electro meters (serial number, type of electro meter, number of systems, records, etc.). Values of energy in certain time or certain time period are recorded into registers. Measured data are stored here in a form of enumeration such as total used or created energy in the previous time period. Measured maxims including time marks also belong here. Range and type of recorded registers depend on parameters of specific meters before placing it at the offtake location. From the transfer point of view registers usually have smaller data capacity than values of the firstly named profiles. Part of the electro meters register telegram is illustrated in Fig. 1.

Historical Profile:

Reset Time From Meter	Reset Counter	OBIS Code	Value	Scale	Unit	Status
01.04.2016 00:00:00.000 DST W. Europe Standard Time	37	1-1:21.8.0	13523594.00	1000.00	Wh	0
01.04.2016 00:00:00.000 DST W. Europe Standard Time	37	1-1:41.8.0	13300953.00	1000.00	Wh	0
01.04.2016 00:00:00.000 DST W. Europe Standard Time	37	1-1:61.8.0	13707545.00	1000.00	Wh	0
01.04.2016 00:00:00.000 DST W. Europe Standard Time	37	1-1:1.8.0	40529682.00	1000.00	Wh	0
01.04.2016 00:00:00.000 DST W. Europe Standard Time	37	1-1:22.8.0	32339.00	1000.00	Wh	0
01.04.2016 00:00:00.000 DST W. Europe Standard Time	37	1-1:42.8.0	31114.00	1000.00	Wh	0
01.04.2016 00:00:00.000 DST W. Europe Standard Time	37	1-1:62.8.0	30393.00	1000.00	Wh	0
01.04.2016 00:00:00.000 DST W. Europe Standard Time	37	1-1:2.8.0	92144.00	1000.00	Wh	0
01.04.2016 00:00:00.000 DST W. Europe Standard Time	37	1-1:23.8.0	3077569.00	1000.00	varh	0
01.04.2016 00:00:00.000 DST W. Europe Standard Time	37	1-1:43.8.0	2928120.00	1000.00	varh	0
01.04.2016 00:00:00.000 DST W. Europe Standard Time	37	1-1:63.8.0	2999941.00	1000.00	varh	0
01.04.2016 00:00:00.000 DST W. Europe Standard Time	37	1-1:3.8.0	8991257.00	1000.00	varh	0
01.04.2016 00:00:00.000 DST W. Europe Standard Time	37	1-1:24.8.0	98045.00	1000.00	varh	0
01.04.2016 00:00:00.000 DST W. Europe Standard Time	37	1-1:44.8.0	100802.00	1000.00	varh	0
01.04.2016 00:00:00.000 DST W. Europe Standard Time	37	1-1:64.8.0	103700.00	1000.00	varh	0
01.04.2016 00:00:00.000 DST W. Europe Standard Time	37	1-1:4.8.0	289742.00	1000.00	varh	0
01.04.2016 00:00:00.000 DST W. Europe Standard Time	37	1-1:25.8.0	3061682.00	1000.00	varh	0
01.04.2016 00:00:00.000 DST W. Europe Standard Time	37	1-1:45.8.0	2911669.00	1000.00	varh	0
01.04.2016 00:00:00.000 DST W. Europe Standard Time	37	1-1:65.8.0	2981416.00	1000.00	varh	0

Fig. 1. Example of part of the meter register telegram

2.2 Overview of Meters Used During Testing

General marks used in practice were used for labelling of meters. Individual type series differ only in details that are insignificant for testing, such as difference in accuracy grade, number of tariffs, or if the meters is used for primary/secondary reading. Following meters were used for the testing:

- **ZxD (ZxD3xx/4xx)** – electro meters by Landis&Gyr company are represented by ZMD405CT44.0457 1A, ZFD410CT44.0459B and ZMD410CT44.2407 types. Meters feature profiles and registers. Part of the electro meters communicated through DLMS protocol and part through VDEW. Reading took place with the help of GSM/GPRS technology. 11 electro meters communicated in multi-master operation with DLMS protocol and GSM/GPRS communication.
- **Type SL7000** – electro meters by Itron (Actaris) company are represented by SL7C71_100V2_1A10 and SL7 B71_58V3_1A10 types. These electro meters also have profiles and registers. Protocol DLMS is exclusively used for communication. All devices used GSM/GPRS technology for remote data gathering.
- **Type E700** – are older electro meters by Enermet company. Registers and profiles are stored in the electro meters. Meters of E705DJZ and E705DNJZ type were used through communication protocol SCTM and GSM technology.
- **Types FAG and FBC** – encoders by Landis&Gyr company used only fifteen-minutes profiles in active/reactive offtake and supply as output values. These devices do not read registers. Readings were taken with SCTM protocol and PSTN technology.
- **Type LZQ** – electro meters by Schrack (EMH) company were LZQJ_100V2_5A6_E8 types. For data gathering VDEW protocol and GSM/GPRS technologies were used. Meters read profiles and registers data.
- **Type EKM647** – meters are not classical electro meters but coders for summative measurement. Unlike FAG and FBC types they can read registers. SCTM protocol and GSM communication technology was used for data reading.
- **Type DC3** – older electro meters DC371D types were originally produced by Schlumberger Industries company and they were read by VDEW communication protocol and GSM communication technology. DC3 type can read profiles and registers values.

2.3   Reading Methods and Statistic Data Collection

According to specifications of individual meters the readings were done by GSM/GPRS and PSTN communication technologies. With some meters reading was possible only with GSM technology given by a possibility of installed modem and device. In all occurrences the meters were of older manufacturing date. Virtual electro meter with pre-defined protocol types and number of profiles was created in Converge data central. Readings took place once a day from 1.9.2016 to 31.12.2016. During every reading the values of individual telegrams, therefore values of profiles and registers, were downloaded, and simultaneously check of the time unit was executed. All profile values had a fifteen-minute period. Value reading always started at the last recorded time mark so the data would not override each other or stored profiles. During the register readings the remote data collection was different. A part of the data is overwritten (enumerations of immediate values), changed (phase voltage) or added (maximal values, values from the past period). During the data reading the time control with meter time was realized in reading central. If the time gap reaches up to two second synchronization with time in the reading central happens automatically. If the time gap is longer than two seconds, the synchronization does not happen and it is necessary to adjust the time manually. Reason for the time desynchronization can be too long a time period between individual readings caused for example by operator signal being out of reach, weak battery in electro meter or error in electro meter's memory. In the last two cases service maintenance is necessary at the offtake site.

2.4 Reading Course

In GSM mode the communication with electro meter is very similar to a regular phone call. In the reading central virtual electro meter with data number is created. Using this number the central calls to specific electro meter. GPRS communication is very similar to a network connection between two devices. Both devices identify each other with an IP address. Every place with GPRS remote reading has SIM with an IP address assigned. This address is registered in the system of reading central. Converge data central uses exclusively static IP addresses for remote readings. Except for IP addresses a data phone number is filled in communication. That is so in order to choose between GSM and GPRS modes. Communication in multi-master operation is used only in case of cascade connection when all electro meters are connected through one data number. Every electro meter in cascade has specific identification number (ZDUE Password, Physical address) that guarantees its uniqueness. Most of the time they are serial numbers of individual electro meters either in their full or partial form. Meters in cascade cannot be mixed. PSTN communication is similar to GSM. All tested devices used SCTM protocol at the same time. Every meter has specific address in the central, which is not kept in practice and the passwords are set collectively.

3   Operation Evaluation

All meters were chosen to be situated in the same or close locations to eliminate possible influence of mobile operator signal accessibility during testing. During data reading the reading success in everyday operation was compared, therefore the execution of all predefined and planned tasks, such as already mentioned profile and electro meters registers readings, including control or synchronization of time unit. A part of the testing was also one the offtake site working in multi-master operation in order to analyse negative influences of this meter group to common reading.

3.1 Reading Times Comparison

In Fig. 2 average data volumes between data central and individual meters are depicted. From the picture it is clear that the values of tasked profile have the largest share and the smallest one is the time.

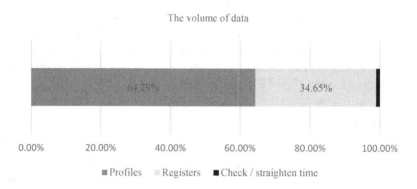

Fig. 2. The average volume data for remote reading

From the analysis of acquired values the time period of individual reading jobs was discovered. In the Fig. 3 reached times during observed period are depicted. There is a distinct difference between the time of profile and register readings. In this relative small test the differences do not seem to be very essential from the practical point of view, however, in the general use these transition time parameters play an important role. SL7000 type electro meters need the longest and with a distance the ZxD is the same which is given by DLMS communication protocol use. ZxD type electro meters were read by two types of communication protocols (DLMS and VDEW) and because of that the time difference was shorter in average. FCB type device and FAG do not feature registers and therefore they are not mentioned in the graph. Very similar time came from profile values reading because there is not a great difference in the data volume. All older devices had higher time demand at the beginning and also the end of connection. From all tested meters E700 electro meters had the greatest problem with establishing and terminating the connection. On the other hand, LZQJ, SL7000 and ZxD had the least difficulty with establishing and terminating the connection. All three electro meters fall in the group of newer devices than E700.

3.2 Operation Evaluation According to Data Readings

In Fig. 4 average data readings of every day remote collection are depicted. Successful electro meter reading includes transferring of all necessary telegram values such as profile data and electro meter register including time unit control with data central. In partial readings data transition was not successful in one or two items. For example, register values were read and time control was successful. However, profile reading failed etc. Errors are best analysed on the basis of interrupted telegrams during the communication. In a case of telegram interruption data central initiated new transfer after 30 s. Five tries in total were set and if used up the transfer was evaluated as failed. The highest percentage of successful data reading had FAG and FBC coders because this device does not feature registers therefore lowering the possibility of problems with data reading. Despite a high percentage of successful data collecting in several cases the readings were successful after new transfer. DC3 and E700 types showed higher number of interrupted telegrams during the testing. During data registers reading interruption of connection with data central came about and with that time delays connected with repeated transfers. ZxD, SL7000 and LZQJ electro meters have similar values despite using different communication protocols. Communication results showed that GPRS technology is problematic. Data readings in GPRS mode have worse readings than GSM or PSTN. Main reason for this was bad signal. Problems did not happen during the whole testing period, they came in irregular and unexpected intervals. However, when the connection in GPRS mode was established it was stable during the whole data reading. Between 1.9.2017 and 31.12.2017 there were only few occasions when the GPRS data collection was not possible. When the communication technology was unavailable the readings were done manually in data central through GSM Backup Line tool. Because of this possibility LZQJ, ZxD and SL7000 electro meters have average data reading over 80%. During this testing the cascade (multi-master operation) connected group of meters was added. Readings of ZxD meters group was influenced minimally by this.

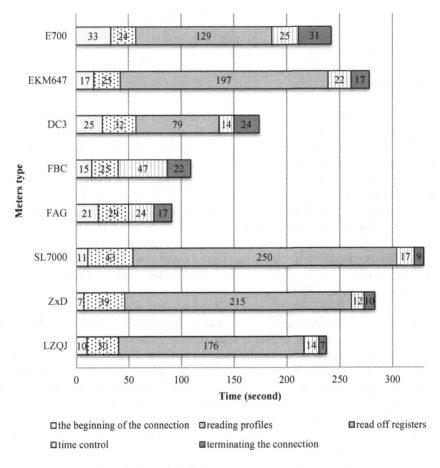

Fig. 3. Times readings for various types of gauges

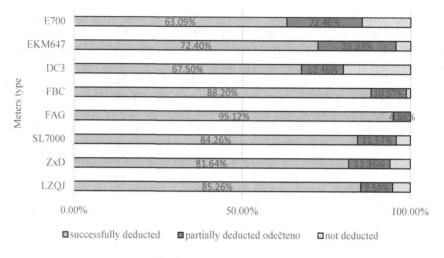

Fig. 4. Total reading of data

4 Conclusion

The aim of this study was to analyse available and used technical devices for remote readings of AMR system electro meters. The behaviour of selected technological devices in AMR operation was tested and analysed in real operation in period between 1.9.2016 and 31.12.2016 focused on reliability, reading effectivity and communication with used protocol and volume of transferred data. Selection of theoretical criteria based on intern data of ČEZ Distribuce, a.s. company was done at the beginning of testing. That was followed by a practical test between meters selected in theoretical part and data (reading) central Converge by Landis&Gyr company. Some meter types do not meet selected criteria and in electro-energetic networks, therefore they should not serve as devices for collecting invoice values. In the future they can be used for example as secondary meters controlling collected data from electro meters installed by distribution companies. This applies to FAG, FBC and EKM types of coders that still can carry out some of the tasks but the only reason they are still used at reading sites or transmitting sites is reluctance of entrepreneurs to change the contract between the customer and the distributor of electric energy. In the current technical solution these coders collect data from electro meters that meet all requirements of the present-day invoice meter. Unlike said coders electro meters DC3 and E700 meet some of the requirements but they are morally old and their next use cannot be recommended due to their unbalanced performance and relatively high error rate. Devices mentioned also do not meet requirements for Smart Metering that will probably replace current remote data collection in the future. Only devices that meet basic standards if the full Smart Meeting system is established are LZQJ, SL7000 and ZxD electro meters.

In the general evaluation it can be said that all electro meters showed very similar results in practical testing. Individual differences were based for example on used communication protocols or technical support. Communication protocol DLMS had advantage during the testing due to missing drivers in Converge central that was by the same producer/supplier as type ZxD electro meters, despite DLMS being thought standard in the world, while his concurrent VDEW is overshadowed and can be found only in older devices or electro meters from Landis&Gyr company that support them. Older meters (except FAG) had higher error rate during the testing mostly in responses and errors in exceeding maximal waiting time for telegram. They also connected and disconnected. The worst was E700 electro meter that had the worst results in all tests. On the other hand FAG coder reached the best results despite belonging in older meters category. FBC devise can be found in load profiles without registers which is in accordance with current legislative that uses load profile for invoice values. It seems like a paradox that only register values undergo demanding testing in metrological testing room. From the register values progress of the electric use reading cannot control unlike in the profile with 15-min intervals. The important aspect is whether during the testing the results were not influenced. An open question for the future is the use of GPRS communication technologies that lacks some qualities and advantages of remote data collecting. During the analysis of real operation problems with availability of this service were recorded and additional reading with GSM technology was necessary. Therefore the demand from the electro meters producer for LTE technology support seems logical. Another possible testing variety is using PLC (also BPL) technologies in distribution companies because they are accounted for in Smart Grid area and Smart Metering area. The main reason for their use is a full control of energy companies such as ČEZ Distribuce over most of the network and minimal expenses when the new network will not have to be built. One of the possible ways to replace the current AMR technology is to unite it with AMM (Advanced Metering Management) or with AMI (Advanced Metering Infrastructure). However, for this realization it is necessary to obtain the long-term analysis of usability of diverse technical devices for remote readings of electro meters because their mass replacement in the short-term is technically and financially impossible. Therefore, the aforementioned implementation of currently used remote electro meter reading technical devices into AMM or AMI systems analysis was carried out. This work and the contribution were supported by project of specific science "Computer networks for cloud, distributed systems, and Internet of Things", Faculty of Informatics and Management, University of Hradec Kralove, Czech Republic. We would like also thank to students Lubos Mercl and Pavel Blazek.

References

1. Tan, H.G.R., Lee, C.H., Mok, V.H.: Automatic power meter reading system using GSM network. In: International Power Engineering Conference (IPEC 2007), Singapore, pp. 465–469 (2007). ISSN 1947-1262
2. Khalifa, T., Naik, K., Nayak, A.: A survey of communication protocols for automatic meter reading applications. IEEE Commun. Surv. Tutor. 13(2), 168–182 (2011). https://doi.org/10.1109/surv.2011.041110.00058. Accessed 16 Mar 2018. ISSN 1553-877X
3. Geetha, A., Jamuna, K.: Smart metering system. In: International Conference on Information Communication and Embedded Systems (ICICES), pp. 1047–1051. IEEE (2013). https://doi.org/10.1109/icices.2013.6508368. Accessed 16 Mar 2018. ISBN 978-1-4673-5788-3

Smart Tourism Platform Based on Microservice Architecture and Recommender Services

Laura Martínez Garcia[1](✉) (iD), Silvana Aciar[2](✉) (iD),
Raynel Mendoza[1](✉) (iD), and Juan José Puello[1](✉) (iD)

[1] Fundación Universitaria Tecnológico Comfenalco, Cartagena, Colombia
{lmartinezg,rmendoza,jjpuellob}@tecnologicocomfenalco.edu.co
[2] Universidad Nacional de San Juan, San Juan, Argentina
Silvana.aciar@gmail.com

Abstract. Smart tourism platforms have made it easier for travelers to plan and manage their trips as a decision support. This paper is focuses on three applications in tourist intelligent (tourism marketplace, trip planning and heritage education), integrated in a microservice architecture as a suite of small services. Each microservice exposes a small set of functionalities and runs in its own process, communicating with other external services.

Keywords: Smart tourism · Recommender system · Microservices
Route planning · Heritage education · Marketplace

1 Introduction

The evolution of the technology associated with innovation process is an important step in the development of tourism in any city. For example, the use of smart tourism technologies such as travel websites, social media, and smartphones has been pervasive and growing.

Smart tourism can be seen as a logical progression from traditional tourism [1]. Authors in [2] define the smart tourism as an innovative tourist destination, built on an infrastructure of state-of-the-art technology guaranteeing the sustainable development, accessible to everyone, which facilitates the visitor's interaction, increases the quality of the experience at the destination, and improves residents' quality of life.

One of the technological approach focused on smart tourism are recommender systems. Recommender systems are software tools and techniques that provide relevant suggestions to a user, helping with the problem of information overload. They filter information, products, services, people from a set of thousands of options based on the interests, tastes and needs of users [3–5]. In travel recommender systems, there are many applications of recommendation system, most of them, learns the user preferences to recommend places of attractions according to the user interests.

This paper described a suite of small application in tourism using recommendation approach and supported in a microservice pattern, which consist of a set of independent deployable services. This architecture is extensible and can be adjustable in a future.

© Springer International Publishing AG, part of Springer Nature 2018
M. Younas et al. (Eds.): MobiWIS 2018, LNCS 10995, pp. 167–180, 2018.
https://doi.org/10.1007/978-3-319-97163-6_14

Each Microservices support the next functionalities: (1) suggest routes and point of interest to users with respect to the choice of tourism activities; (2) strengthen and position not only the cultural resources and natural scenes of the city, but also strengthen the suppliers in tourism through a Tourist Market; (3) preserve in time the historical memory of the tourist attractions and the same time show the tourists in an interactive way the evolution of cultural heritage; and (4) enabling tourist to share their travel experiences to help other travelers in their decision making process.

The paper is organized as follows: Sect. 2 shows the state of the art; in Sect. 3 presents the results of the proposal, finally, some conclusions and future research directions are outlined.

2   Related Work

Tourism is one of the domains where the use of recommender systems has been exploited, there are many applications that filter destination, hotels, attractions, packages and presentation of personalized guides using the recommender systems [9–11]. The application of traditional recommendation methods such as content-based and collaborative filtering becomes more complicated in this domain. The complexity is caused by the diversity of preferences, diversity of tourist services and especially the number and variety of profiles to recommend in a group of people. Prediction techniques that used a ratings matrix as input are not easily applied in the tourism domain [5, 11]. The context at the time of requesting a recommendation greatly influences the decisions to be taken by tourists. For example, planning a vacation involves a combination of several interconnected services such as hotels, transportation, restaurants, tourist and heritage attractions and other activities. Besides the company of other people, the profiles and tastes of those people, the climate, and the money available are other factors that influence the decisions of the people when planning a trip [11–16]. In the tourism domain, the recommender systems are applied for the recommendation of points of interest [13–17, 19, 20], tour packages [12, 14], accommodation [8, 10, 11] among others. To predict tourism recommendations, researchers faced different challenges to obtain and analyze user preferences and predict recommendations.

Regarding the acquisition of user preferences, the user of a tourist service has certain distinctive characteristics of the customers of an online book store or an online music store. There is a great variety of variables such as the number of companions, age of the companions, preferences of climate and seasons, availability of economic resources, etc. These variables are restrictions to take into account when predicting recommendations. For the acquisition of this information, the user directly enters their tastes, preferences and needs explicitly, either through the login to the system or through the boxes where it enters their needs and preferences [9, 10, 12, 13, 17–19]. This way of acquiring information is intrusive to the user. Many times, users do not want to enter certain information in the systems. Other systems acquire information from users in a less intrusive way, for example, by monitoring user behavior, analyzing the history of purchases and reservations, analyzing opinions written in text format, or through a conversational system. Text mining techniques, Bayesian networks, decision trees, association rules, are used for the analysis and classification of such information [16–22]. As mentioned above, the simple representation of a user ratings matrix is not easily applicable to this domain. Artificial intelligence models such as ontologies, rule-based systems, Bayesian networks and fuzzy logic are used to represent preferences [9, 13, 15, 23, 27–30]. However, the analysis of tourists' preferences is not enough to predict good recommendations, it is necessary to analyze contextual information that influences the acceptance of recommendations. Information such as weather, social relationships and mood is necessary to take into account for the prediction of recommendations. Different methods, techniques and tools are used to obtain this information, such as the analysis of social networks or geo-location [10, 16, 21, 22, 31].

Regarding the methods used to predict the recommendations, metrics used in traditional methods are not easily applicable in the tourism domain. Hybrid recommendation methods, incorporating content-based filtering, collaborative filtering and demographic filtering are used to make the recommendations. Artificial Intelligence techniques are used in such methods such as: Clustering, decision-making algorithms based on constraints, Vector Support Machine techniques and Multiagent Systems are applied in the different methods. Clustering techniques are used to group users in collaborative filtering, where similarity metrics such as cosine cannot be applied. Users are grouped based on demographical information or similar preferences [4, 28, 32–34]. Techniques of optimization and processing based on constraints are used to deal with the problem of constraints imposed by users and context information. Genetic algorithms, neural networks, meta-heuristics, are applied to manage these constraints [19, 22, 24, 29, 33, 35, 36]. Multi-Agent systems are used to deal with the diversity of interconnected services to make recommendation of tourist packages; each agent represents a tourist service component of the package. [37–40]. Support Techniques Vector Machines (SVMs) is used when tourist items and user profiles are modeled as vectors [28, 31, 41–43].

3 Microservices Architecture

Microservices architecture [6] is a pattern that divides the solution into a component parts and treat them as separate development efforts; which increase the speed of development and go down the cost of making changes [7]. This pattern is used to architect large, complex and long-lived applications [8] and is appropriate when it is necessary to ensure compatibility with a different platforms and type of devices.

The development of a project under this method is an application through the conjunction of independent services that are deployed as needed. Therefore, it becomes a modular application based on "small pieces", expanding or reducing as required. It's important that every instance of each microservice would have complete autonomy over the environment [7]. Many websites have decided to invest in the evolution towards microservices in a future, where the maintenance and scalability of the products is much simpler, more effective and faster. Some of these companies are Netflix, Amazon, Ebay, etc.

The Smart Tourism Platform proposed uses a modular architecture that provides a set of applications or microservices, in which each one runs a unique process through an orchestrator or gateway. In this architecture, each microservice can be independently deployed, upgraded, and replaced, with a complete autonomy over the integrated environment. The applications have dependency by the process but not from applications. It allows modify, update and change easily a component (microservice) for other.

The tourism platform is composed with multiple small microservices that use RESTful to communicate with other similar services. The platform is composed by different distributed subsystems that are connected to each other in order to provide recommendations in trip planning, tour packages and heritage learning. This means, although each application has its own domain, all have in common to invoke the services in: recommendation, providers, points of interest and authentication to offer smart tourism services. Each service has their own database, data and structure.

The architecture is composed by front-end services and back-end services. Front-end services are designed to provide a single and secure interface trough the API Gateway, responsible to the requests from authorized apps, executing REST calls. Backend services: are the services that provided endpoints for CRUD operations and the authentication services made by SSO (Single sign-on) that permits a user to use one set of login credentials to access in all applications with the same username and password.

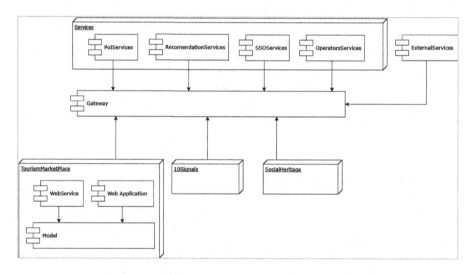

Fig. 1. Microservices architecture for smart tourism platform

A detailed description of the components displayed in Fig. 1 is given below in Table 1:

Table 1. Components description

Component	Type	Functionality
PoI	Services	Internal services providing point of interest to recommend in trip planning route, learning heritage routes and tours package
Recommendation	Services	It's a recommender algorithm based on KNN. The algorithm compares a JSON Object of user profile with similar tastes using Euclidean distances, returning top K closest objects according to his/her preferences. (managing user preferences)
SSO	Services	Services secures access to all the apps. A user logs in with a single ID and password
Operators	Services	Services that permits obtains data about tourism operator
Gateway	Runtime	It's a proxy to receive all the request to the correct service and transmit the response back to client
ExternalServices	External services/ Data Provider	External service providing connection to third parties applications
Tourist Marketplace	Application	Mobile application that represents the user interface to get the access in the tourism marketplace
10 signals	Application	Mobile application that represents the user interface to obtain a planning route for travelers
Social Heritage	Application	Mobile application in learning heritage

4   Smart Tourism Platform

Smart tourism represents a new direction implying a significant influence on tourist destinations, enterprises, and also tourists themselves. Our applications incorporate at first instance the city of Cartagena de Indias, Colombia, one of the cities most visited by tourists in the world. The functionalities of each applications or microservices are defined below:

4.1   10 Signals: Trip Planning

Tourists generally have an agenda in mind of different places to visit in a city to attend. The main tasks of this application are: Pre-Trip planning, generation of activities in the destination city, generate customized automatic routes and be guided to Point of Interest in the map [44] (Figs. 2, 3, 4 and Table 2).

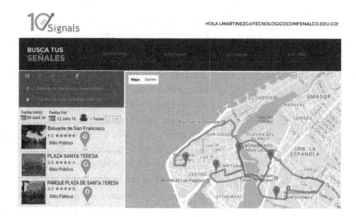

Fig. 2. 10Signals app

The first screen of the application is a form in which users are asked to provide the socio-demographic data necessary for determining their stereotype. After filling out the form (username, password, age and gender), the application computes the most relevant stereotypes based on information previously provided by the user. The algorithm iterates through all stereotypes available and adds up the likelihood for each property. In order to recommend city tours routes even in the cold start phase, a user modeling approach based on stereotypes is appropriate. So, when a new user is registered into the system, a new empty row is added to the rating matrix and the system is unable to generate any rating predictions for this user. In our case, user needs to select some images (related with type of tourism and point of interest) to refine their user profiles and get better recommendations [45].

Consequently, the best rated is performed, ordering the recommended POIs list by user preference in descending order in a map using Google Maps API. Finally, the output is a sequence of attractions or spots to be visited, through a map, filtered to the tourist's according to the user preferences.

Fig. 3. Route trip planning

4.2 Social Heritage Application

In heritage education process, the learner is referred as a Citizens/Visitor who is interested in learning about his/her heritage. The citizen is known as a person who was born or inhabits a specific place. Visitors are referred to people who are temporarily in a particular place. The main purposes of Recommendation System of Heritage Routes are proposing a route of heritage that Citizens/Visitor can visits according their preferences and motivations [46].

The Individual behavior is stored in terms of interests, consulted heritage, selected routes, viewed and aggregated content, etc. This system initially implements a recommendation scheme based on contents, comparing available information about the heritage content. When the Behavior Database counts with a considerable amount of data, recommendations will be implemented based on collaborative filtering. Delivery System (Delivery in LTSA) is in charge to present the content to learners in different formats: audio, video, text, animations, etc. These contents should be accessible from different types of mobile devices such as phones, eyeglasses and tablets, as well as desktop.

On the other hand, the heritage content is stored as Heritage Learning Resources establishing a large repository of resources to support heritage education which increase while the Citizens/Visitor creates new content. Heritage Learning Resources feed the augmented reality perspective of the heritage, and that permits contextualize heritage education in real scenarios.

Fig. 4. Social heritage app

4.3 Tourism Marketplace

A Marketplace is a business model where one or several sectors (clusters) converge on a single platform in order to promote and sell products and/ or services. SRT is a Marketplace in tourism to acquire and offer different types of services and products from different suppliers. This platform has the purpose to:

(a) Offer products and services in tourism integrating all companies in the sector in a single portal. For each of the companies will have a content management system, friendly and intuitive, which gives autonomy and agility when updating the virtual store; (b) Personalization in the acquisition of tourist services and products to users in order to guide him/her in the satisfaction of his/her purchase process; (c) Offer a comprehensive range of tourism services through a multi-channel platform with the possibility of online shopping, optimized for search engine positioning and connected to social networks; and (d) Integrating of third-party services to create a communication channel with other applications of the tourism sector and social networks (TripAdvisor, Booking, Trivago). Actually, this app is under construction.

5   Evaluation

5.1   Usability Evaluation

The first evaluation corresponds to the planning app: 10 signals, where the information was collected through the following questionnaire:

Q1 was it easy to use the application?
Q2 is the navigation provided by the application easy to use?
Q3 Am I satisfied with the point (s) of suggested interest (s)?
P4 Am I satisfied with the planning (s) route (s) suggested (s)?

The survey was answered using a 5-point scale according to the following criteria: totally disagree, disagree, neutral, mostly agree and totally agree. The results in general were positive, considering it useful and interesting. However, question 4 does not follow the same distribution as the other questions, because it implies a negative assumption regarding the planning of the suggested route. However, almost all users agreed with the recommended stereotype and suggested points of interest.

The second evaluation was for the social heritage app. The application was developed for two categories of users in the context of heritage education. The first category is for citizens/tourists, who would use the platform in order to carry out informal heritage education and also the collaborative management of contents. The second category refers to heritage managers, as expert users who support various activities in the framework for the validation of the contents and heritage interest points, Citizens/Tourists can access all the augmented information for each point of interest geo-located. Once the user starts his/her route, he/she has different options to interact, such as personalized search through organized lists, content loading and content qualification and data visualization points with augmented reality.

For the evaluation, a mixed approach was considered: quantitative and qualitative. The first one, have the intention of identifying the level of acceptance and the second one with the intention of observing the interests and behavior of users when they use the application.

Two instruments were used, one for quantitative analysis and the other for qualitative analysis. Regarding the quantitative study, a survey was applied to the users. The survey consisted of 4 questions that could be answered using a scale of 5 possible values: "Strongly agree", "Partially agree", "Indifferent", "Partially disagree" and "Strongly disagree". The questions were oriented to identify if the users considered that the application helped them to learn about the heritage and also about the usability of the system.

Regarding the results of the survey, we can conclude that the majority of users consider that the process of learning about heritage in Cartagena was assertive.

Regarding the interest and behavior when using the application, most, were very interested and showed the desire to continue working with the application in its comprehension and use. 76% of surveyed indicated they "strongly agree" regarding the idea of prototype support in the process of learning about heritage in Cartagena, meanwhile, 24% of surveyed reported being "somewhat agree". 88% of the surveyed were "totally in agreement" that the developed prototype would help others in the heritage education process. Regarding usability, 81% of people indicated that they considered the application easy to use, while 19% partially agreed.

On the contrary, the instrument for the qualitative analysis was used by people in the area of psychology who observed the behavior of users while interacting with the application. The instrument provides the observer a set of categories of analysis, and for each one of them, the observer was drawing conclusions according to the behavior and interaction of Citizen/tourist. With the instrument it was possible to confirm that most of the users showed a high level of interest, which was demonstrated in the positive attitude they had when they used the application and the attention they showed while it interacts with them. It is also important to highlight the recommendations done about the application. For example, including more heritage interest points in the city of Cartagena, or users can define their own personalized content.

5.2 Contributions with Respect to Other Solutions

In order to clearly demonstrate the contribution with respect to other proposals in literature by comparing the presented in this article, a comparative table is shown, between 10 Signals and two of the most important applications in tourism in the world at present: Minube (https://www.minube.com/) and Google Trips (https://get.google.com/trips/). Google Trips is an application to create itineraries, which includes information such as scheduled daily plans and hotel reservations. One of the novelties of this application is to obtain personalized suggestions based on the location and the climate where the person is. For its part, Minube is an application that presents user suggestions on sites of interest from 180 countries and more than 15,000 cities, where travelers share extensive and complete travel guides to assemble personalized itineraries, choosing the places they want to visit.

If the previous table is analyzed, it is appreciated that 10Signals is at a good level, taking into account the applications with which it was compared. Therefore, the most important contribution is the recommendation service of heritage routes. This method of recommendation is based on the interests of users to present a learning path that allows people to develop the Heritage Education process based on a recommendation. The foregoing is evidenced in the system evaluation where the use of the application facilitates the assimilation, accommodation and understanding of knowledge in relation to the tangible and intangible assets that are presented. Therefore, it is important to define alternative methods that allow motivating the people of a specific city towards the patrimonial education.

Table 2. Comparative with other proposals

Criterio	10Signals	Google Trips	Minube
Offers travel recommendations	X	X	X
Personalization of daily plans	X	X	
Offers processes of recommendation of routes in patrimonial education.	X		
Apply different approaches in the recommendation process	X	X	
Offers precision in the recommendation offered to the tourist	X	X	X
Integration of third-party services		X	X
Usability and responsive design	X	X	X
Multiplatform application		X	X

** The (X) represents that the application has the functionality.

6   Discussion

We analyze the reasons behind our architectural choices. Until recently, most of the developments have been made using standard methods. Microservices are opposed to the traditional philosophy of application architecture. Recently the usual was to have an application with a large core, large applications, with heavy and expensive developments, where there are no facilities to adapt to the changing needs of current projects. Different to monolithic applications this architecture builds small applications capable of developing concrete tasks, and collaborates with each other to realize a common purpose. This point was crucial for adopt microservices architecture: 3 applications in tourism with different goal, but need work together and invoke common web services to offer personalized services in tourism for travelers.

A positive point when selecting microservices is that mobile applications depend on services and these services must be deployed in isolation. Without this approach, the work of systems will become more complicated every day. In microservices you have the freedom to choose the technology to be used in each of the small services that form an application; you simply choose the one that best suits the needs you have to solve. So, in a microservice platform, each service can fail and heal independently with a possibly reduced impact on the overall platform's functionalities [8].

MicroServices have many issues to clarify, transactionality, modularity, transversal services, etc. However, they have become an excellent solution they are a useful and agile alternative for the development of an application.

7 Conclusion

In conclusion, two principal challenges in tourism recommender systems were found which was given a solution through the tourist services offered by the smart tourism platform presented in this article: *Optimal itinerary planning for tourists* and *improve the recommendation accuracy for new items and new users to provide recommendations when rating data is sparse or entirely missing*.

Today's tourists demand more information focused to his/her preferences. This paper presents a platform for tourism services based on Microservices patterns. The application has many features in order to facilitate the tourists their trips.

Preliminary tests carried out on the platform are encouraging, but there is still much work to do in many aspects. In particular, our future steps will include the deployment in a real scenario in order to validate the applications of the platform under different conditions.

References

1. Gretzel, U., Sigala, M., Xiang, Z., et al.: Smart tourism: foundations and developments. Electron Mark. **25**, 179 (2015). https://doi.org/10.1007/s12525-015-0196-8
2. Lopez de Avila, A.: Smart Destinations: XXI Century Tourism. Presented at the ENTER2015 Conference on Information and Communication Technologies in Tourism, Lugano, Switzerland, 4–6 February 2015
3. Bobadilla, J., Ortega, F., Hernando, A., Gutiérrez, A.: Recommender systems survey. Knowl. Based Syst. **46**, 109–132 (2013). ISSN 0950-7051
4. Ricci, F., Rokach, L., Shapira, B., Kantor, P.B.: Recommender Systems Handbook, 1st edn. Springer, Boston (2010). https://doi.org/10.1007/978-0-387-85820-3
5. Beel, J., Langer, S., Genzmehr, M., Gipp, B., Breitinger, C., Nürnberger, A.: Research paper recommender system evaluation: a quantitative literature survey. In: Proceedings of the International Workshop on Reproducibility and Replication in Recommender Systems Evaluation (RepSys 2013), pp. 15–22. ACM, New York (2013)
6. Baresi, L., Garriga, M., De Renzis, A.: Microservices identification through interface analysis. In: De Paoli, F., Schulte, S., Broch Johnsen, E. (eds.) ESOCC 2017. LNCS, vol. 10465, pp. 19–33. Springer, Cham (2017). https://doi.org/10.1007/978-3-319-67262-5_2
7. Cherradi, G., El Bouziri, A., Boulmakoul, A., Zeitouni, K.: Real-time HazMat environmental information system: a micro-service based architecture. Procedia Comput. Sci. **109**, 982–987 (2017)
8. Ciavotta, M., Alge, M., Menato, S., Rovere, D., Pedrazzoli, P.: A microservice-based middleware for the digital factory. Procedia Manuf. **11**, 931–938 (2017)
9. Borràs, J., Moreno, A., Valls, A.: Intelligent tourism recommender systems: a survey. Expert Syst. Appl. **41**(16), 7370–7389 (2014). ISSN 0957-4174
10. Gavalas, D., Konstantopoulos, C., Mastakas, K., Pantziou, G.: Mobile recommender systems in tourism. J. Netw. Comput. Appl. **39**, 319–333 (2014)
11. Braunhofer, M., Ricci, F.: Selective contextual information acquisition in travel recommender systems. Inf. Technol. Tour. **17**, 5 (2017)

12. Santos, F., Almeida, A., Martins, C., Oliveira, P., Gonçalves, R.: Tourism recommendation system based in user's profile and functionality levels. In: Desai, E. (ed.) Proceedings of the Ninth International C* Conference on Computer Science & Software Engineering (C3S2E 2016), pp. 93–97. ACM, New York (2016)

13. Lorenzi, F., Loh, S., Abel, M.: PersonalTour: a recommender system for travel packages. In: Proceedings of the 2011 IEEE/WIC/ACM International Conferences on Web Intelligence and Intelligent Agent Technology - Volume 02 (WI-IAT 2011), vol. 2, pp. 333–336. IEEE Computer Society, Washington, DC (2011)

14. Wang, Y., Chan, S.C.-F., Ngai, G.: Applicability of demographic recommender system to tourist attractions: a case study on trip advisor. In: Proceedings of the the 2012 IEEE/WIC/ACM International Joint Conferences on Web Intelligence and Intelligent Agent Technology - Volume 03 (WI-IAT 2012), vol. 3, pp. 97–101. IEEE Computer Society, Washington, DC (2012)

15. Nunes, H., Almeida, A., Martins, C.: Gathering data for professional tourism points of interest. In: Desai, E. (ed.) Proceedings of the Ninth International C* Conference on Computer Science & Software Engineering (C3S2E 2016), pp. 125–126. ACM, New York (2016)

16. Silamai, N., Khamchuen, N., Phithakkitnukoon, S.: TripRec: trip plan recommendation system that enhances hotel services. In: Proceedings of the 2017 ACM International Joint Conference on Pervasive and Ubiquitous Computing and Proceedings of the 2017 ACM International Symposium on Wearable Computers (UbiComp 2017), pp. 412–420. ACM, New York (2017)

17. Braunhofer, M., Ricci, F., Lamche, B., Wörndl, W.: A context-aware model for proactive recommender systems in the tourism domain. In: Proceedings of the 17th International Conference on Human-Computer Interaction with Mobile Devices and Services Adjunct (MobileHCI 2015), pp. 1070–1075. ACM, New York (2015)

18. Savir, A., Brafman, R., Shani, G.: Recommending improved configurations for complex objects with an application in travel planning. In: Proceedings of the Seventh ACM Conference on Recommender Systems, pp. 391–394. ACM (2013)

19. Umanets, A., Ferreira, A., Leite, N.: GUIDEME – a tourist guide with a recommender system and social interaction. In: Conference on Electronics, Telecommunications and Computer (CETC), Lisboa, December 2013

20. Kurata, Y., Hara, T.: CT-Planner4: toward a more user-friendly interactive day-tour planner. In: Xiang, Z., Tussyadiah, I. (eds.) Information and Communication Technologies in Tourism 2014, pp. 73–86. Springer, Cham (2013). https://doi.org/10.1007/978-3-319-03973-2_6

21. Garcia, A., Vansteenwegen, P., Arbelaitz, O., Souffriau, W., Linaza, M.T.: Integrating public transportation in personalised electronic tourist guides. Comput. Oper. Res. Spec. Issue Transp. Sched. 3, 758–774 (2013)

22. Braunhofer, M., Elahi, M., Ricci, F., Schievenin, T.: Context-aware points of interest suggestion with dynamic weather data management. In: Xiang, Z., Tussyadiah, I. (eds.) Information and Communication Technologies in Tourism 2014, pp. 87–100. Springer, Cham (2013). https://doi.org/10.1007/978-3-319-03973-2_7

23. Meehan, K., Lunney, T., Curran, K., McCaughey, A.: Context-aware intelligent recommendation system for tourism. In: Proceedings of the 11th IEEE International Conference on Pervasive Computing and Communications, pp. 328–331 (2013)

24. Oh, K.-J., Kim, Z., Oh, H., Lim, C.-G., Gweon, G.: Travel intention-based attraction network for recommending travel destinations. In: International Conference on Big Data and Smart Computing (BigComp), Hong Kong, pp. 277–280 (2016)

25. Yu, Z., Xu, H., Yang, Z., Guo, B.: Personalized travel package with multi-point-of-interest recommendation based on crowdsourced user footprints. IEEE Trans. Hum. Mach. Syst. **46**(1), 151–158 (2016)

26. Nguyen, T.N., Ricci, F.: A chat-based group recommender system for tourism. In: Schegg, R., Stangl, B. (eds.) Information and Communication Technologies in Tourism 2017, pp. 17–30. Springer, Cham (2017). https://doi.org/10.1007/978-3-319-51168-9_2

27. Chu, W.T., Tsai, Y.L.: A hybrid recommendation system considering visual information for predicting favorite restaurants. World Wide Web **20**, 1313 (2017)

28. Ravi, L., Vairavasundaram, S.: A collaborative location based travel recommendation system through enhanced rating prediction for the group of users. Intell. Neurosci. **2016**, 7 (2016)

29. Valliyammai, C., PrasannaVenkatesh, R., Vennila, C., Krishnan, S.G.: An intelligent personalized recommendation for travel group planning based on reviews. In: 2016 Eighth International Conference on Advanced Computing (ICoAC), Chennai, pp. 67–71 (2017)

30. Afzaal, M., Usman, M., Fong, A.C.M., Fong, S., Zhuang, Y.: Fuzzy aspect based opinion classification system for mining tourist reviews. Adv. Fuzzy Syst. **2016**, 14 (2016)

31. Herzog, D.: Recommending a sequence of points of interest to a group of users in a mobile context. In: Proceedings of the Eleventh ACM Conference on Recommender Systems (RecSys 2017), pp. 402–406. ACM, New York (2017)

32. Delic, A., et al.: Observing group decision making processes. In: Proceedings of the 10th ACM Conference on Recommender Systems (RecSys 2016), pp. 147–150. ACM, New York (2016)

33. Moreno, A., Valls, A., Isern, D., Marin, L., Borràs, J.: SigTur/E-destination: ontology-based personalized recommendation of tourism and leisure activities. Eng. Appl. Artif. Intell. **26**, 633–651 (2013)

34. Nilashi, M., Bagherifard, K., Rahmani, M., Rafe, V.: A recommender system for tourism industry using cluster ensemble and prediction machine learning techniques. Comput. Ind. Eng. **109**, 357–368 (2017)

35. Lucas, J., Luz, N., Moreno, M., Anacleto, R., Figueiredo, A., Martins, C.: A hybrid recommendation approach for a tourism system. Expert Syst. Appl. **40**(9), 3532–3550 (2013)

36. Farokhi, A., Nima, A., Vahid, M., Nilashi, M., Ibrahim, O.: A multi-criteria recommender system for tourism using fuzzy approach. J. Soft Comput. Decis. Support Syst. **3**(4), 19–29 (2016)

37. Othmane, A.B., Tettamanzi, A., Villata, S., Le Thanh, N.: Towards a spatio-temporal agent-based recommender system. In: Proceedings of the 16th Conference on Autonomous Agents and MultiAgent Systems (AAMAS 2017), International Foundation for Autonomous Agents and Multiagent Systems, Richland, SC, pp. 1664–1666 (2017)

38. Batet, M., Moreno, A., Sánchez, D., Isern, D., Valls, A.: Turist@: agent-based personalised recommendation of tourist activities. Expert Syst. Appl. Int. J. **39**(8), 7319–7329 (2012)

39. Chen, C.-C., Tsai, J.L.: Determinants of behavioral intention to use the personalized location-based mobile tourism application: an empirical study by integrating TAM with ISSM. Future Gener. Comput. Syst. (2017)

40. Jia, Z.Y., Gao, W., Shi, Y.J.: An agent framework of tourism recommender system. In: MATEC Web of Conferences; Les Ulis, vol. 44. EDP Sciences, Les Ulis (2016)

41. Fang, G.-S., Kamei, S., Satoshi, F.: A Japanese tourism recommender system with automatic generation of seasonal feature vectors. Int. J. Adv. Comput. Sci. Appl. **8**, 347–354 (2017)

42. Bahramian, Z., Abbaspour, R.A., Claramunt, C.: A context-aware tourism recommender system based on a spreading activation method. Int. Arch. Photogramm. Remote Sens. Spat. Inf. Sci. 333–339 (2017)

43. Bahramian, Z., Abbaspour, R.A., Claramunt, C.: A context-aware tourism recommender system based on a spreading activation method. In: ISPRS - International Archives of the Photogrammetry, Remote Sensing and Spatial Information Sciences. XLII-4/W4, pp. 333–339 (2017)

44. Garcia, L.M., Serna, J.M., Codutti, V.: 10 SIGNALS: a personalized city tours prototype. In: 2017 IEEE Colombian Conference on Communications and Computing (COLCOM), Cartagena, pp. 1–6 (2017). https://doi.org/10.1109/colcomcon.2017.8088207

45. Garcia, L.M.: A user modeling approach to personalized sightseeing tours. In: Proceedings of the XVIII International Conference on Human Computer Interaction (Interacción 2017), Article 47, 8 p. ACM, New York (2017). DOI:https://doi.org/10.1145/3123818.3123875

46. Mendoza, R., Baldiris, S., Fabregat, R.: Framework to heritage education using emerging technologies. Procedia Comput. Sci. **75**, 239–249 (2015)

Autism Sohayika: A Web Portal to Provide Services to Autistic Children

Muhammad Nazrul Islam, Muimmah Kabir$^{(\boxtimes)}$, Jakia Sultana,
Chowdhury Nawrin Ferdous$^{(\boxtimes)}$, Afsana Zaman, Ummey Habiba Bristy,
Priyanka Kundu Moumi, and Iffat Tamanna

Department of Computer Science and Engineering,
Military Institute of Science and Technology, Dhaka, Bangladesh
nazrulturku@gmail.com, muimmahkabir@gmail.com,
jakiajyoti@gmail.com, bipashachowdhury03@gmail.com,
afsana2013nipa@gmail.com, ummeyhabibabristy30@gmail.com,
priyankamoumi13@gmail.com, iffat.tamanna@gmail.com
http://www.mist.ac.bd

Abstract. Autism is increasing at a significant rate in the whole world as well as in Bangladesh. It is unfortunate that, there is major lacking of awareness and support system for autism in Bangladesh. As a consequence of the advancement of technology, Internet is accessible to more people. Internet based support system for autism is the demand of the day for autistic children and their parents. The purpose of this research is to design and develop an online support system (Autism Sohayika<Autism Help>) for autistic children and their parents in context of Bangladesh. In this paper, the need of all possible stakeholders (e.g., donors, autistic kids, and parents) is demonstrated and reviewed the existing online applications to develop a conceptual framework and then materialize the framework by implanting the online portal, named-Autism Sohayika<Autism Help>. The portal was evaluated with 19 participants. The evaluation results show that the developed system is effective, efficient, useful and acceptable to all users.

Keywords: Autism · Web portal · Autism detection
Autism Spectrum Disorder · ICT

1 Introduction

Autism Spectrum Disorder (ASD) is a lifelong developmental disability that affects how people perceive the world and interact with others. Autistic people see, hear and feel the world differently to other people. If it is detected at an early stage of life, the condition of autistic people may get better with proper therapy and love and care from others [2]. ASD is reported to occur in all racial, ethnic, and socioeconomic groups [3]. Research has shown that a diagnosis of autism at age 2 can be reliable, valid, and stable.

© Springer International Publishing AG, part of Springer Nature 2018
M. Younas et al. (Eds.): MobiWIS 2018, LNCS 10995, pp. 181–192, 2018.
https://doi.org/10.1007/978-3-319-97163-6_15

In Bangladesh, one child in every 500 has autism [1]. In spite of this huge number, people are still unaware of the disability considering autism children as mental illness or just mischievous kid. There is a lack of knowledge about ASDs even among doctors. So, proper support system and awareness about autism is the demand of the day.

There are many schools, therapy centers are being built at different corner of our country. But therapy center and consultants charge a lot of money which may be affordable for upper and upper middle class. But middle or lower class may be unable to treat their children [4,5]. Most of the parents are unaware of the symptoms of autism and depth of the levels of autism. Moreover, questions may arise in parents mind regarding their children which they cannot share with anytime or ask anyone. Though sometimes, autism related workshop, seminars are arranged but parents may not be aware of them. Above all, as the costing for taking-care of autistic children is huge, so they often require donation. But people willing to donate cannot find proper platform to donate and the autistic children remain deprived of the donation.

Therefore, the objective of this paper is to design and develop a web portal 'Autism Sohayika' <Autism Help> for autistic kids as well as their parents to support in several ways. The rest of the paper is organized as follows. Background studies related to this work are stated in Sect. 2. In Sect. 3, need findings, conceptual framework and development of the portal are discussed briefly. Evaluating of the web portal is discussed in Sect. 4. Finally discussion and idea of future is presented in the final Sect. 5.

2   Literature Review

This section provides an overview of the ICT related work focusing to autistic children.

Berument et al. [6] proposed a system which can screen a people through different types of questions to detect autism. This system consists of 40 questions to screen the people which are based on ADI-R (Autism Diagnostic Interview). In [7], an online survey was carried out among people with autism and their family to understand the usages behavior of software and technologies related to autism. As outcome, they found that only 25% responders reported experience with software and technologies designed for people with cognitive disabilities. Many applications are developed for the specific needs of the autistic people. Most of these applications are for children. The list of some tools which are used for betterment of autistic children are summarized in Table 1.

In sum, throughout the world, many applications/web portals have been developed focusing on autistic children. Some of them are focused on detecting the level of autism by conducting some interview of the children and some are developed to provide information about how to take proper care of these special children. There are also some applications developed in this regard in context of Bangladesh. They mainly focus on providing information about resources such as special school, diet plan, etc. for the children. However, to the best of our knowledge, no research work has been conducted thoroughly to bring out

Table 1. List of ICT tools for Autistic child

Serial	Tools/Application	Purpose/Objective
1	Autism Parenting Magazine [8], Autism Parent Behavior Support [9]	Developed to help parents to understand how to behave with their autistic child
2	Autism Test [10]	This app is made for educational purposes in order to raise awareness of some common Autism signs
3	ABA Therapy Aphasia Autism [12]	Helps to improve communication, cognitive skills through our real life picture cue cards for oral language practice
4	Troc@s [13]	Allows tutors and peers to prepare a unique setup for a child's need.
6	Autism Speak [14]	It is a website where autism related information and detecting autism through questionnaires are available
7	Autism Test (R-ISSA) [11]	Helps to test the level of autism which are based on ISSA (INDIAN SCALE FOR ASSESSMENT OF AUTISM)
8	Autism BD [15]	Provides forum where people can share their experiences about autism

the desires of the autistic children as well as their parents in context of our Bangladesh. This research work will focus on the autistic child and their parents to find out what kind of help they are in need for handling this situation in an enhanced way.

3 Design and Development of Web Portal

In this section, the design and development of the portal is represented. The three consecutive steps were followed to develop this portal: (a) Need findings, (b) Conceptual Framework, (c) Developing the Web portal.

3.1 Need Findings

A semi-structural interview was conducted to understand the parents and teacher of autistic children and some general peoples opinion towards autistic children. Interview was conducted in three parts. Firstly, basic information of the interviewees such as their name, age, gender, profession and relationship with an autistic kid were collected. Total 17 people of age limit 31.625 ± 10.703 were interviewed. Among them, 8 people were parents, 6 people were teachers of autistic kids and rest 3 people were general people. Secondly, they were asked if they are interested

Table 2. Summary requirements

Serial	Requirements	Frequency
1	Autism detection or screening	16
2	Discuss and share experiences among parents of the autistic kids	17
3	Event or workshop management tool for autism	11
4	Donation information and a reliable platform to donate for autistic	10
5	Information about school, hospitals, doctors and therapists	10
6	Availability of scholarly articles and books related to autistic kids	5
7	Provide online support (or availability) for 24/7	8
8	User friendly application	12
9	User interface of the portal should be in Bengali language	16

to use any kind of ICT tools to get or provide support to the autistic kids. If they replied in affirmative, the interview was continued asking them what kind of features they think will be necessary for autistic child in an ICT tool. Among interviewees were agreed to use ICT tools as a means of providing support to autistic children. The summary of their requirements are presented in Table 2.

A market analysis of ICT tools developed in context of Bangladesh is also carried out to understand that what are the featured they already providing for autistic kids, the results are summarized in Table 3.

Table 3. Market analysis

Serial	Features	Autism BD [Web Application]	Autism [Android Application]	AutismBarta [Android Application]
1	Detect autism	×	×	✓
2	Manage donation	×	×	×
3	Provide forum support for parents	✓	×	×
4	Create or Manage events	×	×	×
5	Provide institution information	✓	×	✓
6	Achieving related articles and books	×	×	×
7	Easy to use	✓	✓	✓
8	UI in Bengali language	✓	✓	✓

Through some of the tools have already been developed for autistic child but requirements received through need finding study are not presented integratedly in a single web platform on app and few requirements are completely missing. For example, Online Care, Donation, related research papers, books and Event management related to autism are not available in any application in Bangladesh. So, developing a web portal in Bengali language which will integrate all these features is a buzzing need according to stakeholders demand. Thus this work focus to develop such a platform as a named Autism Sohayika <Autism Help> to cover these features.

3.2 Conceptual Framework

The conceptual framework to develop a web portal is depicted in Fig. 1. Parents or guardians can use this portal for detection of autism of their children by answering several questions. They can also access the forum to ask questions and share experiences. The feature of giving donation for the special children is included here and creation of events like workshops, seminars,competitions etc. are also possible this portal.

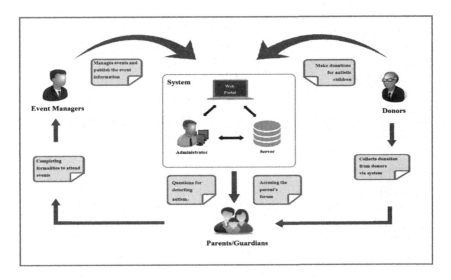

Fig. 1. Conceptual framework of Autism Sohayika

3.3 Developing the Portal

This section represents the portion how the portal is developed. The development phase is divided into three parts.

Fig. 2. Home page of Autism Sohayika

Database and Server End. At first, an E-R (Entity Relationship) diagram of the database according to the requirements of the system is designed and implemented the database in MYSQL server. Security constraints are maintained to prevent unauthorized access. Two separate databases (admin and user) are used in this system so that no one can easily hack or destroy the existing top level information of admin panel. Admin panel ensures the requirements of the system that coming from the user database and keep the whole system updated.

User Interface. In the system, secured access point is provided to personalize the information of the users where content of the web portal is unique based on the user criteria. It has device and browser compatibility at the same time it is designed in a user friendly way so that it is easy to accessible for authenticated user. Th notification system is implemented to notify the users through mail integration using PHP mailer (SMTP server) so that they can remain up-to-date about the web portal. For technical development of the system we used HTML, CSS, JavaScript, JQuery, PHP etc. that make the system more interactive for the users.

Security Aspects. Users need to register first to get the facilities of the web portal and their registration will be completed after verifying all the required information. We have used HTTP Basic authentication (using password_hash() function of PHP) which confirms the encrypted strong password for user that is verified with the existing email address through encrypted message. The session based login will be valid until the user will logged out or system will automatically logged out after a specific time when the session will be ended. Thus implementing these types of security aspects, we have tried to make the web-portal trustworthy and secured for the users.

The main features of this portal are detection of autism of children, Provide parents forum, Creation of events related to autism, Manage donation for autistic children. A screen shot of the homepage of the 'Autism Sohayika' is showed in Fig. 2.

For better understanding of the system's workflow, we have depicted the activities of detecting autism process through an activity diagram shown in Fig. 3.

At first the homepage will appear to the users where the navigation bar, side bar and slide show contains the attractive and important features are also being shown in slide show at the top of our homepage. People can switch language at any time from sidebar widget. Afterwards, if the parents select "detection of autism" from the homepage, they will be directed to age detection page. Here, three age categories are present.

Parents have to select according to their childrens' age. After the above procedure, parents will be redirected to detection page. After clicking start button, parents will view questions. After completing answering the questions, parents will be viewed level of autism of their children as result of the questionnaires.

Figure 2 depicts that parents have answered most of the questions negatively with respect to autism. Here the result says that the children is autism free.

4   Evaluation

The assessment of Autism Sohayika <Autism Help> portal was carried out through an experiment to evaluate its effectiveness, efficiency and satisfaction. This section will briefly discuss the participants profile, the study procedure and the results of the evaluation.

4.1   Participant's Profile

To conduct the evaluation study, a total of 19 participants were recruited. Among them only two don't use computer or Internet. Rest of them are using internet

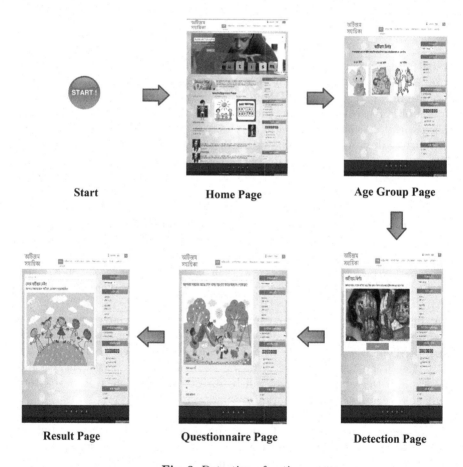

Start   **Home Page**   **Age Group Page**

Result Page   **Questionnaire Page**   **Detection Page**

Fig. 3. Detection of autism

Table 4. Usability test

Participants	Task	TCT (mins)	Wrong Navigation (frequency)	Asking Help (frequency)	Input Error (frequency)	System Error	Task Completion Status
Parents (n = 6)	Determine whether children are autistic or not	3 ± 2	0.4 ± 0.2	0.5 ± 0.15 (3 part. ask for 1 times, 1 part. ask for 2 times	0	0	Successfully completed (everyone needed single trial)
Parents and Teachers (n = 12)	Access parents forum to view and post and put comments	1 ± 1	2.2 ± 0.5	1.7 ± 0.4 (3 part. ask for 3 times, 2 part. ask for 2 times, other ask for 1 times)	1 (3 persons login info were wrong)	0	Successfully completed (5 part. needs 2 trials, others need single trial)
Donor (n = 3)	Fill up form for donation	1.5 ± 0.5	0.6 ± 0.1	1 ± 0.2 (2 part. ask for 1 times)	1 (amount of money less than lowest amount)	1 (internet failure)	Successfully completed (1 part. needs 2 trials, others need single trial)
Event Organizer (n = 2)	Organize events	1.3 ± 0.3	0.8 ± 0.1	1 ± 0.3 (2 part. ask for 1 times)	1 (info of place was not accurate)	0	Successfully completed (1 part. needs 2 trials, others need single trial)
Total		1.50 ± 0.95	0.84 ± 0.25	0.84 ± 0.23	3	1	

for about 2.73 h in average per day. Among participants, 6 people were parents, 6 people were teachers of autistic kids, 3 people were donor and rest 2 people were interested to organize related events. The age variation of the participants was within 23 to 55 years.

4.2 Study Procedure

At first, participants are notified about the purpose of this study and their need requested them to perform tasks as listed in Table 4 and collect the data related to TCT (Time Completion Time) and frequency of wrong navigation, asking help, input error and system error. Finally, all types of participants are asked to complete a set of questionnaires. The questionnaires include 5 questions: (1) satisfaction level, (2) recommendation of the portal to others and (3) willingness to use the portal in future. The others are open questions: (4) Any extra features to enrich the portal and (5) any other comments. The first three questions were closed questions and ask to rate into a scale of 1 (strongly disagree) to 5 (strongly agree).

Evaluation and Results. The resultant outcome is shown in Tables 4 and 5. The study data showed that all participants completed the respective task successfully within a short time (1.50 ± 0.95 min) and most of the participants completed in single trials. No system error except internet failure occurred and input error frequency was comparatively less which all shows a good level of effectiveness. Required TCT, wrong navigation and asking help frequency were less; therefore, they completed the task very smoothly and efficiently.

Table 5. Summary of result of user satisfaction

Participants	Average Satisfaction Level (Avg frequency with Stdv)	Whether he/she will recommend this portal to others? (Avg frequency with Stdv)	Willing to use it in future? (Avg frequency with Stdv)
Parents (n = 6)	4.6 ± 0.15	4.4 ± 0.2	4.6 ± 0.2
Teachers (n = 6)	4.4 ± 0.2	4.4 ± 0.17	4.0 ± 0.1
Donor (n = 3)	4.4 ± 0.1	4.4 ± 0.1	4.5 ± 0.18
Event Organizer (n = 2)	4.6 ± 0.1	4.7 ± 0.15	4.8 ± 0.1
Total (n = 17)	4.5 ± 0.14	4.43 ± 0.15	4.48 ± 0.15

In case of satisfaction (Table 5), the overall score gathered from all users (parent, teacher, donor and event organizer) was comparatively high. They were highly intended to recommend this portal to others and their willingness to use it in future was also overwhelming which represents a good level of satisfaction. From the open questions, the study found that all are agreed to say that the tool will introduce an innovative means to support the parents whose children are autistic. They also highlight the following benefits:

1. **Reduce cost in primary checkup:** 4 Parents and 3 teachers thought that autism detection feature reduces the cost for primary checkup. If parents find that there is a probability of having autism in their child, then they can go to the doctors.
2. **Knowledge and Experience Sharing:** 5 parents and 4 teachers thought that it's a good platform for the parents to share their experience and knowledge to other parents.
3. **Getting financial help:** Parents thought that raising an autistic child is expensive. Many low-income people can't afford this cost. Donor can help them financially to raise them.
4. **Increasing awareness:** To increase awareness this platform may help many people to organize autism related events like seminars, rally discussion etc.

In a nutshell the outcome of the evaluation study showed that the system is effective, efficient, useful as well as satisfiable to end users.

5 Conclusion

Autistic kid is really special ones. So support system for them should be also special and developed with extra care. Therefore, in most of the cases they are being ignored by our society as well as their parents. This paper provides a brief overview of the design and development of a web portal, which will be very effective for taking care of these children. The light weighted evaluation study also highlighted the portal as a useful and innovative means of proving help to the kids. Future work of this support system would be to carry out an extensive empirical study with a large number of real-users to improve portal's usability and technical features.

References

1. Shebi. http://www.shebi.org/Autism_in_Bangladesh.html. Accessed 11 July 2017
2. The National Autistic Society. http://www.autism.org.uk/about/what-is/asd. aspx. Accessed 11 July 2017
3. Morbidity and Mortality Weekly Report (MMWR). https://www.cdc.gov/mmwr/ volumes/65/ss/ss6503a1.htm. Accessed 7 May 2017
4. Medical expenditures for children with an autism spectrum disorder in a privately insured population. https://www.ncbi.nlm.nih.gov/pubmed/17690969. Accessed 10 May 2017
5. Amendah, D., Grosse, S.D., Peacock, G., Mandell, D.S.: The economic costs of autism: a review. In: Amaral, D.G., Dawson, G., Geschwind, D.H. (eds.) Autism Spectrum Disorders, pp. 1347–1360. Oxford University Press, Oxford (2011)
6. Berument, S.K., Rutter, M., Lord, C., Pickles, A., Bailey, A.: Autism screening questionnaire: diagnostic validity. Br. J. Psychiatry 175(5), 444–451 (1999). RCP
7. Putnam, C., Chong, L.: Software and technologies designed for people with autism: what do users want? In: Proceedings of the 10th International ACM SIGACCESS Conference on Computers and Accessibility, pp. 3–10. ACM (2008)
8. Autism Parenting Magazine - Android Apps on Google Play. https://play.google. com/store/apps/details?id=com.bdfffaiidj.ebcbdfffaiidj&hl=en. Accessed 10 Nov 2017
9. Autism Parent Behavior Support - Android Apps on Google Play. https://play. google.com/store/apps/details?id=com.conduit.app_f764ec89d9ca40a8a97c51dc5c ff133a.app&hl=en. Accessed 7 May 2017
10. Autism Test-Android Apps on Google Play. https://play.google.com/store/apps/ details?id=com.consurgo.autismtest&hl=en. Accessed 12 Feb 2018
11. Autism Test-Android Apps on Google Play. https://play.google.com/store/apps/ details?id=com.autism.assessment.assessmentautism&hl=en. Accessed 12 Feb 2018
12. ABA Therapy Aphasia Autism - Android Apps on Google Play. https://play. google.com/store/apps/details?id=appinventor.ai_coolbhavana1.Kids_Picture_ Dictionary_Aphasia_autism_speech_language&hl=en. Accessed 19 Feb 2018

13. Da Silva, M.L., Gonçalves, D., Guerreiro, T., Silva, H.: A web-based application to address individual interests of children with autism spectrum disorders. Procedia Comput. Sci. **14**, 20–27 (2012)
14. Autism Speaks. https://www.autismspeaks.org/. Accessed 15 Jan 2018
15. One Stop Autism Resource of Bangladesh. http://www.autismbd.com/. Accessed 15 Jan 2018

Improving Driver Behavior
Using Gamification

Simge Helvaci⊙, Aras Senova⊙, Gorkem Kar⊙, and Sezer Gören$^{(\boxtimes)}$⊙

Department of Computer Engineering, Yeditepe University, Istanbul, Turkey
{simge.helvaci,aras.senova}@std.yeditepe.edu.tr,
{gkar,sgoren}@cse.yeditepe.edu.tr
https://cse.yeditepe.edu.tr

Abstract. This work proposes a gamification approach to measure the driving behavior using the in-vehicle data and score drivers. Existing work largely focus on one functionality: either displaying vehicular info or scoring the driver. And some other work just provides navigation or Point of Interest (POI). In our work, we combine these features with minimal distraction for the driver. With this goal, we consider a system that interfaces to the vehicle bus and find the errors of the driver during the drive using multiple criteria. Furthermore, by providing achievements and leader boards, the driver is motivated to have a good score while driving. To facilitate this analysis and to evaluate the system, we recorded two trips in real traffic. The results show that we achieve more than 95% accuracy between real-world scenario and the simulation. We also present POI feature that finds nearest preferred locations which are restaurants, hospitals, gas stations, pharmacies, car repair shops.

Keywords: Vehicular sensing · Gamification

1 Introduction

Vehicle accidents are the most common factors that lead to deaths all around the world. In fact, nearly 3 thousand people die everyday due to vehicle accidents [1]. For decades, intensive research in the field of road safety has been conducted in the world with the fundamental objective of establishing the mechanisms of occurrence of traffic accidents and the development of new processes, methods, and systems for their prevention. The proportion of human factors that cause traffic problems is not negligible. For this reason, it is necessary to carry out studies that will offer people a safe traffic environment, warn them of their wrong movements, and improve their driving behavior.

Driver Behavior and Gamification. As vehicles become programmable and with the connected vehicle technology, they are capable of supporting new applications by computing the data available coming from the engine.

© Springer International Publishing AG, part of Springer Nature 2018
M. Younas et al. (Eds.): MobiWIS 2018, LNCS 10995, pp. 193–204, 2018.
https://doi.org/10.1007/978-3-319-97163-6_16

One sample application to use this data is to measure the driver behavior. How to evaluate the performance of the driver and how to improve that? The answer to this question will help in understanding to build an application that can provide the driving score of each driver in a game-like manner. The OpenXC [2] framework was used to gather vehicle data in real time which then triggers algorithms to infer the driver behavior errors. After each trip, the drivers score is added to the overall score. Gamification involves incorporating elements of this application such as scores, leaderboards, and badges to motivate drivers.

Existing Work. Today, there are innovative solutions that involve smartphone based GPS tracking and driver scoring. However, due to GPS limitations, those methods do not work well in metropolitans. There are some other methods to estimate the road conditions, driver behavior using wearables and traffic management. Those will be discussed in the next section.

The salient contributions of this work are summarized below.

- Accessing a rich set of in-vehicle sensor data using through a CAN bus interface and examine the driving performance
- Measuring the drive on real time and notify the user about the errors during the drive
- Including a leaderboard and badges to motivate the driver to drive carefully in a game-like environment
- By using POI feature, the driver can go to favorite locations with the help of Google Maps

2   Background and Applications

Modern vehicles are equipped with many Electronic Control Units (ECUs) that control and monitor different vehicle modules, such as the engine, doors or AC. These ECUs are accessible through Controller Area Network (CAN) bus. Many sensor data can be listened from the CAN bus. Recently, car makers make this sensing information accessible through smart phone applications [3].

2.1   Accessing the In-Vehicle Data

This data is accessible through the On-Board Diagnostics II (OBD II) port[1]. OBD II is a standard interface for vehicles to provide self-diagnostics and data reporting capabilities, and has been mandatory for vehicles sold in the United States since 1996 [4].

2.2   Previous Works

In the realm of driver distinction, the work [5] provides an app that can access the in-vehicle data to either decide on driver characteristics or road features. The authors manage to identify drivers with more than %90 accuracy.

---

[1] www.obdii.com.

Predicting human behavior is another subject that is investigated by scientists. In [6], the authors achieved 95% accuracy at predicting automobile driver's actions from their initial preparatory movements.

In [7,8], authors studied on understanding the driver behavior using smartphone sensors. They use accelerometer, gyroscope and magnetometer to understand the driving habits and provide recommendations for a safer drive.

Driver performance measuring has been studied by [9]. The authors use phone sensors to measure the vehicle dynamics. Details about the drive such as made maneuvers, average speed info is shared with the driver at the end of the trip. Similar work has been done by [10]. They provide road types, vehicle mileage, speed and collisions. In another work [11], the app specific to Mercedes cars show some useful information such as tire pressure, fuel level, battery charging level etc. They also provide the feature of locking/unlocking the vehicle through the app.

Researchers have been exploring wearable devices to measure driver behavior as well. In works [12,13], authors used smart watched to detect steering wheel angle and rate drivers using that.

There are some other works that involves GPS tracking as in [14–17]. However, the performance of these works are limited with the GPS performance, which is poor in metropolitans.

There has been some work on systems for traffic monitoring, rather than driver monitoring both in commercial companies and research facilities. Many of them leverage GPS units on cars(OnStar [18] system) to track the vehicle's movements and analysis can be done at the server. In another work, the authors [19] investigate the fleet management package that covers maintenance and monitoring for businesses.

3   Design

We seek to find the most common error types of drivers that can lead to dangerous driving. With this purpose, we propose to design a mobile application that can measure the driving behavior using in-vehicle data that are closely related with driver mistake habits. By using the vehicle accident reports [1], we observed that we need to focus on aggressive acceleration, harsh braking and signaling before making turns. We access this data using OpenXC. By deducting points from each error that the driver makes, we propose to score the overall drive.

In the proposed application, we have 9 features as shown in Fig. 1. These features are achievements, leaderboard, location POI, fuel info, score, errors, emergency button, pedal position and settings. Each feature will be explained in detail in the next section.

3.1   Selection of Events

We propose to find the minimum set of events that can lead to dangerous driving. With that reasoning, we focus on accelerating and decelerating patterns of drivers, and the habit of using a signal before turning. Of course, excessive

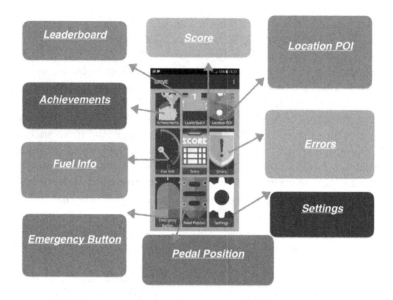

Fig. 1. Application screen

speeding could be another field to examine. If the driver goes over 10 km/h over the speed limit, we deduct a point from the overall score.

For manual geared vehicles, driving with the neutral gear can also be a dangerous act. We also examine if drivers do that during the drive, and deduct another point for that case.

3.2 System Overview

Based on the aforementioned insights, we consider a system that seek to identify the mistakes in driving style and rate the driving with a score. The system primarily consists of three components, vehicle bus data capture, identify mistakes and present score for the drive as shown in Fig. 2.

4 Implementation

We have implemented the entire system using a custom OBD-II scan tool (dongle), a smartphone and a remote server. We place a smartphone in the vehicle that can communicate with the dongle over Bluetooth and record incoming data in the database. When we start the vehicle (e.g., ignition status is ON), the application starts. The initial score for each driver is 100. If any of the errors is encountered, the driver loses a point. When the ignition status is OFF, the application stops and provide the trip score to the driver. We also record the driver info with the score in our remote server using Firebase database in real time. With the help of Google

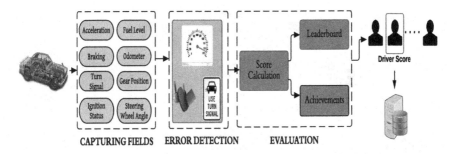

Fig. 2. System overview

Play Services, we can use achievement and leaderboard features. Before using the application, the user should be authenticated with the google play account.

Achievements Activity. We have three main achievements which are perfect driving, long road driver candidate and long road driver master. Perfect driver accomplishment is achieved when the driver finishes the trip with no driving behavior error. When 1 km. is traveled, the long road driver candidate accomplishment will be achieved. Similarly, when 100 km. is traveled, the long road driver master achievement will be achieved.

Leaderboard Activity. The scores of the leading competitors are displayed. It motivates drivers to drive their vehicles by following rules carefully to get higher scores.

Location POI Activity. Nearest restaurants, hospitals, pharmacies, car-repair shops or gas station can be found using this activity. After selecting a destination, required path would be shown in the screen via Google Maps.

Fuel Information Activity. Using this activity, fuel level, speed, ignition status, distance, turn signal status, accelerator pedal position can be shown.

Score Activity. The score of the driver for that trip is shown here. The driver loses a point each time he made a mistake. A maximum of 100 points and a minimum of 0 points are possible. When a certain distance (e.g., 10 km.) is traveled with no mistake, the driver accumulates a point.

Errors Activity. We show the quantity and type of driver errors. The errors are: aggressive acceleration, harsh braking, throttling neutral position, left turn-signal misuse, right turn-signal misuse.

Emergency Button Activity. We send the last known location to the predefined phone numbers. We define contact numbers using the setting activity.

Pedal Position Activity. Similar to the fuel information activity, different vehicle information from the OpenXC dongle is transmitted to the driver through this screen. Consequently, gear position, accelerator pedal position, brake pedal position, steering wheel angle, engine speed are shown in the screen.

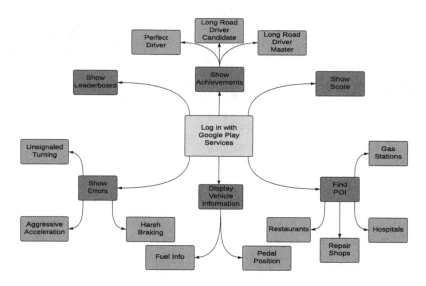

Fig. 3. Use case diagram

4.1 System Details

Proposed system has many features including displaying vehicle information, showing achievements during the drive, showing mistakes of the driver and finding POI.

The use case diagram of our application can be seen in Fig. 3. The application displays the activities which are achievements, leaderboard, location POI, fuel info, score, errors, emergency button, pedal position, settings. Also, inner activities contents and features are shown. In achievements screen, there exist three achievements that are perfect driving, long road driver candidate, long road driver master. In find location POI, there exist five icon-based buttons that have the functionality of finding nearest restaurant, hospital, pharmacy, car repair and gas station. In show fuel information, fuel level, speed, ignition status, accelerator pedal position, turn signal status and distance are shown. In show errors activity, aggressive acceleration, harsh braking, throttling neutral position, left turn-signal misuse, right turn-signal misuse are shown in the main screen. When button pressed emergency messages with current location will be sent to the preset telephone numbers. In pedal position activity, gear position, accelerator pedal position, brake pedal position, steering wheel angle, engine speed are shown in this screen. In the settings screen, phone numbers of the people you want to be notified when an emergency occurs.

Sequence Diagram. When we start the application, Android device and OpenXC Dongle should be paired via Bluetooth. If the pairing is successful, two blue lights become active. In order to use this app on a car, connection type as Bluetooth should be selected from OpenXC Enabler Application settings.

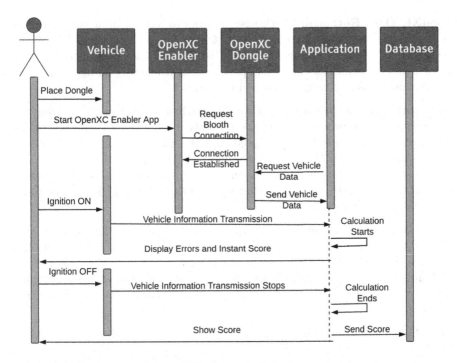

Fig. 4. UML diagram of the system

Enabler requests data from the dongle and gets a response. Subsequently, the application requests data and get the response. Afterward, data-set such as pedal positions, fuel level sent through the dongle. Application displays each data changes periodically. Algorithms are applied during the trip and scores are calculated regarding errors. Sequence diagram of the android application is shown in Fig. 4.

4.2   Software Implementation

In this paper, we have obtained access to several car sensors on late model Ford vehicles. Table 1 lists the sensors and the frequency of each signal.

Table 1. List of Vehicle CAN sensors

	Vehicle sensor frequency
Brakes active	100 Hz
Vehicle lateral acceleration	50 Hz
Vehicle speed	10 Hz
Left/right turns signal	Event
Throttle position	10 Hz
Steering wheel angle	100 Hz

OpenXC Data Retrieval Methods. In order to retrieve data, we use the listener methods that are provided by OpenXC code. These listeners include engine speed listener, ignition listener, fuel level listener, vehicle speed listener, accelerator pedal position listener, brake pedal position listener, odometer position listener and transmission gear position listener.

Aggressive Acceleration Detection Algorithm. In vehicle speed listener we received speed measurement at regular intervals. There exist an array list named List takes two inputs which are speed and the current time as milliseconds. Average acceleration is the change of velocity in given time.

If average acceleration is greater than 5, we classify this as an aggressive acceleration. The driver loses one point for each time the aggressive acceleration is detected.

Harsh Brake Detection Algorithm. As in the aggressive acceleration algorithm, if the average acceleration is less than -4, we classify this as harsh braking. In such a case, the driver loses another point.

Through accelerator pedal status listener, we can observe the accelerator pedal pressed birth time. If gear position is neutral neutralGasDetected() method is called.

Turn Detection and Signal Misuse Detection Algorithm. In order to detect turns, we continuously monitor the steering wheel angle. When the absolute value is greater than a certain threshold, the turn event is detected. Depending on the angle is greater or less than 0, we can identify the vehicle has turned right or left, respectively. This algorithm is designed by [20]. If the driver is not using the correct signaling before the turn starts, we deduct a point from the score.

Gamification. We propose to motivate drivers to get high scores using gamification. We include features such as achievements and leaderboard. In Google Play Console, there exist both of the features for developers.

Emergency Button. When button is pressed, the emergency message with the current location will be sent to the preset telephone numbers.

Find Nearest Specific Location. Based on the driver's location and the selected POI, we list the nearby positions of the selection on a map. Although such an information can be gathered from many different applications, we create a single application that includes all the information about the drive that a driver might need.

5   Performance Evaluation

We conduct our experiments in two different routes in Turkey. Both routes includes an highway with 3 lanes in each direction and a freeway with 2 lanes in each direction. We use a Ford Focus ST Line model vehicle, a custom OBD-II dongle and a Samsung Android phone. During the tests, the mobile phone was kept inside the vehicle to collect data from vehicle in real time as shown in Fig. 6. When the phone is paired with the dongle, the application starts.

Apart from the real-world tests, we include some simulation results. The OpenXC Simulator is used to simulate the incoming vehicle sensor data as it was collected from an actual vehicle. The OpenXC Simulator is shown in Fig. 5. We add following conditions to our system:

Fig. 5. OpenXC Simulator.

When the pedal percentage is above 30, a warning is given after 7 seconds and it indicates an aggressive acceleration. With the same logic, when the brake pedal is pressed for 7 seconds, it gives the "brake pedal overused" warning. Throttling in neutral position test cannot be done in the simulator. This is because there is no neutral in the gear position value in the simulator.

In the field test, we observed that when the driver uses the accelerator pedal over 70% for duration of a few seconds, the speed reaches more than 120 km/h and the aggressive accelerator mistake is observed using the application. Similarly, when the brake pedal is used over 70% for duration a few seconds, harsh braking mistake is observed and the user loses a point. The field test is shown in Fig. 6.

Fig. 6. Field test.

We use low pass filtering [21] to get rid of the noise in longitudinal acceleration over the last 11 samples.

For both the simulator and the field test, average acceleration and harsh brake results are shown in Fig. 7. We have more than 95% match between two methods (Table 2).

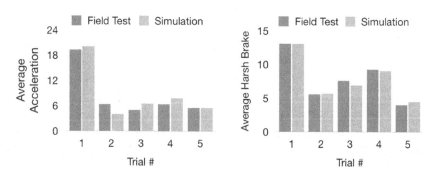

Fig. 7. Acceleration and harsh brake performance for both the field test and the simulator in m/s^2

Table 2. Aggressive acceleration and harsh braking performance comparison in m/s^2

Trial #	Simulator	Field Test	Trial #	Simulator	Field Test
1	19.31	20.07	1	-13.07	-13.08
2	6.41	4.07	2	-5.58	-4.69
3	5.04	6.57	3	-7.60	-6.91
4	6.42	7.89	4	-9.27	-9.05
5	5.58	5.62	5	-4.02	-4.51
Average	8.55	8.84	Average	-7.91	-7.65

6 Conclusion and Future Work

We have shown that driver mistakes can be detected and presented to the driver in real time. We used vehicle sensor data from CAN bus and presented the score of each drive at the end of the trip using gamification. With this way, improving the driver behavior is possible. During tests, we asked two drivers to drive as they do in their daily lives with no restrictions. We did real-world experiments and observed more than 95% accuracy between real drives and the simulator.

With a larger number of sensors and electronic control systems in newer vehicles and luxury vehicles, one can expect even higher accuracy.

One relevant question could be what will be the incentive for the drivers to use such an app? Insurance agencies and car companies could make discounts or give out some rewards for the drivers that use such an application and get good scores.

Acknowledgement. We want to thank to Mine Kandil, Burak Koc, and Yanki Insel for their constant supports and contributions to the project.

References

1. Association for Safe International Road Travel (2017). http://asirt.org/initiatives/informing-road-users/road-safety-facts/road-crash-statistics. Accessed 29 May 2018
2. OpenXC. http://openxcplatform.com/. Accessed 30 May 2018
3. Qiu, H., et al.: Towards robust vehicular context sensing. IEEE Trans. Veh. Technol. **67**(3), 1909–1922 (2018)
4. OBD-II Regulations. https://www.arb.ca.gov/msprog/obdprog/obdregs.htm. Accessed 30 May 2018
5. Kar, G., Jain, S., Gruteser, M., Bai, F., Govindan, R.: Real-time traffic estimation at vehicular edge nodes. In: Proceedings of the Second ACM/IEEE Symposium on Edge Computing, p. 3. ACM (2017)
6. Pentland, A., Lin, A.: Modeling and prediction of human behavior. Neural Comput. **11**, 229–242 (1995)
7. Eren, H., Makinist, S., Akin, E., Yilmaz, A.: Estimating driving behavior by a smartphone. In: Intelligent Vehicles Symposium (IV), 2012 IEEE, pp. 234–239. IEEE (2012)

8. Wang, Y.: Determining driver phone use by exploiting smartphone integrated sensors. IEEE Trans. Mob. Comput. **15**(8), 1965–1981 (2016)
9. DriveWell on the App Store (2015). https://itunes.apple.com/us/app/drivewell/id655601647?mt=8. Accessed 29 May 2018
10. Cambridge Mobile Telematics (2015). https://www.cmtelematics.com/blog/. Accessed 29 May 2018
11. mercedes-benz.com. Mercedes-Benz Apps (2007). https://www.mercedes-benz.com/en/mercedes-benz/lifestyle/mercedes-benz-apps/. Accessed 29 May 2018
12. Liu, L., et al.: Toward detection of unsafe driving with wearables. In: Proceedings of the 2015 Workshop on Wearable Systems and Applications, pp. 27–32. ACM (2015)
13. Karatas, C., et al.: Leveraging wearables for steering and driver tracking. In: IEEE INFOCOM 2016-The 35th Annual IEEE International Conference on Computer Communications, pp. 1–9. IEEE (2016)
14. Brown, A.K., Sturza, M.A.: Vehicle tracking system employing global positioning system (GPS) satellites, 6 July 1993. US Patent 5,225,842
15. Brown, A.K., Sturza, M.A.: GPS tracking system, 3 January 1995. US Patent 5,379,224
16. Chadil, N., Russameesawang, A., Keeratiwintakorn, P.: Real-time tracking management system using GPS, GPRS and Google earth. In: 5th International Conference on Electrical Engineering/Electronics, Computer, Telecommunications and Information Technology, 2008. ECTI-Con 2008, vol. 1, pp. 393–396. IEEE (2008)
17. Kar, G., et al.: Detection of on-road vehicles emanating GPS interference. In: Proceedings of the 2014 ACM SIGSAC Conference on Computer and Communications Security, pp. 621–632. ACM (2014)
18. OnStar. OnStar by GM (2015). https://www.onstar.com/us/en/home/. Accessed 30 May 2018
19. Fleetio Review. https://reviews.financesonline.com/p/fleetio. Accessed 29 May 2018
20. Turk, Y., Ozcan, B., Gören, S.: Precise vehicle positioning for indoor navigation via OpenXC. In: Proceedings of the 4th International Conference on Vehicle Technology and Intelligent Transport Systems, VEHITS, vol. 1, pp. 440–445. INSTICC, SciTePress (2018)
21. Department of Electrical Engineering Linkopings universitet. Detection of Critical Events Using Limited Sensors (2012). http://www.diva-portal.org/smash/get/diva2:570048/FULLTEXT01.pdf. Accessed 29 May 2018

Transformation of Human Labour
from Stone Age to Information Age

Michal Beno[(✉)]

VSM/City University of Seattle, Panonska cesta 17, 851 04 Bratislava, Slovakia
michal.beno@vsm-student.sk

Abstract. Over the past few years, the labour market in general has been caught up in different financial and economic crises worldwide. Unemployment has grown to record levels. Our life is an odd mixture of different moments of action and inaction, work and rest. Work provides us with inner creative joy. Usually, it saves us from the dullness and boredom of life, puts our energy to proper use, provides us with money for our livelihood, and makes our lives meaningful and peaceful. We think that two things are necessary for really useful and happy work: skill and constructiveness. Work is not only an important part of our daily lives, but we have come to a point where it has taken over our lives. It is also an important political issue at the present time. Human labour is changing according to socio-ecological and technological transitions. These transitions are expected to have many far-reaching implications for human labour. To understand this situation, we have evolved a simple scheme that can be applied to the timeline of human evolution from the Stone Age to the Information Age. Using this device, we have tried to explore the historical relationships between changed regimes and the changes in human labour.

Keywords: Work · Labour · Stone age · Information age

1 Introduction

Generally, work constitutes two separate activities: "paid" and "unpaid" work. Unpaid work can be understood to comprise all productive activities outside the official labour market done by individuals for their own households or for others [1]. This means that it occurs in a domestic context, such as housework (cooking, washing, ironing), care of children or members of the family, voluntary community work, help in family business and similar work. On the other hand, if the work is done in exchange for a salary or wage, it is usually called "labour".

Work is not only an integral part of our lives, but also one of the most important topics of human concern throughout the world [2–5]. The future of labour history research has been discussed a great deal, for example through regime changes and demographic changes, oil crises and the transition from the use of fossil fuels, globalisation, the history of technology, and other milestones [6–8]. The majority of labour historians have occupied themselves with the era of industrialisation [9, 10], but we have to begin to focus on earlier periods.

M. Younas et al. (Eds.): MobiWIS 2018, LNCS 10995, pp. 205–216, 2018.
https://doi.org/10.1007/978-3-319-97163-6_17

We think that employment in the next decade will not only depend on demographic dynamics, the increasing or decreasing of active age, but also on macroeconomic conditions (GDP), technological advances (ICT development), education systems, and the transition away from fossil fuels (energy prices) and environment changes.

We emphasise the nature of changes in the workplace too. We believe that innovation in the workplace is a driving force for changes towards sustainable forms of increasing productivity e.g. flexible work, remote work, e-Work, alternative payment schemes, greater autonomy, job rotation, multi-skilling, teamwork and others. This brings about advantages not only for the economy, but also for society as a whole and for individuals, such as employees and employers.

To understand this phenomenon, we evolved a simple scheme that can be applied to the timeline of human evolution from the Stone Age to the Information Age. Historically, doing lots of backbreaking work is the way countries have become rich, and being rich means to do more pleasant work. Using this device, we tried to explore historical relationships between changed regimes and the changes in human labour e.g. the industrial revolutions in the 1760s, 1860s and 1990s [11], capitalism, democracy, globalisation [12] and digitisation [13]. We target the regimes, human lifetime spent on labour and institutional forms. Changes in technology, culture and economies are having an impact on the way people work at all levels around the world [14]. Generally, work became more pleasant for skilled workers. Getting work done is a fundamental concern for any business, and modern digital and communications technologies are changing this in different ways [15]. We believe that in the modern age of information technology and the Internet, artificial intelligence, computerised algorithms, mobile sensors, 3-D printing and other developments, virtual reality will play an important role in different organisations.

In the following sections, these two core questions will be addressed: (1) How is the world of human work evolving? (2) What could labour look like after the ongoing socio-ecological and technological transitions?

2 Meaning of Work and Labour

Work is a specific, complex activity of human beings, exclusively a human phenomenon that has been detached from the animal world. It is an economic, sociological and psychological category. Work is not a human raison d'être, yet we consider it a very important issue in our lives.

The term is a vague concept without a clear definition. The understanding of the aim and impact of work varies among individuals. Primarily we have to understand what work is, paid or unpaid. Under unpaid work we include work that usually occurs in the home environment (cooking, cleaning, washing, ironing or childcare) including also volunteer work. If the work activity is paid, it means it is done in exchange for salary and wages, and then it is usually called labour. This concept also includes independent business ranging from the simplest self-employment to international banking.

Generally, it is easier to define what work is not. When a person wakes in the morning and prepares for the day ahead, it is generally considered that he/she has not done any work activity during this day yet. Morning hygiene, breakfast, and other personal rituals are not considered work, but for those who have to dress children, prepare their breakfast and take them to school, the workday has begun.

Giddens [16, p. 176] says, "most pre-modern societies seem to have no word for work, presumably because working wasn't readily distinguishable from other activities". Chris and Charles Tilly [17, p. 22] described work as follows, "work includes any human effort adding use value to goods and services". More precisely, the personal use of one's own free time would also be included, and Tilly and Tilly [17] took this aspect into consideration in their definition. Therefore, the alternative to work would be personal care, where sleep would be included, but both leisure and personal care should definitely differ from work. Schwimmer [18, p. 287] emphasises that "work as a concept is based on the assumption that, from a certain view-point, all economically useful activities are fully comparable by a yardstick transcending their diversity, in other words, that labour has become a commodity and that the technical and administrative direction of that labour become part of the same kind of commodity".

Giddens [19, p. 505] identified six key characteristics of paid work, which are essentially connected with the economic and professional achievements of human beings: *money (wages, salary), activity level, diversity of life, temporal structure, social contacts* and *personal identity*. The degree of saturation of human needs subsequently affects an individual's relationship with work, and his/her impact is wide-ranging (relationship with colleagues, relationship with clients, workplace relationships, relationship with the organisation and others).

3   From Stone Age to Information Age

As most people would no doubt agree, the world of human work is an extremely multi-faceted and dynamically changing field of study. In a first, extremely simplified approximation, we may model the historical development of human labour evolution trying to set out some of the important milestones. Hands, hand tools, machines, computers, digitisation, smartphones, cloud computing and virtual organisation are the main features of the evolution of work.

Stone Age began at the beginning of what would become human civilization till the discovery of smelting. Smelting allowed people to create tools made out of metal and stone tools become obsolete. In Table 1 we summarized the main Stone Age Technologies.

Stone Age humans satisfied their basic needs by hunting, gathering and preparing the food for consumption, which did not require much time, and constructing human artefacts such as hand tools. As humans lived in social groups (at most a dozen or so people), they cooperated to survive by implementing various forms of division of labour. The increase in working time under such conditions, however, could be self-defeating, because the increased hunting and gathering in the same area would tend to exhaust the food resources, thereby forcing the community to migrate. As documented in cultural anthropology research, the hunting/gathering regime requires the least amount of human work from its members [20, 21]. Polanyi [22] stressed that the first human work relations

Table 1. Stone age technology.

Technology	
Stone	Most tools were created to help humans to survive using the technique flint knapping;
Fire	It may seem primitive but million years ago it was necessary to survive, allowed early humans to control the environment;
Wheel	Used this to move more quickly through the use of wheeled vehicles;
Clothing	Used the pelts of animals;
Bow and Arrow	Was a very useful tool allowed to kill the food from longer ranges much easier and safer;
Boat	Created primitive boats for short distance;
Pottery	Allowed prehistoric humans to store food for longer periods.

Source: Author

were in this sense direct, and thereby reciprocal. The people of this regime worked according to a timescale norm reminiscent of the work of animals in order to survive.

The evolution of agriculture (farming) through modern technology tools and mechanisation, the exchange of goods and services between people, an increase in the amount of work and an increase in the intensification of traditional agriculture [23, 24] then started. Farmers produced surpluses, made possible the formation of substantial reserves and achieved progress with work specialisation. The industrialisation of agriculture helped people to reduce working time using fossil-fuel technologies. In the agricultural period, work became a much more significant feature of human existence, both quantitatively and qualitatively.

In the period of Aristotle and Xenophon in Ancient Greece and Cicero in Ancient Rome, it may have been considered unworthy for a free man to be working, because all men valued a life of leisure and service to the polis as a free self-determined citizen, and working under somebody else's command was incompatible with personal dignity However, the concept of work depends on social formation and differs throughout the genesis of human society. We illustrate the following broad historical classifications of the various institutional forms:

- *family work* with interdependent systems and mutual obligations, such as survival and subsistence agriculture.
- *first professionals* such as potters, spinners, weavers, carpenters, brick makers, masons, transporters, smiths and priests began to make their appearance in Neolithic evolution [25].
- the beginning of the exchange of goods and services between specialists, which led to the formation of arrangements and models, such as the *jajmani system* which was founded in Indian villages, where goods and services were exchanged for grain at roughly constant exchange rates [26]. We understand this system to have been a durable relation between a land-owning family and the landless families that supply it with goods and services. According to Wiser [27], this system served to maintain the Indian village as a self-supporting community. Beidelman [26] is of the opinion that the jajmani system maintained the higher caste's prestige.

- *creation of first cities* in Eridu, Uruk in Southern Iraq, Hemudu in China; the cities of the Nile and Indus valley created tributary labour relations [22], documented in Eurasia and in South and Central America.
- with the emergence of states, two models of working relationship developed: *slavery* and *wage labour*. We believe that both originated contemporaneously, as recorded in the examples of soldiers. At the same time, slaves were taken as hostages who were not killed, as is later described explicitly in the inscription on the statue of Justinian written in 528–534: *"Servi autem ex eo appellati sunt, quod imperatores captivos vendere iubent ac per hoc servare, nec occidere solent; qui etiam mancipia dicti sunt, quod ab hostibus manu capiuntur"* [28, pp. 18], (*Slaves are called by that name, because it is customary that commanders order the prisoners to be sold and in that way save them and do not kill them*, author's translation). Obviously, wars occupied a central place in the history of labour. Sargon of Akkad (2334-2279 BC) was the first ruler who established a large state in world history with recorded slaves and professional soldiers, namely in Mesopotamia [29].
- *labour markets* emerged next to the cities, states and temples, and subcontractors began to act as employers of labour. Meanwhile, commodity markets were needed on a regular basis [30]. In these markets, we can find two kinds of buyers: independent producers who bought and sold from and to each other, and professional soldiers or others who produced food partly or not at all, or used money for buying.
- *independent labour* included family business arrangements in which women already played an early role [31].
- from the subcontractors of the temples and other central organisations there also emerged the first *employers of labour.*

Physical power was the main feature of human labour during the agrarian epoch. The ruling classes were not interested in the majority of the population who were engaged in agricultural production, nor were they interested in improving the skills and knowledge of this sector of the population as long as they fed themselves and paid their tithes and taxes. During the course of industrialisation, the working time needed for production was very much reduced, allowing for the development of a highly differentiated labour market, together with the further development of the division of labour within and between countries. According to Geser [32], the concept of industrialisation denotes the fusion of mechanisation and bureaucratisation (Fordism and Taylorism), and mechanised and formalised plants.

Work in the coal-based industrial age multiplied the demand for labour characterised by physical power and development of modern technologies (e.g. steam engines). In this period, the reduction in daily working hours and the introduction of child labour were established [33]. Most countries started to offer public-funded compulsory school education for children [34], which created a demand for professional teachers. One can also observe an increasing cultural differentiation by gender.

After World War II, the use of oil and other fossil-fuel sources became dominant. This era is characterised by a rise of energy consumption in the economy, decreasing working hours, and rapidly rising energy intensity. In households, we can observe the same changes, e.g. electrical equipment, which substitutes for physical effort at home, raises the intellectual requirements for handling it. Technological development, increasing consumption of fossil fuels and electric motors have replaced a large portion of physical labour.

Information and communication technology (ICT) of the 1970s has acted as a substitute for the knowledge work component of human labour. ICT has replaced the knowledge-based human labour component. Replacing knowledge is basically less energy consuming than replacing physical work. Nevertheless, the production of knowledge and the control of knowledge remain a key feature of human labour. At the same time, with the First-World oil crisis of 1973, there was a structural change in the relationship between energy and labour. The industrial revolution brought employees from their homes to the factories. With ICT, the reverse is possible, with employees now able to move back to their homes [35].

Telework, also known as telecommuting, can be defined simply as when employees work at some place other than the traditional workplace. The concept of telework, more precisely telecommuting, was born during the oil crisis in the early 1970s, when American Jack Nilles and colleagues published their calculations on the savings to the national economy that would result from reduced commuting [36].

In Table 2 we compare the evolution of work from the past to the future for an understanding of how the world of work is changing.

Table 2. The evolution of work.

The past	The future
Hierarchy	Flattened structure
Fixed working hours	Flexible working hours
Hoarded information (top secret)	Shared information
Command & control and fear-based leadership	Engaging, empowering, and inspiring leadership
On-premise technology	Cloud technology
E-mail is primary form of communication	E-mail is secondary form of communication
Corporate ladder	Create the ladder
Siloed and fragmented company	Connected and engaged company
Work at office	Work from anywhere

Source: Author's own compilation according to [37]

At present, workplace innovation refers to a number of specific actions, such as teleworking, telecommuting, remote-work, networking, digital nomadic work, flexiplace, networking and many other variants [38, 39], alternative payment schemes, employee empowerment and autonomy, task rotation, multi-skilling, teamwork and team autonomy. We believe that technology is an important enabler of workplace innovation.

The flexibility for jobholders to be able to work at any time in any place is technically feasible for many employees and has been for many years. In the literature, there seems to be an accepted category now: subject, working anywhere, for over forty years [40–42].

Using technological innovations, more and more organisations have started to redesign their approach to work. We feel strongly that central to this new approach is the fact that employees are asked to organise their work flexibly.

E-Work was defined by the PRISM Center as any collaborative, computer-supported and communication-enabled productive activities in highly distributed organisations of humans and/or robots or autonomous systems [43–45]. Basically, e-Work is based on e-activities, e.g. e-Business, e-Commerce, e-Government, e-Logistics, e-Learning and other, which rely on ICT. Some have defined e-Work as telework [39, 46], several conferences on e-Work as telework have taken place [47, 48].

The designation e-Work is a relatively new term, replacing different terms such as teleworking, telecommuting, networking, digital nomads, flexi-work, and various other variants that describe how ICT has made remote work possible. Huws [39] emphasises that although this term does not specifically refer to distance, it has the benefit that it avoids over-specificity and can apply across a range of activities without being restricted to a particular form (homeworking or mobile working).

We feel that the classic definition of remote work is actually obsolete. These days it is almost impossible to imagine any kind of office work that does not make use of one or other telecommunication medium. In our opinion, e-Work is no longer an exception, but is becoming more and more standard in the working process. E-Work is associated with working at a distance. We think that this term extends the definition of teleworking in all activities through information processing with the utilisation of ICT. This may involve individual or collective forms, internal corporate decentralisation and classic outsourcing. The scope of e-Work ranges from call centre or software development companies in decentralised locations to mobile working, homeworking and e-lancers [49].

In a very broad definition, e-Work "encompasses any work which is carried out away from an establishment and managed from that establishment using information technology and a telecommunications link for receipt or delivery of the work" [39, p. 22]. Eichmann et al. [50] define e-Work as "any mode of work organization within a country or between countries practicing: telemediated, controlled, remote work (individualized/ isolated or office-based and telemediated, collaborative work (tele-cooperation, virtual teams))". When we use this definition, e-Work can be distinguished from similar concepts that are either more restricted or more widespread, such as **telework, e-Work, online work, knowledge-based work, and white-collar work.** We understand the concept of e-Work as a way to be an employee as well as a method and mechanism for performing a job in the modern, digitalised world because "to Do Good e-Business, Somebody Has to Do the e-Work" [51].

The workplace was merely a physical space employees occupied during regular office hours. Today's permanently connected, instant-access environment has blurred the lines between the physical office and the place where work actually happens. The workplace has become a digital environment, and employees are communicating and collaborating in different ways. The green workplace is simply defined as a workplace that is environmentally sensitive, resource efficient and socially responsible [52]. The digital workplace encompasses all the technologies people use to get work done in today's workplace – both the ones in operation and the ones yet to be implemented [53].

The virtual workplace is one in which employees operate remotely from each other and from managers [54]. It means virtual work in different types of virtual workplaces (home office, teleworking centres, mobile office, office hotelling, etc.) is done in whole or in part via electronic communication requiring little or no daily face-to-face contact with co-workers or supervisors. It does, however, requires technology such as telephones, Internet tools and computers, and creates a work environment without geographical boundaries. In Table 3, we summarise the main differences between traditional and virtual work.

Table 3. Traditional work versus Virtual work.

Traditional work	Virtual work
Recruit and utilise employees at one location only	Recruit employees in any geographical location, to support projects
Communicate face to face and brainstorming	Communicate via telephone, e-mail/chat, videoconferencing, IM, blogs, social networking
Workdays defined	Flexibility of workdays
Work hours fixed	Work hours flexible
Work limited to the workplace	Work performed online from any location at any time

Source: Author

A global increase in alternative forms of work and employment is currently observed, entailing alternating working at home and in the main office. Flexibility profoundly changed the character of the modern workplace. Employers can benefit from flexi-time in a variety of ways. It is conceivable that individuals who are more open to new experiences will profit from working in the virtual world, experiencing more work, while spending less energy to adopt this new work design. Mobility in the workplace is increasingly emerging. By 2015, the results from IDC research showed that the world's mobile working population had reached 1.3 billion, i.e. 37.2% of the total workforce, which is 300 million more than in 2010 [55].

Human work and energy policy are closely connected, therefore a new energy transition from fossil fuels will have an important role in shaping the future of work. Human labour is highly dependent on the fossil-fuel-based energy age. Technological and social forces are transforming how work gets done, who does it and even what work looks like. In our opinion, the effect of technology is that work will become increasingly more interesting and more creative, thereby offering a freer market for human skills. Generally our attitudes to work and to the changing the quality of it depend as much on our own disposition and the alternatives available on the market as on the jobs themselves.

4   Conclusions

All over the world, work is the most important source of income in modern society with its social role and its role in the lives of human beings. Human work has always been a fundamental need, an indispensable social bond and a source of ego. In the history of work up to the present time, almost all the attention has been focused on work relations between slaveholder and slaves and employer and employee.

We often relate the world of work to making money. But work is perceived as an activity requiring effort, being autonomous and creative, paid employment, time spent finishing tasks, a tool that enables individuals to express themselves, establish contacts with others, develop human skills.

The historic milestones which we have discussed are obviously connected but are not self-explanatory. Of course the first market developed enormously at the expense of other institutions, such as trade unions, employers' organisations and the socio-economic policy of national states [56]. The global crisis during the evolution, globalisation and unification of Europe and other countries played an important role in this development too.

Across history, the longest period of time spent on labour was in the agriculture industry. The industrialisation of agriculture relieved labour time using modern fossil-fuel technologies. Physical power was the main key of human labour during the evolution. Since the 1970s, ICT has substituted for the knowledge work component of human labour. With the availability of liquid fossil fuels and electricity, physical human and also animal labour was replaced in economic sectors.

In conclusion, we can sum up by saying that the evolution of labour through the ages has been characterised by the following features:

(1) Movement of the workplace from the home to the office/factory and back to the home. This, more recently, includes the fact that business owners can outsource certain tasks and no longer have to provide facilities such as office space, canteens, medical aid and pensions for employees. The workers, on the other hand, now not only have to take responsibility for these former benefits of fixed employment, but also have to act as their own "managers" by ensuring that the work is completed and that all the requirements for doing it are available.

(2) Some jobs are lost, e.g. wainwright, wheelwright, farrier, and new jobs appear in especially ICT demanding new skills, which creates a demand for training for new job-seekers, but also for existing workers who have to move from one field to another (proving the truth of the saying that "most people will have three different careers during their lifetime"). This is also tied up with the move away from the use of fossil fuel.

(3) Change in gender distribution. The traditional role of the man as the breadwinner and the woman staying at home to do the housekeeping and look after the children changed, and women entered the workplace too. This trend continued, and in later decades women started doing work that had traditionally been the preserve of men (bankers, doctors, senior managers) and even the more "masculine" jobs, such as in the police, army, firefighting, motor mechanics, bullfighting.

References

1. Swiebel, J.: Unpaid work and policy-making towards a broader perspective of work and employment. DESA Discussion Paper No. 4, ST/ESA/1999 DP.4 (1999)
2. Burgmann, V.: The Strange Death of Labour History, Bede Nairn and Labor History, pp. 69–81. Pluto Press, Sydney (1991)
3. Irving, T.: Challenges to Labour History. University of New South Wales Press, Sydney (1994)
4. Moody, C.J., Kessler-Harris, A.: Perspectives on American Labor History – The Problems of Synthesis. Northern Illinois University Press, DeKalb (1989)
5. Van der Linden, M.: The End of Labour History?. Cambridge University Press, Cambridge (1993)
6. Van der Linden, M., Lucassen, J.: Prolegomena for a Global Labour History. International Institute of Social History, Amsterdam (1999)
7. Van der Linden, M., Lucassen, J.: Workers of the World: Essays toward a Global labor History. Brill, Leiden & Boston (2008)
8. World Economic Forum: Future of Jobs Report. http://www3.weforum.org/docs/WEF_FOJ_Executive_Summary_Jobs.pdf. Accessed 21 May 2018
9. Bairoch, P., Kozul-Wright, R.: Globalization myths: some historical reflections on integration, industrialization and growth in the world economy. UNCTAD/OSG/DP/113. http://citeseerx.ist.psu.edu/viewdoc/download?doi=10.1.1.473.4259&rep=rep1&type=pdf. Accessed 12 Feb 2018
10. Rees, J.: Industrialization and Urbanization in the United States, 1880–1929, Oxford Research Encyclopedia of American. http://americanhistory.oxfordre.com/view/10.1093/acrefore/9780199329175.001.0001/acrefore-9780199329175-e-327?print=pdf. Accessed 12 Feb 2018
11. Henry, J.: Workplace transformation: intel's vision for embracing change and innovation. https://www.intel.com/content/dam/www/public/us/en/documents/white-papers/workplace-transformation-vision-paper.pdf. Accessed 21 May 2018
12. Doogan, K.: New Capitalism?. The Transformation of Work. Polity, Cambridge (2011)
13. OECD. https://www.oecd.org/mcm/documents/C-MIN-2017-4%20EN.pdf. Accessed 21 May 2018
14. ADP: The Evolution of Work: The Changing Nature of the Global Workforce. https://www.adp.co.uk/assets/vfs/Domain-3/evolution-of-work/eow-ebook-uk-vf.pdf. Accessed 21 May 2018
15. Stockton, H., Filipova, M., Monahan, K.: The evolution of work: new realities facing today's leaders. https://www2.deloitte.com/insights/us/en/focus/technology-and-the-future-of-work/evolution-of-work-seven-new-realities.html. Accessed 21 May 2018
16. Giddens, A.: Beyond Left and Right: The Future of Radical Politics, 284 pp. Polity Press, Cambridge (1994)
17. Tilly, Ch., Tilly, Ch.: Work Under Capitalism, 336 pp. Westview Press, Boulder (1998)
18. Schwimmer, E.: The self and the product: concepts of work in comparative perspective. In: Wallman, Sandra (ed.) The Social Anthropology of Work, pp. 287–315. Academic Press, London (1979)
19. Giddens, A.: Sociology, 815 pp. Polity Press, Cambridge (1989)
20. Gowdy, J.: Limited Wants, Unlimited Means: A Reader on Hunter-Gatherer Economics and the Environment. Island Press, Washington, DC (1998)
21. Sahlins, M.: Stone Age Economics. Aldine Atherton Inc., Chicago & New York (1972)
22. Polanyi, K.: The Great Transformation. Farrar Rinehart, New York & Toronto (1944)

23. Boserup, E.: The conditions of agricultural growth. The Economics of Agrarian Change under Population Pressure (1965). https://www.biw.kuleuven.be/aee/clo/idessa_files/boserup 1965.pdf. Accessed 12 Feb 2018
24. Ringhofer, L.: Fishing, Foraging and Farming in the Bolivian Amazon. Springer, Netherlands (2010)
25. Whittle, A., Cummings, V.: Going Over: The Mesolithic-Neolithic Transition in North-West Europe. Oxford University Press, Oxford (2007)
26. Beidelman, T.O.: A Comparative Analysis of the Jajmani System, 86 pp. J.J. Augustin, New York (1959)
27. Wiser, W.H.: The Hindu Jajmani System. Lucknow Publishing House, Lucknow (1936)
28. Rossberger, W.M.: Die Institutionen des Kaisers Justinian in vier Büchern, Berlin, p. 18 (1829)
29. Freewalt, J.: Sargon the great of akkad: the first empire builder of mesopotamia (2014). http://www.freewalt.com/freewaltfamily/jason_erika/documents/SargontheGreat-JasonFreewalt.pdf. Accessed 12 Feb 2018
30. Hofmeester, K., Van der Linden, M.: Handbook Global History of Work, 612 pp. Walter de Gruyter, Berlin/Boston (2017)
31. Barber, E.J.W.: Women's Work: The First 20,000 Years: Women, Cloth, and Society in Early Times. W. W. Norton, New York & London (1994)
32. Geser, H.: The three-dimensional evolution of human work: some methodological consequences for social and historical research. In: Prof. Hans Geser. Online Publications, Zürich (2011). http://geser.net/arbeit/t_hgeser8.pdf. Accessed 13 Feb 2018
33. ILO: International Labour Standards on Working time. http://www.ilo.org/global/standards/subjects-covered-by-international-labour-standards/working-time/lang-en/index.htm. Accessed 12 Feb 2018
34. Gellner, E.: Plough, Sword and Book. The structure of Human History, 288 pp. Collins Harwill, London (1988)
35. Simitis, S.: The Juridification of labour relations. Comp. Labor Law 93, 93–142 (1986)
36. Nilles, J.M., Carlson, R.F., Gay, P., Hanneman, G.J.: The Telecommunications-Transportation Tradeoff: Options for Tomorrow. Wiley, New York (1976)
37. Morgan, J.: The Evolution of Work (2013). https://www.forbes.com/sites/jacobmorgan/2013/09/10/the-evolution-of-work/#777c4b528067. Accessed 12 Feb 2018
38. Bates, P., Bertin, I., Huws, U.: E-Work in Ireland, 72 pp. IES Report 394, Brighton (2002)
39. Huws, U.: Statistical indicators of eWork, A Discussion paper, 30 pp. IES, Report 385, Brighton (2001)
40. Nilles, J.M.: Telecommunications and organizational decentralization. IEEE Trans. Commun. 23(10), 1142–1147 (1975)
41. Wilkes, R.B., Frolick, M.N.: Critical issues in developing successful tele-work programs. J. Syst. Manag. 45(7), 30 (1994)
42. Hunton, J.E.N., Strand, C.: The impact of alternative telework arrangements on organizational commitment: Insights from a longitudinal field experiment. J. Inf. Syst. 24(1), 67–90 (2010)
43. Nof, S.Y.: Robot ergonomics: optimizing robot work. In: Nof, S.Y. (ed.) Handbook of Industrial Robotics, 2nd edn, pp. 603–604. Wiley, New York (1999)
44. Nof, S.Y.: Models of e-Work. In: Proceedings of the IFAC/MIM-2000, Rio, pp. 521–527 (2000)
45. Nof, S.Y.: Intelligent collaborative agents. In: Moore, C., et al. (eds.) Encyclopedia of Science and Technology, pp. 219–222. McGraw Hill, New York (2000)

46. Chiozza, E., Stanford-Smith, B.: E-Work and E-Commerce: Novel Solutions and Practices for a Global Networked Economy, Volume 2, Section 2.1 Mobile Applications for Business and Work, pp. 644–650. IOS Press (2001)

47. Adaptland.it, International Conference "E-Work As A Model For Flexibility, Work-Life Balance And Productivity In Spanish And Comparative Law" (United Kingdom, France, Germany, Italy, Argentina and Spain). https://moodle.adaptland.it/pluginfile.php/21441/mod_resource/content/3/programa_santiago_2015_en.pdf. Accessed 12 Feb 2018

48. E2003: eChallenges Conference: E2003-eChallenges Conference, 22–24 October 2003, Bologna, Italy (2003). http://www.cheshirehenbury.com/ebew/e2003.html. Accessed 12 Feb 2018

49. Flecker, J., Kirschenhofer, S.: Jobs on the Move: European Case Studies on relocating eWork. The Institute for Employment Studies, IES Report 386, Brighton (2002)

50. Eichmann, H., Saupe, B., Schwarz-Wölzl, M.: Critical Issues Pertaining to the Code of Practice for Global E-work, CSI, D11 Impact Analysis (IST-2000-25463), 167 (2002)

51. Purdue News: Purdue's new Lifetime University debuts with e-biz workshop (2000). http://www.purdue.edu/uns/html4ever/0804.Chaney.lifetime.html. Accessed 12 Feb 2018

52. SHRM: Green Workplace (2008). http://web1.ctaa.org/webmodules/webarticles/articlefiles/18_SHRMsurvey.pdf. Accessed 12 Feb 2018

53. Deloitte: The digital workplace: think, share, do. Transform your employee experience (2011). https://www2.deloitte.com/content/dam/Deloitte/mx/Documents/human-capital/The_digital_workplace.pdf. Accessed 12 Feb 2018

54. Cascio, W.F.: Managing a virtual workplace. Acad. Manag. Perspect. 14(3), 81–90 (2000)

55. The Rise of Mobility: The Rise of Mobility (2018). http://cdn.idc.asia/files/5a8911ab-4c6d-47b3-8a04-01147c3ce06d.pdf. Accessed 13 Feb 2018

56. Hu, A., Manning, P.: The global social insurance movement since the 1880s. J. Glob. Hist. 5(01), 125–148 (2010)

Author Index

Printed in the United States
By Bookmasters